Best

★ *Fallen Stars*

SWAIM-PAUP-FORAN
SPIRIT OF SPORT SERIES

Sponsored by

James C. '74 & Debra Parchman Swaim

Nancy & T. Edgar Paup '74

Joseph Wm. & Nancy Foran

Fallen Stars

FIVE AMERICAN ATHLETES

WHO DIED IN

MILITARY SERVICE

Carson James Cunningham

TEXAS A&M UNIVERSITY PRESS
COLLEGE STATION

This paper meets the requirements of ANSI/NISO Z39.48-1992
(Permanence of Paper).

Binding materials have been chosen for durability.

Manufactured in the United States of America

LIBRARY OF CONGRESS CATALOGING-IN-PUBLICATION DATA

Names: Cunningham, Carson, author.
Title: Fallen stars : five American athletes who died in military
    service / Carson James Cunningham.
Other titles: Swaim-Paup-Foran spirit of sport series.
Description: First edition. | College Station : Texas A&M
    University Press, [2017] | Series: Swaim-Paup-Foran spirit of
    sport series
Identifiers: LCCN 2017000915 (print) | LCCN 2017005680
    (ebook) | ISBN 9781623495602 (cloth : alk. paper) |
    ISBN 9781623495619 (ebook)
Subjects: LCSH: Athletes—United States—Biography. | War
    casualties—United States—Biography. | Soldiers—United
    States—Biography. | Fish, Hamilton, -1898. | Baker, Hobey. |
    Kinnick, Nile C. (Nile Clarke), 1918-1943. |
    Kalsu, Bob, 1945-1970. | Tillman, Pat, 1976-2004.
Classification: LCC GV697.A1 C86 2017 (print) |
    LCC GV697.A1 (ebook) | DDC 796.0922 [B] —dc23
LC record available at https://lccn.loc.gov/2017000915

To freedom lovers far and wide,
past, present, and future,
especially Sugar Nup, Birdie,
Rooney, DeLa, Popper, and Mae Mae.

Contents

Acknowledgments

THANK YOU TO THE UNIVERSITY OF IOWA LIBRARIES (Nile Kinnick collection), to Princeton University, its Seeley G. Mudd Manuscript Library in particular (Hobey Baker collection), and to Columbia University and its archives library (information on Hamilton Fish II). I drew upon many other libraries for this project, including the University of Chicago, Purdue University, DePaul University, the University of Nevada Las Vegas, and the University of Utah. Thank you. The opportunity to interview Jan Kalsu, wife of the late Bob Kalsu, was deeply moving. I am grateful for it. I am also thankful to have interviewed a great-grandnephew of Hobey Baker, Christo Morse, who I met with in Manhattan and who shared family letters that Hobey wrote as a boy to his mother. Thank you as well to the Pat Tillman Foundation, the City of Las Vegas and Rough Rider Memorial Collection, and to the Utah Division of State History. A slew of folks helped edit the manuscript: the good folks at Texas A&M University Press, Janet Butler, Eric Furman, Justin Smith, Chris Dodge, Christy Cunningham, and more. Thank you all. Thank you to the various historians who took my calls and emails to offer insight into this project. Much appreciation to the journalists, embedded or otherwise, and authors whose work I have drawn upon for *Fallen Stars*. Finally, what an honor to spend time with the men featured in this book: Hamilton "Ham" Fish II, Hobart "Hobey" Baker, Nile Kinnick, James Robert "Bob" Kalsu, and Patrick Tillman. Thank you.

★ *Fallen Stars*

Introduction

IN THE SPRING OF 2002, motivated by the 9/11 terrorist attacks, football stalwart Patrick Daniel Tillman turned down a multimillion-dollar National Football League (NFL) contract and instead joined the US Army. Two years later, he died serving his country in the mountains of Afghanistan. In the process, he became an American icon.

Sports Illustrated put Tillman on its cover. His NFL jerseys sold in record fashion.[1] Five years after Tillman's death, author Jon Krakauer published an authorized biography of him that was a best seller.

People across the country and the world have wondered what motivated Tillman to leave the NFL for the army, marveled at the public's response to his death, and tried to figure out what his life reflected about America.

Given America's love for sports and the importance of heroes, the Tillman story made me wonder about not only him but other standout athletes who died in military service to their country. Who were they, and what were their lives like? How did the American media respond to their deaths? What might it all say about America, then and now?

This book, then, captures the lives and times of five war-hero athletes: Hamilton "Ham" Fish, Hobart "Hobey" Baker, Nile Kinnick, James Robert Kalsu, and Patrick Tillman, all of whom died while serving in the US military. These men's lives are filled with drama, sacrifice, and jaw-dropping physical feats. Their stories give us a kaleidoscopic picture of America over the course of more than one hundred years. Through these men, we learn about the wars that America has participated in, the values that Americans have celebrated, and what it has meant to be an American hero.

Celebrated historian Roderick Nash maintained that figuring out what captured the enthusiasm of ordinary people at a given period in history, examining what has been popular, and probing how people's tastes in heroes have changed can tell us "more about the climate of opinion in any era than does standard political history."[2] *Fallen Stars* strives to better see America through these five men.

All five athletes featured in *Fallen Stars* played football. That didn't happen by initial project design, but in a way it makes sense. Baseball might claim to be the national pastime, but football, as sports historian Michael Oriard has argued, counts as America's "war game." Just consider terminology: from referring to the "generalship" of quarterbacks in the 1890s to the more modern use of the phrase "war in the trenches." There's the blitz and the bomb. It happens in reverse, too. Consider World War II's Operation Goalpost or Vietnam's Operation Linebacker.[3]

Connections between war and sports, especially football, reveal themselves when looking at all five athletes in *Fallen Stars*, most notably in the cases of Baker, Kinnick, and Tillman. (During the Spanish-American War some Rough Riders generated commentary on their football backgrounds, but most of the attention on Fish's athletic prowess highlighted his rowing and boxing, although he played class football at Columbia. In the case of Kalsu, his wartime death simply didn't generate the coverage one might expect. But thirty years later it did.)

Stephen Crane, embedded as a journalist with Hamilton Fish and the rest of the Rough Riders during the Spanish-American War, once said he could write about war because he'd written about sports. On the eve of World War I, Hobey Baker participated in perhaps the first-ever military flyover at a college football game. In his wartime diary, he wrote about the similarities between preparing for and competing in a big football game at Princeton and preparing for and participating in a firefight in the sky. The combination of his football exploits and willingness to take to the skies riveted folks. In 1939, Kinnick, a pilot as well, attracted more media attention than any other college athlete, and his gridiron exploits figured prominently in the coverage of him during the war. Later, more clearly than any other athlete in American history, the in-depth coverage of Tillman's life and wartime service captured the connection between war, sport, and American culture.

One might ask why a focus on fallen war-hero athletes, and why these five? Because here we have a century's worth of heroes who faced the fears and uncertainties that come with life, and in doing so gave the ultimate sacrifice. The men in *Fallen Stars* weren't perfect. But they were strivers, men who represented the hopes of their fellow citizens—men who believed that some justice, some meaning, or, at the very least, some recognizable order could be brought to things. And their sacrifices have reverberated through time.

They were traditional, carrying with them the values of citizenship, honor, courage, and justice. Yet they were forward-thinking, living in times in which scientific knowledge steadily improved and society steadily changed. They were romantic and pragmatic. These men radiated, then, the continuity and change that has marked American culture since the country's inception.

HAMILTON "HAM" FISH JR.

In the late 1800s Hamilton "Ham" Fish registered with the American public in a big way. He was tall, strong, and handsome, a member of one of America's most distinguished families, and one of America's most eligible bachelors. He was also a great athlete. In 1895, in front of thousands of spectators, he led Columbia to an unlikely victory at the famed Poughkeepsie crew race. He played class football at Columbia and was considered the best boxer in his 1895 class. A romantic and Nathaniel Hawthorne fan, he joined Theodore Roosevelt's now legendary Rough Riders in 1898. Months later, out in front in Cuba, Ham Fish became the first Rough Rider killed in combat in the Spanish-American War.

Through Ham Fish we see a patriotic country that valued courage, fought wars on foot and horseback, and celebrated both the rugged West and the gilded East. We see a country that wanted to feel unified across economic classes and saw Ham Fish as a chance to show unity. And we learn about how this war put America on a path toward global prominence, a role that brought with it new kinds of challenges.

HOBART "HOBEY" BAKER

There was no NFL until 1922, no National Basketball Association (NBA) until 1946, and no widespread sports television coverage until the 1950s. But sports did attract considerable attention in the early 1900s, and there certainly were sports heroes. Hobey Baker, perhaps his era's most famous athlete, demonstrates this. Known for selling out collegiate football and hockey stadiums, he remains the only person inducted into the NCAA's football *and* hockey halls of fame.[4]

Baker not only excelled, he played cleanly. Throughout his entire hockey career at Princeton, he reportedly registered just *one* penalty. After a hard football game or hockey match, he was known to go into the opposing team's locker room and shake hands. The press loved it.[5] To them, he embodied the Victorian model for manliness just as America was transitioning from a Victorian-minded culture to a modern one driven largely by consumerism and entertainment.

However, as readers will see—through his torrid love affair with a Newport heiress during World War I and through his penchant for risk-taking as a fighter pilot, which factored into his untimely death in a plane crash shortly before returning from the war—Hobey was both traditional and modern, layered in ways that were not captured by the press.

NILE KINNICK

In June 1943, America and the world looked quite different than a couple of decades prior. The United States had been attacked at Pearl Harbor, was embroiled in World War II and developing the atomic bomb, and had become the world's far and away leading power. Radio coverage had swept the nation, knitting together more tightly a national popular culture. Commercial airlines and television were emerging, in tune with the surging popularity of major sports, especially college football.

In *King Football*, college football historian Michael Oriard stated that while the 1920s have been known as the Golden Age of Sports, the 1930s "are more truly the Gold Age of Football." By the end of this decade local radio stations all over the country had started to broadcast college football games each week. In many communities, "football was just about the only thing to be found on the radio dial on Saturday afternoon." In the 1930s the *Saturday Evening Post* and *Collier's* began to publish regular fall football articles. Hollywood tapped into football's popularity, too. If you went to the movies on an autumn evening, football had a good chance of being featured in the newsreel footage, which was a staple feature of going to a show in the 1930s, a record-setting decade for movie attendance. Football, Oriard wrote, could work as "shorthand to establish the heroic masculine character."[6]

In 1939, the year Germany invaded Poland, plunging a chunk of the globe into World War II, perhaps America's most celebrated sportsman was Heisman Trophy winner Nile Kinnick of the Iowa Hawkeyes. That year, Kinnick, president of his class and a Phi Beta Kappa student, led a group of unheralded Hawkeyes from Big Ten bottom-feeders to national sensations known as the "Iron Men." In a time of economic woe and global military crisis, people celebrated those Hawkeyes. It was as if they were asking, "If the Hawkeyes can do it, why can't we? Why can't America?"

In 1943, while serving as a pilot in the US Navy, Kinnick died in a plane crash at sea. Memorials poured in. To this day, Kinnick graces the special coins used at the start of every Big Ten football game. Iowa's football stadium bears his name.

Kinnick is the only Heisman winner to lose his life in World War II. His legend has become such that it doesn't just represent one man's sacrifice. The tributes, the books, the articles about him, reflect the celebration of a generation which, even as times change and issues shift, held values that still resound.

JAMES ROBERT "BOB" KALSU

Twenty-seven years after Kinnick died at sea, Bob Kalsu of the Buffalo Bills died in the Vietnam War—a war that could hardly have been more dissimilar to World War II, both in how it came about and how the country reacted to it, especially by the time of Kalsu's death.

Kalsu was the only professional American athlete to die fighting in the Vietnam War. Just a couple of years prior, he'd completed a stellar rookie campaign with the Buffalo Bills, earning the team's Rookie of the Year award. A year before that, as an offensive tackle at Oklahoma, he had capped his senior season with an Orange Bowl victory over Tennessee and taken home All-American honors.

Of all professional athletes, only six football players and a bowler saw active duty in the war. Kalsu, even though the Tet Offensive had taken place a year earlier and public sentiment had turned increasingly against the war, didn't try the Army Reserve or National Guard route common in his time. "I gave 'em my word. I'm gonna do it," he told his teammate John Frantz.[7]

Kalsu died defending a base that the US Army would abandon two days later. The battle that took his life marks the last major military engagement between the United States and North Vietnam in the frustrating, convoluted history of the Vietnam War. By this time, July 1970, the United States media and its citizens had largely turned against the war. Unlike the other athletes featured in this book, the media barely even covered Kalsu's death. It's as if everyone wanted to forget the war even happened.

PATRICK "PAT" TILLMAN

Unlike Kalsu, after his 2004 wartime death, Pat Tillman figured prominently in headlines, and his name stayed there for years. On 31 March 2007, readers of MSN.com were greeted with a front-page picture of Tillman. ESPN.com carried a Tillman headline, too. If you were an ESPN.com subscriber, you could read a three-part series about Tillman with the titles "An Un-American Tragedy," "Playing with Friendly Fire," and "Death of an American Ideal."[8] His story moved people, and his death showed the ability of technological advancements to give common Americans easy access to an array of information.

While both edges of the political aisle tried to claim Tillman, something about him struck a common chord among a wide swath of Americans. Regardless of party, Americans respected his volunteerism and physical prowess, much like with the coverage of Fish, Baker, and Kinnick. His intellectual curiosity and willingness to question American leaders registered with many Americans, too, things that in earlier times would not have been probed as deeply by the media. The widespread admiration Americans expressed for Tillman suggests he came as close as most anyone of late to being an authentic, universally admired American hero, not an easy thing in these tumultuous times.

We can see America—and much more, if we look closely—in the lives and valiant deaths of Ham Fish, Hobey Baker, Nile Kinnick, Bob Kalsu, and Pat Tillman.

ONE

Hamilton "Ham" Fish Jr.

1

IN 1898 IN SAN ANTONIO, shortly before breaking training camp for the Spanish-American War, future president Theodore Roosevelt and his famed Rough Riders staged a drilling exhibition. It was a hot day in May—Texas hot—yet thousands of San Antonians had come out to watch. They wanted to see in person the Rough Riders, this motley group of men who had animated the nation.

With the crowd looking on and the sun scorching the dry ground, the Rough Riders lined up at the bottom of a slight hill, looking strong and rough-hewn atop their horses. When all were ready, Lt. Col. Roosevelt ordered them to charge ahead, and the Rough Riders hurtled forward in a powerful surge. But just as the impressive sight was unfolding, a young Mexican girl scampered out in front of the rushing column. Realizing what she'd done, she looked up at the horses coming toward her and froze. The horrified crowd gasped, expecting the worst. Terror struck the charging Rough Riders. Getting their horses to stop before trampling her seemed impossible. Hoping for a miracle, they yanked their reins up with all their might.

One Rough Rider, however, took a different approach. Rather than carry out a futile attempt to pull up, he spurred his horse ahead even faster to get out in front. Hundredths of seconds separated the young girl from death, and yet, with his horse in full gallop, this man reached down and pulled her up to safety, making an extraordinary rescue look easy.

For a moment or two, the shocked onlookers were silent. Once it fully registered with them what had happened, an approving roar erupted from the crowd. Soon "the save" was the talk of the town, indeed the nation, as newspapers across America ran stories celebrating it.[1]

★ AS IF SCRIPTED, the man who saved the young girl that day was one of America's best-known bachelors, Hamilton "Ham" Fish Jr. A member of one of America's most distinguished families, he had led Columbia University crew to an unlikely title over the University of Pennsylvania and Cornell at the famed Poughkeepsie race in 1895. He was known to box. And, as widely reported, he had passed up "the easy life" to volunteer for Roosevelt's Riders.

Tall, broad-shouldered, and blue-eyed, with light, curly hair, Ham Fish wasn't just known for his volunteerism, athletic pursuits, and distinguished pedigree, however. He also had a rowdy streak that got him into fights with "coachmen, cooks, and policemen." He was a restless man with a romantic bent. The press might describe him, within the same paragraph, as among the best-natured of men, with scores of friends, and yet as someone whose "prowess was displayed on several occasions while he was in this city [New York] in fist fights which he had, in most of which he was victorious." In short, he was "one of the boys" in an era when manhood was in ways returning to its virile, rugged roots.[2]

As fate would have it, in June 1898 Ham Fish also became the first Rough Rider killed in action in the Spanish-American War. Just a few days removed from his twenty-fifth birthday and almost exactly a month after he saved the young Mexican girl in San Antonio, he was killed by a bullet on a dangerous trail to Santiago, Cuba. That bullet, had Ham not positioned himself to block it, would have likely killed a poor, unknown, part-Cherokee volunteer from Muskogee Territory, Ed Culver. Instead, it took Ham and ricocheted into Culver's shoulder.

Across the nation, newspapers carried front-page reports of Ham Fish's death. People were fascinated by his story. A member of one of America's most elite families, an athletic standout and Columbia man, had died in voluntary service to his country during a war that the public broadly supported, alongside a group of soldiers the likes of which the nation had never seen, and while saving the life of a man with virtually no worldly possessions or status.[3] It was indeed the stuff of legend.

In reporting his death, local papers often ran wire stories. The *Logansport Journal* of Indiana ran a story that highlighted Ham's athleticism, handsomeness, and patriotism. His sacrifice, the article asserted, showed that there was class unity in America. The *Weekly Gazette and*

Stockman out of Reno, Nevada, ran a front-page letter that credited him with further glorifying "a name that shines in American history," while Ohio's *Republican News* printed an article titled "Patriots Form His Family Tree," in which it was written, "It may be said of this family that its sons are typical of all that is best in American manhood."[4]

The Fish family really did enjoy an illustrious past. Fish's great-grandfather, Nicholas Fish, was a Revolutionary War hero, a well-known Federalist, and had married a Stuyvesant—one of the earliest and most formative families in the history of New York City. Nicholas Fish was also good friends with Alexander Hamilton. In fact, you can credit this friendship for the Fish tradition of naming their sons Hamilton. Ham's grandfather was named Hamilton, and during his career Grandpa Fish was the governor of New York, a US senator, and the US secretary of state, from 1867 to 1875, under President Ulysses S. Grant.[5] The Fish name was

Sketch of Hamilton Fish the Rough Rider, surrounded by well-known family members: his great-grandfather Nicholas Fish, American Revolutionary War soldier, first adjutant general of New York, and friend of Alexander Hamilton; Ham Fish's grandfather Hamilton Fish, governor of New York, a US senator, and secretary of state under President Grant; and Nicholas Fish Jr., Ham's father, former US minister to Belgium and member of the Harriman and Co. banking house. This sketch ran in papers across the United States after Ham Fish's death in Cuba.

right up there with Astor. This helped make Ham Fish one of America's most eligible bachelors in the late 1890s, and it helps explain why his death generated such attention.

Following Ham's death, the *Boston Herald* maintained that, the night after he'd saved the young girl in San Antonio, the girl's mother sought him out to give him a small, pewter-based image of St. Joseph, which her daughter had worn around her neck. The child had received the image as a baptismal gift, and it was said to protect against danger, particularly of a violent kind. As the story goes, the mother told Ham Fish not to lose the image or he would be more vulnerable than before receiving it. While still in training in San Antonio, however, Fish either lost the pendant or, as one story has it, threw it into nearby brush one night. (Fish, who was Protestant, wouldn't have venerated St. Joseph as a Catholic did.)

Regardless, shortly after losing possession of the St. Joseph pendant, the *Herald* story maintains that Ham talked about it to a group of Rough Riders while they unwound from the rigors of camp at a bar. Musing on the warning the girl's mother had given him, Ham is reported to have said, "I have never amounted to much in this world, and I suppose it is well I should be killed in battle. My family will have the consolation that at least I died honorably."[6]

And yet it is rather ironic that a Fish became the first Rough Rider killed in combat the Spanish-American War—not just because the name was so well known, but because as secretary of state, Ham's grandfather, fending off intense pressure from interventionists, had helped keep the United States *out* of war in Cuba in 1873. Twenty-five years later his grandson, motivated not by empire-building but by humanitarianism, honor, and a vague notion of battlefield glory, would die there in a war that in its aftermath would become associated with American expansion as the United States gained the Philippines, Puerto Rico, and Guam, annexed Hawaii, and became an imperial power with strategic bases ranging from the Caribbean to Asian Pacific trade routes.

2

STRIKING SIMILARITIES exist between turn-of-the-nineteenth-century America and contemporary America. Then, as now, the US political scene was dominated by two parties, the Democrats and Republicans. And, like today, Americans loved their sports—in fact, through them they found heroes to rally around. People, much as they do today, also sensed something special about the American experiment, and this sense brought with it a marked optimism, a willingness to take risks, and fierce individuality.

Still, the differences are pronounced. In the late 1800s, life expectancy stretched a mere forty-seven years, and the US population stood at just seventy-five million. The "flying machine," or "aeroplane," was a figment of human imagination, and Ford's Model T did not exist. Hollywood didn't make movies, and a vast majority of homes did not have a bathtub.

In rural areas in the late 1800s, with mechanization leading to low crop prices, farmers struggled to get ahead. In urban areas to which people flocked, clean water, sufficient housing, and good wages were hard to find. In New York City's Lower East Side, for example, dumbbell tenements—named for their shape—with whole families crammed into one room became all too common.

Yet the opulence of American elites at this time was staggering—whether in Manhattan, where Ham's parents lived, or in Newport, Rhode Island, where Ham's aunt and uncle, Stuyvesant and Mamie Fish, had a mansion and where the staging of a summer gala could cost hundreds of thousands of dollars. In 1897, for instance, with America mired in an economic Depression, Mr. and Mrs. Bradley Martin staged a ball at New York's Waldorf-Astoria, decorated to resemble the French palace at

Versailles, at the cost of over $300,000 (well over $7 million in today's dollars). At one of many legendary parties hosted by the family of William Astor, guests relaxed after coffee by smoking cigarettes rolled in hundred-dollar bills. To regular Americans, this seemed unfathomable. To the super-rich, though, such outlandish displays of wealth signaled status, as did being named in Louis Keller's *Social Register*, which used as its template the roughly 400 people—known as "Mrs. Astor's 400"—who would receive invitations to Mrs. William Astor's fabled "Patriarch Balls." The families on Keller's register were the types of families that the Fishes had run with since before Ham was born.

The excess, the lavishness, and the opulence, however, created a backlash among some elites. As the vibrancy of cities grew, as technological advancements transformed daily life and "democratized" society, young elites like Ham Fish yearned for authenticity more than exclusivity.

Related to this, odd as it might seem, Ham Fish saw it as a kind of badge honor that he did not actually graduate from Columbia in 1895, despite having spent the previous four years attending the school. He did not need a diploma from an elite university—at a time, when only 2 percent of Americans went to college—to show he had worth.

★ IT IS DIFFICULT TO TRACK HAM in the years leading up to the 1898 Spanish-American War; what is clear is that Ham Fish's legend mushroomed on 24 June 1895—shortly before he left Columbia just short of a degree—when he helped steer Columbia crew to that upset victory at Poughkeepsie. By the time of this dramatic performance, the Cuban insurrection that would eventually pull him into war was well under way, but it was not registering much with most Americans. People, in Poughkeepsie at least, were focused on the big race.

With the sun shining down, that race-day afternoon in Poughkeepsie rolled along smoothly, much like the Hudson itself, as thousands of racegoers leisurely descended upon the river's banks in preparation for the contest between the shells from Columbia, Penn, and Cornell. The summer scene that day reflected crew's striking popularity, a time when the sport's big races were covered by newspapers across the land and the sport's stars were known nationwide.

As race time neared later in the afternoon, a sizable portion of the thousands that had filtered in had found spots on the river's west bank to sit and watch the race. Space was tight, indicated by the fact that a group of clever children took to climbing atop a church to catch the action. Across the river from the church, hundreds upon hundreds more piled on top of a long observation train, which had purposefully come to a stop upon a rail line that hugged the Hudson at Krum Elbow, the race's starting point.

Although the day had dawned nicely and provided plenty of sun into the afternoon, shortly before the race was set to begin, the wind whipped up, clouds rolled in, accompanied by thunder and lightning, and heavy rain started pouring down, causing a considerable delay.[1] Most of the spectators, not prepared for rainfall, took cover. But a group of collegiate fans from Columbia, perched atop train car 11, took the downpour in stride, singing and joking as they got soaked. These students even had the nerve to rib millionaire John Jacob Astor IV as he arrived at the race by way of an "electric launch," a commercially viable electric motorboat that had debuted a couple of years earlier at the Chicago World's Fair. Like the drenched students from Columbia, Mr. Astor (the same Astor scion that would die in 1912 aboard the *Titanic*) found a spot upon the train to watch Ham Fish and the other rowers compete.[2]

At 6:53 in the evening, under a thick haze, the race finally got under

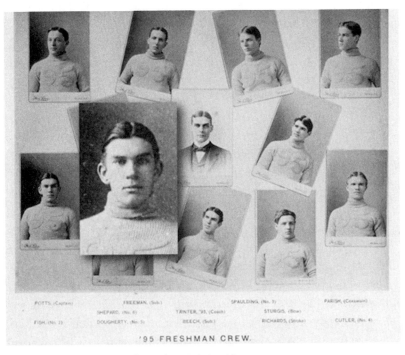

POTTS, (Captain)   FREEMAN, (Sub.)   SPAULDING, (No. 7)   PARISH, (Coxswain)
                    SHEPARD, (No. 6)   TANTER, '93, (Coach)   STURGIS, (Bow)
FISH, (No. 2)   DOUGHERTY, (No. 5)   BEECH, (Sub.)   RICHARDS, (Stroke)   CUTLER, (No. 4)

'95 FRESHMAN CREW.

Columbia yearbook image of Hamilton Fish Jr. with crew mates.

way. The first mile finished with all three boats virtually even. Columbia gained during the early portion of mile two, even with "wind against
tide" causing the oarsmen to splash. Fish's vaunted strength helped pull
Columbia ahead in this rough stretch and ultimately powered the Blue and
White to a five-length win, a win that few prognosticators had foreseen,
and which set off raucous celebrations among Columbia's supporters.[3]

Indeed, in short order, 500 or so Columbia fans paraded down Poughkeepsie's main streets. They set up a base of celebratory operations at the
Nelson House Inn, and these Columbia "boys," as Pulitzer's *World* would
explain the following day, proceeded to give Poughkeepsie a "shaking
up" the likes of which the sedate old town had never experienced.[4]

Crewmen from Columbia's last championship squad of 1886 were
on hand, as were Walter B. Peet and Joe Lawrence of the 1884 and '85
squads. Lawrence was credited with drumming up a brass band that
played riffs on "college airs" and popular fare, helping to make the night
"fully hideous." *The World* reported that the "rumpus" was full of fireworks and general mayhem, and it taxed the policemen mightily.[5]

Ham Fish, it turns out, celebrated a little too much. Before sunup,
he'd find himself in a Poughkeepsie pen for brawling. His father Nicholas, a Manhattan banker, was summoned. Eventually, Mr. Fish would
send money upriver to help cover the costs of his son's rowdiness. Recall-
ing the scenario decades later, a cousin of Ham's—who also happened to
be a member of the US Congress from 1920 to 1945—wrote:

> He [Ham] was as tall as I am, but in those days they were a little wilder,
> and he went up to my district when they won the races at Poughkeep-
> sie and arrested the police force and tore up the bar, cost his father two
> or three thousand dollars, and they [citizens in that area of New York]
> always thought it was me. I don't know whether it won me votes or not.[6]

The Poughkeepsie arrest might have contributed to Fish not getting
a degree from Columbia. He was already known, however, for giving
"little attention" to his studies, even though he did so much else while
at Columbia.[7] In addition to his four years of crew, he served for a year
as the vice-president of his class, played freshman football, managed
Columbia's musical society, and was a member of its Fencers' Club.[8]
He joined two literary societies as well: the Peithologian Society, formed

in 1877 to rival Columbia's hallmark literary society of the nineteenth century, the Philolexian, of which Ham became a member as a senior.[9] Given all that, it seems odd that he wouldn't finish.

At the same time, though, this was an era when people debated whether college was necessary. For Ham, who wanted to bridge the gap between the gilded life and the lives of regular Americans, *not* graduating could show that the elite didn't need special honors to separate themselves. In the 1895 Columbia yearbook, Ham's fellow classmates ribbed him for coming perilously close to actually graduating—as if this were something to avoid. There was concern among "college men," as Roosevelt once expressed in a speech at Harvard, that universities, if allowed, could turn men into mere critics and opinion-makers by making them cliquish, "oversensitive," and "overeducated"—in short, mollycoddles, left without the courage to act.[10]

While it's not clear exactly why Fish did not graduate, within several months of the Poughkeepsie race he set out west, bound for Utah, to work on the railroads. He chose this over working in the banking or financial sectors, which he surely could've gotten into through his family's connections (Ham's father worked for the banking firm of Harriman & Co.). Rather than sit behind a desk poring over bond spreads and the like, Ham chose an industry that would allow him to work with his hands and be outdoors. And the railroad industry was booming. Rail titans like Cornelius Vanderbilt—and, to a lesser degree, Ham's uncle Stuyvesant Fish, who presided over the Illinois Central—were some of the era's most powerful men. Rail work had a kind of rugged allure.

Ham arrived in Salt Lake City, Utah, in the fall of 1895, having drawn on his uncle Stuyvesant's standing to help him find work with the Rio Grande Western railroad company. In the ensuing months, he worked in just about every capacity that a railroad man could: in the freight house, the local shops, and as a brakeman on the main line. He was even sent to Provo Canyon for a bit to carry chain for surveyors. He didn't much go for that, though—too much standing around—so he returned to Salt Lake.[11]

The railroad that Ham worked for was a standard-gauge offshoot of the Denver and Rio Grande Western Railway, which made up a portion of a large family of lines that together were simply called the "Rio Grande." This collection of lines was known for majestically rip-roaring through mountain passes, as evidenced by its tagline, "Through the Rockies, Not

Around Them." In particular, the Rio Grande's Tennessee Pass, which cut through the Rocky Mountains in central Colorado, was one of the awe-inspiring engineering feats of the nineteenth century.

★ NOW, IF YOU LET THE *New York World* tell it, Fish traveled to Utah alone, eager to make it on his own, even though he could have gotten a berth from his uncle to travel in style. The *World* also claimed that Ham didn't use his uncle's influence to land a position in Utah; that instead he found the work independently. But Salt Lake City's *Daily Tribune* did what it could to refute this by stating plainly that Ham Fish arrived in Salt Lake with letters from his uncle, flush with cash, and with several trunks of clothes.

Soon after arriving, Fish cut a salient figure. Salt Lake's *Daily Tribune* would write later that his "powerful physique" and fine looks, along with his makings of a soldier and "college-bred" background, helped him become the center of a "collegial" group of new friends in Utah.[12]

As it were, he'd come to an area, settled in 1847 by Brigham Young and his fellow Mormon pioneers, brimming with economic possibility. It had been only twenty-six years since the final spike connecting the Transcontinental Railroad was pounded into Utah ground, a mere forty miles from downtown Salt Lake. The Transcontinental catapulted the growth of Utah's mining industry and attracted a more varied lot to the predominantly Mormon state.

Still, in the 1890s, Utah remained quite exotic to the average American, what with its western location and Mormon background. Not until 1896, the year after Ham came to Salt Lake City, did Utah become America's forty-fifth state. And it was only seven years before this that the Mormon Church had officially ended the practice of polygamy. Thus, it's quite consistent with Ham Fish's personality that he made his way there and found a group of like-minded adventurers to cavort with.

As fate had it, though, even with all the economic possibility, Fish ended up staying in Utah for only about a year. Exactly why he lasted such a short time there is a bit murky. Again, if you got your news from the *New York World*, you'd have thought he returned east because he injured a finger in a rail accident and needed to get the finger amputated in New York. But Salt Lake's *Daily Tribune* reported that Utah's Dr. Samuel Pinkerton had amputated the digit in Salt Lake and that Fish was "perfectly well before he left this city."[13]

In fact, according to Salt Lake's *Daily Tribune*, a few days after Dr. Pinkerton amputated the finger, Ham went to a saloon and got quite drunk. While at the saloon, so the story goes, at least two guys offered to "dope" him—apparently a reference to morphine, which at the time was the world's most abused narcotic painkiller and was not a controlled substance in America (not until 1914, with the passage of the Harrison anti-narcotics act, would morphine become controlled). Fish, as reported in the press, didn't take kindly to these fellas' overtures and, although his injured hand was in a sling, "picked up a chair with his other hand and smashed one man over the head." The other fellow responded by grabbing a beer bottle and successfully chucking it at Fish's head. Ultimately, Fish was forced outside the bar, where he took a seat on the sidewalk.

While Fish was sitting on this sidewalk, a policeman, Sergeant Wire, happened by and tapped him on the shoulder. Fish, inebriated, turned toward the copper and said, "Don't you hurt my hand or I'll tell Pinkerton on you," presumably meaning Dr. Pinkerton.[14] However, apparently Sergeant Wire took this to mean that Ham was threatening him by claiming to be a member of the nation's leading private law enforcement agency, the Pinkerton National Detective Agency. Not in a trifling mood, Wire saw the reference to Pinkerton as an attempt by Ham to pull rank.

A different version of this encounter holds that a hotheaded Fish did indeed tell Sergeant Wire that he was a Pinkerton, and also told Sergeant Wire, "I'll have your head, too, before this thing is over." However it went down, Fish went to jail.

Late the next morning, Ham was released, only to get arrested again a few hours later.[15] This arrest occurred when Ham, walking past the Bower residence, encountered a dog that came running at him, barking loudly. Now, Ham was usually an animal lover. He'd cherished his childhood dog, Charlie. As a Rough Rider training in San Antonio he worked fondly with his cavalry mount. And also while training in San Antonio, he pushed through a crowd to break up a dog fight, then took the smaller dog back to his tent, cared for his wounds, and gave him a hearty supper. That dog became a kind of mascot for the Rough Riders. But on this night in Salt Lake City, he thought someone had set the dog after him, and he got so mad about it that he decided to put his head through a side door of the Bower home and unleash a tirade on whoever was in earshot. A maidservant took the brunt of it, and she found Fish's language so appalling that she called headquarters. Ham tried to hide, but eventually two detectives fished him out of a bush in the Bower yard and took him back to the station. The erratic nature of this episode makes you wonder if Ham actually did let the men at the bar "dope" him, and then either became upset because what they gave him wasn't what he expected or he reacted adversely to it, or both.[16]

Shortly after this unfortunate string of events, Fish traveled back east. By the time he did, it's fair to surmise, a lot of folks in Salt Lake City were happy to see him go. But in a special cover article after Fish's death, the *Daily Tribune* did adopt Ham as one of Salt Lake's own, even if his "escapades," as the paper put it, had been quite numerous while living there. As the paper explained, Ham had made many friends in Utah, and "now that he has met death in fighting for his country nothing will be remembered of him possibly save his good qualities, and they were many."[17]

3

IN THE LATTER PART OF 1896, about the time Ham Fish left Utah and returned to Manhattan, that year's presidential election captured the country's attention. Republican William McKinley, Ohio native and Union soldier in the Civil War, ran against the Democratic Party's populist upstart, William Jennings Bryan of Nebraska, who, at thirty-six years old, remains the youngest major presidential nominee in US history. As an indication of the attention the country gave this election, an astounding 79.3 percent of eligible voters cast a ballot.

Although the political parties of the two candidates are around in name today, they looked a lot different in 1896. Most striking—and in one of the more peculiar developments in US political history—in the late 1800s, the Democrats and Republicans drew their constituencies from basically the opposite parts of America from which they would in the late twentieth and early twenty-first centuries. The Democrat Bryan won virtually every southern state as well as all of the Great Plains states, while Republican McKinley took the Northeast and California and Oregon. This meant that McKinley won twenty-three states to Bryan's twenty-two, but McKinley won a wider margin of the country's most populous states, giving him a 271–176 Electoral College victory.[1]

Historians tend to consider the political scene during the latter third of the 1800s as resting more on personality and patronage than substance—except for the 1896 election. The economic panic of 1893 had wracked the country for several years, and America's continual shift from pastoral living to a more urbane and industrial lifestyle helped lead to a substantive election. This was accompanied, though, by a tendency to view the country's political divides in a grimmer light. As historian Edward Ranson put it, a climate close to national crisis emerged in 1896 to the extent that "men of power and property even pondered the likelihood of a revolution."[2]

Monetary policy, dry as it might seem, was a key issue. Analysis of the 1890 Sherman Silver Purchase Act, a law that called for American money to be redeemable by silver as well as gold (and which many blamed for the 1893 economic panic), caused fissures within both parties, particularly with the Democrats.

Generally, the monetary issue broke along sectional lines: those in the North and East, where manufacturing and finance reigned, wanted American money to be backed only by gold. This would keep inflation down. Folks in the agrarian South and West wanted both silver and gold to underpin the dollar so as to bring about some inflation, which would increase the price of their crops.[3]

Those in favor of bimetallism agreed with Bryan when he railed against corporate interests and tried to stand up for the debt-burdened agrarian. His "Cross of Gold" speech, considered among the greatest in American political history, was given at the Democratic convention in Chicago; in it, Bryan proclaimed, "We shall answer their demands for a gold standard by saying to them, you shall not press down upon the brow of labor this crown of thorns. You shall not crucify mankind upon a cross of gold."[4]

Bryan's message was welcomed by a lot of Democrats because the gap between the super-rich and the poor had widened dramatically, and farmers faced high costs to transport their low-cost goods along rail lines. Meanwhile, the gulf between labor and management in the industrial realm had remained vast: just two examples of this were the outcome of the 1892 Homestead strike, during which iron and steelworkers were upset that management wouldn't even recognize their union, yet alone negotiate with it; and the outcome of the 1894 Pullman rail workers' strike, which also ended in defeat.[5] Still, there was a split among Democrats over monetary policy. Critics of Bryan worried that the Republicans were right to claim that if America turned to silver, the value of the dollar would halve and inflation would skyrocket.

As for the moderate McKinley, with his seeming moral uprightness, his prior Civil War service, and his politically beneficial Ohio background, he represented a Republican Party that was less divided over the silver question. Sure, some western Republicans supported bimetallism.

However, as the election neared, a protective tariff supported by manu-facturers in the North and East looked like a more palatable alternative to Republicans than continuing to bicker over monetary issues. So the party (within which the Fish family for many decades had played a sig-nificant role) rallied around McKinley on the tariff, and McKinley won a hard-fought contest. It was under a McKinley administration, then, that Ham Fish would go to war in Cuba less than two years after the election.

Not that Ham Fish (or most anyone else, for that matter) would have predicted in 1896 that he'd wind up in Cuba. In the fall of 1896, Fish was trying to find himself, settling back into a New York life, reconnecting with the New York social scene. He took a job in finance and was a mem-ber of the Union League and the St. Nicholas Society, both of which give insight into his life and times.

The Union League was founded in 1863, and its selective member-ship, heavily Republican, has included the like of Ulysses S. Grant, Teddy Roosevelt, J. Pierpont Morgan, and John D. Rockefeller. Originally focused on supporting the Union in the Civil War, the Union League in subsequent years helped found the Metropolitan Museum of Art and fund the building of the Stature of Liberty's pedestal, and it played key roles in getting the Lincoln Monument constructed in Lincoln Square and Grant's Tomb built, and in the founding of the American Red Cross.[6] In the mid-1890s, at its headquarters on Fifth Avenue and East Thirty-ninth Street, it maintained an active, elite social scene. Members like Ham Fish enjoyed access to wood-paneled rooms, leather furniture, fine liqueurs, thick cigar smoke, business chatter, and extreme exclusiv-ity—including the option to stay the night inconspicuously.[7] In short, it was the Gilded Age's most exclusive social club, and it functioned as an epicenter of social activity for the society man.

The other social club to which Ham belonged, the St. Nicholas Soci-ety, was created in 1835 by Washington Irving and others as a way to cel-ebrate the history of New York and to cultivate camaraderie, as well as to generate a lively but good-natured exchange of ideas.[8] As with the Union League, membership was exclusive and carried considerable prestige.[9]

While Ham maintained a privileged place within the Manhattan social scene—access to fine dining, membership in heady clubs, and elite friends—he does seem to have been facing a crossroads as the New Year arrived. His earlier fights and general wildness could have been blamed on his youthfulness, but by late 1897 he'd been out of Columbia for over two years and his path still lacked clarity. It makes sense to expect, then, that during this time he underwent a period of maturation, perhaps a figurative and literal sobering up.

Yet the occasional dustup continued to entangle him. One afternoon about this time, for instance, Fish and a friend were riding a standing-room-only streetcar near 34th Street. Fish happened to be standing next to a man who was about his height but heavier. In front of this man was a striking, well-heeled woman who was upset by something. It didn't take long for Fish to figure out that the man he was standing next to had said something to cause the woman offense.

"You ought to be licked!" Fish declared.

"What's the matter with you?" the man replied.

Fish suggested the pair exit the car to find out, which prompted the affronted woman to say, "It's all right, young man. Please don't quarrel on my account."

A conductor, who had worked his way through the crowd to see to the cause of the commotion, asked about matters.

"This cur has insulted the lady there, and he's got to get off this car right now," Fish explained.

The streetcar came to a stop. As its doors opened, Ham dragged the "cur" by his collar, threw him into the street, and jumped off after him. Fish's friend disembarked the train at that time, too, and on the street a crowd quickly formed around the men. As Fish tried to explain the scenario to the onlookers, the previously collared fellow, who had by then regained his feet, unleashed a powerful blow toward Fish's face. Drawing on his boxing training, Fish dodged the blow and uncorked a wallop of his own. Fish's punch landed, sending his foe back down to the ground and sending both to jail. The next morning, though, Fish was promptly discharged by the Jefferson Market Police Court, while the other man "received a severe lecture from the magistrate."[10]

4

A WATERSHED MOMENT in Ham Fish's path to Cuba occurred on 15 February 1898: the USS *Maine*, at port in Havana Harbor, exploded into a ball of fire and sank to the bottom of the sea, killing 266 of the 350 US servicemen on board.[1] Americans responded with fury directed at Spain. The *Maine*'s presence in Havana Harbor, after all, was a direct result of the ongoing conflict between native Cubans and their Spanish rulers.

As noted, this latest round of war between Cuba and Spain had gotten started a few years earlier, about the time Ham was powering Columbia to its win at Poughkeepsie. Until the *Maine* went down, however, the United States had stayed out of the fray. First President Grover Cleveland, a Democrat, and then President William McKinley, a Republican, had deemed it wise to stay out. To be sure, by early 1898, tensions—indicated by the *Maine*'s presence in Havana Harbor—had escalated between America and Spain, largely because of rampant reports that Spain was forcing hundreds of thousands of Cubans into squalid reconcentration camps, rampant with disease and starvation. But the game-changer in bringing about war was the *Maine* going down.

Before it blew up, the *Maine* had been sitting peacefully in Havana's harbor for three weeks, and Spain had even tried to play nice by hosting dinners for the *Maine*'s officers.[2] But the two sides were wary of each other, and this wariness turned to rage for Americans after the *Maine*. On 18 February 1898, a headline in an extra edition of William Randolph Hearst's *Journal* proclaimed: WHOLE COUNTRY THRILLS WITH WAR FEVER YET THE PRESIDENT SAYS "IT WAS AN ACCIDENT."

McKinley navigated for peace. But as the weeks wore on and McKinley struggled to resolve America's issues with Spain diplomatically, it became more and more clear that those who were against war were losing the argument to those in favor.

Many Americans grew impatient with McKinley's diplomacy. Even Joseph Pulitzer, who, like Hearst, owned an upstart "yellow" paper that had won market share in a cutthroat news environment with colorful, heart-piercing, imagination-stirring, sometimes hyperbolic coverage, joined the war cry. Considered an isolationist, Pulitzer previously was against war with Spain. Ultimately, though, along with his concern for the loss of American lives, Spain's treatment of Cubans and the belief that Cubans had a right to freedom trumped his isolationism.[1]

Still, McKinley worked to avoid war. The environment didn't make this easy. Sure, Hearst's papers and others' had run stories about Spanish mistreatment of Cubans before the *Maine* went down, but afterward more attention to the matter arose. And the reconcentrados were indeed wretched. Historian David Trask estimates that a staggering 100,000 Cubans died from them.[2] Other estimates are higher.

Still, some Americans remained steadfast against war. Ironically, many of these folks were of the business class. They appreciated McKinley's cautiousness and questioned the accuracy of claims that a Spanish-laid mine sunk the *Maine*.[3] (One hundred years later a report commissioned by *National Geographic* and carried out by the Advanced Marine Enterprises concluded, "It appears more probable than was previously concluded that a mine caused the inward bent bottom structure" and therefore the *Maine's* ultimate sinking.)[4]

Oddly, Spain wasn't helping McKinley with matters. Its leaders either did not know how much pressure McKinley faced to go to war or just didn't care.[3] Those leaders, fearful of revolution in their own country unless it held on to Cuba, played tough, not wanting to appear as if they were caving to US demands.

Ultimately, after much jockeying on all sides, Cuban rebels rejected plans for "autonomy" because they thought this would leave them susceptible to Spanish control, while Spain delayed on the diplomatic front in an effort to find a way to appease its anti-American public. And this is why, in late April, President McKinley finally gave up on diplomacy.

For years he had tried to hold the expansionists within his own party at bay, but now with the Spanish government apparently coming to the post-*Maine* political calculation that even losing a war for Cuba would be better than simply giving Cuba up, McKinley asked Congress for a war declaration.

Taken altogether, Ham certainly didn't seem too conflicted about where he stood on matters. One night, presumably after the USS *Maine* went down, he was sitting at an uptown Broadway café with friends when the conversation turned to war. A friend recalled Fish saying, "If war breaks out, I'll be in the first battle if there's influence enough to get me there."[4] The statement proved prescient. He'd soon find himself on a train bound for Texas, where he'd train with fellow Rough Riders.

THE FIRST UNITED STATES Volunteer Cavalry, the official name of the Rough Riders regiment, was not an easy outfit to join. For every one applicant accepted, twenty got rejected. The Fish family, though, knew the Roosevelts well, and this helped Ham Fish land a coveted spot with the Rough Riders.[5]

The regiment was created in response to the looming war to help alleviate the acute manpower needs of the United States, which in 1898 was not considered a military superpower. Two days before Congress declared war, in fact, President McKinley had recognized this manpower need by calling for 125,000 volunteers, a total that dwarfed the ranks of the 28,000-member regular standing army. In addition, McKinley took the rather unusual step of establishing three voluntary regiments "to be composed exclusively of frontiersman possessing special qualifications as horsemen and marksmen," leading to the Rough Riders.[6]

Technically, army doctor Leonard Wood, a friend of Teddy Roosevelt's and a former football coach and captain at Georgia Tech University—and President McKinley's personal physician—led the Rough Riders as their colonel. Teddy was offered the colonelship but declined, citing a lack of experience. Instead, he became Dr. Wood's lieutenant colonel. Though only thirty-nine years old, by this time he had already been a New York state assemblyman, cowboy, author, the president of the New York City police commissioners, and the assistant secretary of the navy, a post he ultimately resigned from so that he could fight in Cuba. However, most people knew that, regardless of title, the Rough Riders would be Teddy's men.[7]

The vast majority of the 1,060 Rough Riders did come from western backgrounds, as called for by President McKinley. But Ham Fish was able to join because Teddy found a way around the "frontiersman"

FISH LIVED AND DIED
LIKE A HERO OF
MEDIEVAL ROMANCE.

HAMILTON FISH JR

AS A POLO PLAYER

AS A SERGEANT IN THE ROUGH RIDERS

AS A YACHTSMAN

AS A FOOTBALL PLAYER

HAMILTON FISH, JR.

He is the young New York man who was killed while fighting with Roosevelt's Rough Riders in a battle with the Spanish near Daiquiri, Cuba, yesterday morning. Mr. Fish was well known in club and society circles in this city, Philadelphia, Newport and Bar Harbor.

Sketches of Hamilton Fish Jr. as a Rough Rider, football player, polo player, and yachtsman. From an article reporting on his death in Cuba, *Boston Sunday Post*, 26 June 1898.

requirement to enlist fifty "gentlemen rankers," men largely from the Ivy League, most of them sportsmen.[8]

In early May 1898, these cowboys and knickerbockers filtered into San Antonio to train for a style of warfare that called for the use of horses and revolvers, unlike the mechanized divisions and machine guns of twentieth-century warfare.

On 10 May 1898, in San Antonio, Ham Fish officially became a Rough Rider. His two-year volunteer papers listed his age as twenty-four years and eleven months, his occupation as railroad man, and his place of birth as Berlin, Germany, where his father had been stationed as secretary of the US Legation.

As with each of the Rough Riders, a recruiting and examination officer certified that Ham was mentally and physically fit for duty and "entirely sober when enlisted," a specification that the *San Antonio Light* pointed out to readers was "peculiarly desirable in the case of Mr. Fish."[9]

Ham had arrived by train with a group of other "gilded youths" wearing high-class clothes, and they'd made it their first order of business to enjoy a fine breakfast at San Antonio's best hotel, the Menger, which abuts the Alamo. After eating, they said the equivalent of "It's all off after this" and changed into their Rough Rider gear.[10]

Rough Riders were expected to arrive with their own horse or be able to secure one in San Antonio, as well as to show up with basic equipment. They would earn thirteen dollars a month and an allowance for clothes and food that worked out to eighteen cents a day—an amount that, the *Light* noted in reference to the wealthy easterners, would contribute to a diet that "will be different from that supplied at Delmonico's."[11]

Gilded easterners like Ham Fish didn't bring horses with them from the city. So they paid for mounts upon arrival, picking from among a pretty wild bunch. Fish had an abiding love for animals, and this showed in his relationship with the horse he chose. As fellow Rough Rider Mason Mitchell recalled, Fish picked a "wild, unbroken animal that no other trooper cared to tackle." It didn't happen overnight, but in time, with Fish working with his unruly charge day after day, the horse became cooperative. Fish spent extra time petting and leading the animal. By the time the regiment would leave San Antonio for Tampa, Mitchell remembered, "there was no better broken or gentler horse."[12]

The initial standard Rough Rider uniform was made of gray, light-textured clothing and featured a sombrero-patterned hat. However, many of the "dudes"—a not-so-flattering term used to describe the wealthy easterners—showed up for roll wearing Abercrombie and Fitch shirts. Rough Rider arms featured a Krog-Jorgensen carbine, which Teddy had worked hard to secure and which his men appreciated, as the Krog-Jorgensen didn't leave a telltale plume of smoke upon firing. In addition to the carbine, each Rough Rider was issued a couple of revolvers, though in practice the cowboys "insisted on carrying their own guns."[13] And in place of a sword, each soldier got a machete.[14]

During the Rough Riders' training in San Antonio, the *Light*, with rhetorical color, ran an article that sketched the backgrounds of several of the volunteers. It was the type of Rough Rider article that people across America loved. There was, the *Light* noted, "Bronco George," supposedly the wildest rider of the West and in control of over 1,000 wild horses. Albuquerque's "Dead Shot" Jim Simpson could "put a rifle bullet through a jack rabbit's eye at a distance of a thousand yards while riding a wild horse," while legend held that Colorado's "Lariat Ned" Perkins could rope steers from as far a distance as any man. He apparently offered to bring his rope with him to Cuba to "pull some of the Spaniards out of the parapets of Havana's fortifications."[15]

The *Light* also highlighted "the roll of honor of gilded youths who have left the clubs and haunts of luxury in New York and the East to fight for their country." In addition to Fish, it wrote about Woodbury Kane, a polo player, cross-country rider, yachtsman, and cousin of John Jacob Astor. William Tiffany, a cousin of the Belmonts, grand-nephew of Commodore Perry, and a "leader of cotillions," was known for changing his clothes several times a day as well as for possessing a sophisticated "taste in raiment."[16] Indeed, Tiffany was "almost as widely known as Hamilton Fish," the *Light* reported, and a "favorite with the younger element."[17]

There was Dudley Dean out of Harvard, whom Teddy Roosevelt called "perhaps the best quarterback to ever play on a Harvard eleven," and Percival Gassett, the "crack polo player" out of Boston. Gassett's grandfather, Commodore "Mad Jack" Percival, is credited with having saved and restored the USS *Constitution*, otherwise known as "Old Ironsides."[18]

Though not mentioned by the *Light*, the "roll of gilded youths" also boasted David Goodrich, who had recently graduated from Harvard, where he had been a standout in crew, too. His father was a surgeon in the Union Army and, in 1870, founded the B. F. Goodrich rubber company. The Rough Rider Goodrich, in addition to fighting in Cuba, would serve on General Pershing's staff in World War I, and from 1927 to 1950 serve as the chairman of the board of B. F. Goodrich.[19]

As distinguished a lot as the Rough Riders made, Ham Fish was probably, after Roosevelt, the best known. And within Ham's first week or so in San Antonio, he made his presence known further not only by working hard but also by doing things like riding furiously on the back of a cab horse and throwing an ottoman at a music hall singer "as a mark of his esteem."[20]

AS THEY WAITED for their dog tents to arrive, during their opening nights of training most of the Rough Riders slept on the floor of San Antonio's exposition building. They'd arise to a 5:30 a.m. wakeup call, with roll thirty minutes later, followed by twenty minutes of caring for the horses and a 6:30 breakfast. Upon watering their horses in a nearby river and saddling them, they'd carry out an hour-and-a-half strenuous, mounted drill during which the horses would kick up thick plumes of dust as the Rough Riders fine-tuned their lines and practiced coordinated maneuvers. "Dinner" came at 1:30 p.m. Then, as the horses rested, the regiment would practice skirmishes on the parade ground, with Roosevelt leading the action. A 4:00 p.m. stable call was followed up by another roll call at 5:00, followed by an hour of "dress parade." "Supper" was at 7:00. The officers had night school until the final assemblage for roll at 8:30, before taps at 9:00.[21] The days were full.

As Roosevelt biographer Edmund Morris put it, "It would have taxed the powers of a Ghengis Khan to place a thousand individualistic riders, accustomed to the freedom of polo, hunting, and the open range, upon a thousand half-broken horses, and then get them to advance, wheel, fan out, and divide in formation," but Wood and Roosevelt managed a notable measure of success. By the end of May, Roosevelt—not one to lack confidence—said that the Riders could "whip Caesar's Tenth Legion."[22] About a week later he took the time to send a telegram to Ham Fish's father, which read: "Dear Mr. Fish: Just a line to say that Hamilton has done excellently."[23]

Other "dudes," however, like Ham's friend Bill Tiffany, struggled to adjust. A couple of days in, Tiffany complained about not having a clean shirt. Eventually he was allowed to go "hunt his washer woman up," but was "unmercifully guyed" for doing so. Tiffany also got sore after a New Mexican cowboy refused an order he'd given. The cowboy apparently told Tiffany to wait until he reached brigadier-general to start giving out orders "in such a high and mighty fashion."[24]

Tiffany wasn't as bad as Ilallett Allsop Borrowe, who caught flack early in training when word broke that he was making daily trips to a hotel, where he was keeping his valet so that he could get shaven and bathed. After this leaked, the valet found himself on a train headed east.

Fish and the other "gentlemen rankers" could have used their money to make things easier on themselves, like Ilallett Allsop Borrowe did, but they took pride in showing that they could fit in as one of the boys. When Ham's mother, for example, directed Alfred T. Brice, a Fish relative and the treasurer of Washington's Riggs Bank, to make a line of credit available to Ham for any needs that might arise at camp, Fish deferred. He told Mr. Brice that "he did not want a cent." (Ham did agree to take a pricier rubber blanket and cholera bands with him to Cuba, but only after being convinced, his mother said, that it would improve his performance in the field.)[25]

There were some tensions between the westerners and gentlemen-rankers. When Fish and several others, Tiffany included, were promoted by Roosevelt a couple of weeks into camp, some of the westerners grumbled. And the western Rough Riders would "curl their lips in disdain" if a reporter mentioned their eastern brethren's multimillionaire status because—or so the *Light* proclaimed—the only currencies that mattered among the men were "brawn and daring."[26] Largely, though, these grumblings quickly passed because the eastern men really did, for the most part, train as equals and work at fitting in.

Still, the differences between the two groups could be comical. When the Rough Riders learned that they would finally get to move from sleeping on the hard floor of the exposition building to the softer ground of the outdoors, one westerner didn't seem too impressed. He said the floor hadn't been all that bad, seeing as he hadn't slept "in a house . . . in six years."[27]

Indeed, unlikely friendships were struck, not the least of which was the one that arose between Ham Fish and Edward Culver, a part-Indian from Muskogee in Indian Territory. From the standpoint of wealth and family stature, a more unlikely pair could hardly be conjured. Culver was about as poor as they came and about as genuine a frontiersmen as you could find. Yet they clicked. They just seemed to "get" each other and to make each other laugh. In little more than a month, Fish would take a bullet for his new friend.

5

FATIGUED FROM TRAINING, the Rough Riders got a significant morale boost in late May, when marching orders to head to Tampa, Florida, finally arrived, eliciting mighty cheers among the ranks—so mighty, in fact, that the embedded journalist Edward Marshall remembered, "No wilder hurrah was heard in Cuba when we learned our victories."[1]

The Rough Riders left San Antonio by horse, bound for a nearby train station where they would load up for a roughly five-day-long ride to Florida.[2] Upon making it to the station, the Rough Riders struggled to get their horses into the stock cars. Perhaps the horses sensed that the next several days of travel would leave them in virtual neglect.

As for the Rough Riders, they enjoyed only minimally better accommodations than their equines. On the sweltering train, "they slept in their seats, if they slept at all" and endured a number of unaccountable delays. The fellows were buoyed, though, by the crowds that met them along the way, crowds full of excited citizens, eager to offer their good wishes. At one 4:00 a.m. stop, young girls clad in white dresses greeted the Rough Riders, offering posies. In New Orleans a crowd of hopeful onlookers swelled at the train station in the early morning and stayed throughout the day to celebrate Roosevelt and his crew.[3] In addition to breaking up the monotony of traveling, the stops along the way gave the Rough Riders a chance to refresh themselves with watermelon and beer, again thanks to the well-wishers.[4]

Hamilton Fish and Woodbury Kane ranked atop the list of Rough Riders that folks at the various stops clamored to catch a glimpse of. At one stop, Fish and Kane let a couple of lesser-known cowboys impersonate them. The Rough Riders got a kick out of watching these cowboys saunter about as if they were two of America's best-known elites.

★ WHEN COLONEL WOOD finally received word that it was time to head to Cuba, it came with a caveat: only eight of the Rough Riders' twelve "troops" would go. And those soldiers who would be going would have to do so without their horses, except for the senior officers.[5] Ham Fish maneuvered to make sure he made the cut by requesting a transfer to Troop L, led by Capt. Allyn Capron—an accomplished sportsman from a well-known military family—and in which was Ham's buddy Ed Culver. As Culver recalled, Fish's request was welcomed by his fellow troopers because "he was a great friend of all of our squad, and we all allowed he was all right. You see, we all in our squad grew up together from boys around Muskogee, Indian Territory, and on the cattle ranges we just naturally judge a man by his looks."[6]

Ham wasn't just giving himself a better chance of getting to Cuba by joining with Captain Capron. Troop L was advanced guard. He was positioning himself to be at the front of the action, as he'd stated he aimed to do nearly two years prior.[7]

Captain Capron respected Fish's work ethic and zeal and therefore not only accommodated Fish's request but also made him a sergeant. Fish was pleased and strove to make a good impression on his men straightaway by shaking hands with each member of his new company. Striking an impressive figure, he told them, "Boys, we eleven must always stand together, no matter what comes."[8]

★ EVEN BY THE TIME ORDERS arrived to head to Cuba, disorganization still characterized matters in Tampa. Teddy, in fact, had to lead his men on an aggressive maneuver just to secure passage to Cuba. The problem arose when it became clear that another regiment, the 71st of New York and the Second Regular Infantry, had been tasked to take the same ship, the *Yucatan*, as the Rough Riders. With his navy background, however, Teddy quickly realized that the *Yucatan* could accommodate only one of the two regiments. Something had to give.

Teddy called his men to action. They marched double-time straight to the ship, arriving before the other regiment.[9] As the Rough Riders poured onto the 342-foot-long, 43-foot-wide iron-laden *Yucatan*, Teddy made certain that a good number of Rough Riders stood guard just outside it to discourage the 71st of New York, or any other regiment that might have come by, from boarding.[10]

Having secured the *Yucatan* and ridden it out to the channel to wait for the rest of the ships to get in line, the Rough Riders then had to endure a four-day delay.[11] When it came time to sleep, the Rough Riders would huddle below deck in the Yucatan's cavernous holding area and pile onto bunks that were built close together and of rough wood.[12] It wasn't pleasant. Down in the *Yucatan's* bowels, not only were the bunks shoddy but the air was stagnant and the rations questionable, especially the "fresh canned beef," which lacked salt and tended to make people sick.

During the day, the Rough Riders would drill on the limited deck space and read available army manuals and the like, but it was mighty hot and crowded. The best diversion was to hop over the side of the ship to bathe in the Gulf's waters; this the Rough Riders did each morning and evening.[13]

On June 13, the *Yucatan*, as part of an entourage of ships, made its way south through the Gulf of Mexico, bound for the Yucatan Channel. The Rough Riders would ultimately make landfall in southeast Cuba as part of a force tasked with taking the city of Santiago.

ON THE AFTERNOON OF JUNE 22, Fish, Culver, and the rest of their troop disembarked from the *Yucatan* on skiffs, headed for the rocky shores of the Cuban village of Daiquiri, about fifteen miles from Santiago. Even this last portion of the trip, though, was poorly planned, seeing as the seas were rough and the area at which the soldiers were to make landfall featured powerful waves crashing into rocks. A nearby pier, which would have otherwise been rather convenient, had had its top boards ripped off by the Spanish. All of this made getting to dry land quite difficult.

A hundred yards or so from shore, the Rough Riders had to disembark from their skiffs and cling to slippery rocks and then thrash through the choppy water, hoping to reach the next rock, and then do it again until they reached shore. Either this, or climb along the treacherous pier's posts and undergirding. Two regular army soldiers drowned trying to reach land. Teddy made his displeasure with the army's decision to make landfall there known.[14] Luckily, in Ham, Fish's skiff had a skilled oarsman to help handle the rough seas, and they all managed to scramble to shore safely.

On land in Daiquiri, tucked in a picturesque valley between two hills that ran along the Daiquiri River, Roosevelt's men set up their dog tents in haphazard fashion. Locals came out to welcome them. Some even offered the Rough Riders royal palm leaves to use for thatched roofing on their tents.

Once squared away, the soldiers settled in and lit campfires. Anticipation filled the air in what became, to the embedded journalist Marshall at least, a beautiful scene. Living up to the action-minded "yellow" credo, Marshall joined a group of soldiers in climbing atop a nearby hill so that they could unfurl an American flag from high above.[15]

With camp squared away and the Rough Riders confident that no Spanish were nearby, another embedded journalist, Burr McIntosh, decided to race tarantulas, which the soldiers had found crawling about. Burr's idea was to make these races like the turtle races that the Rough Riders had put on back in Tampa. Only McIntosh got stung a few times, making it clear that dealing with tarantulas was different.

Not one to miss an opportunity, Ham Fish, in cahoots with several other Rough Riders, decided to locate a salve to ease the sting of McIntosh's tarantula bites. In short, they went looking for whiskey. They weren't able to find any, but they did come across a stock of Jamaican rum and Spanish wine in a storage area. In his bulletin back home, Marshall wrote that he didn't want to name which of the Rough Riders awoke the next morning feeling the aftereffects of the wine. It seems a safe bet that one of them was Ham Fish.[16]

The soldiers stayed put the next day, June 23, and slept well the following night, despite the various terrestrial creatures crawling and slithering on the jungle floor. On June 24, a sense of foreboding and a kind of lonesomeness set in among the men, especially when darkness fell. Their first live action was less than twenty-four hours away, and they could sense it.

A torrential downpour forced the Rough Riders to try to sleep wrapped in ponchos on a night when getting shuteye would have been hard enough, knowing what lay ahead and with the snakes and spiders and the land crabs. As the night wore on and sleep proved elusive, Fish and Culver decided to get up and cover the rations with their ponchos. Then they stood under a tree in a futile effort to avoid the rain. "Old boy, this is soldierin'," Fish said.[17]

When the rain finally stopped, they started a sizable fire to help them dry out, and shortly thereafter Lieutenant Colonel Roosevelt and Captain Capron happened by. They chatted about the previous day's work and the likelihood of action tomorrow. Teddy was moved by the scene—the powerfully built Fish and Capron and the part-Indian Culver, chatting with him late at night on the eve of live action. In a memoir after the war Roosevelt recalled that by the flickering light of the fire, Fish's and Capron's frames "seemed of steel, to withstand all fatigue; they were flushed with health; in their eyes shone high resolve and fiery desire."[18] Neither would survive the following day.

By and by Teddy and Capron moved along, and Fish and Culver were left to converse about family and home. Fish said, "Old boy, I suppose the people at home are thinkin' about us now."[19]

Early the next morning, about 4:40 a.m., the squad received orders to march toward the city of Santiago. During breakfast, Sergeant Fish let his men enjoy extra tomato rations, telling Culver, "We're liable to all be killed today and we may as well have enough to eat." Later, Fish chucked aside an extra pair of shoes that had cost seven dollars. Culver told him he might want to hold on to them because they could come in handy, but Fish somberly replied, "No, I don't think I'll need them anymore." He also gave away clothes.[20]

Breakfast done, the soldiers commenced a roughly three-mile march that would get them closer to Santiago. The first stretch included steep hills several hundred feet high, which the Rough Riders had to traverse carrying some 200 rounds of ammunition apiece, along with their camp equipment.[21] The New York Times reported that as the day wore on "the weather became intensely hot, and the sun beat down upon the cowboys and Eastern athletes as they toiled up the grade with their heavy packs, and frequent rests were necessary." Continuing on, guns drawn as they kept a lookout for Spaniards, they had to march in single file on parts of the narrow route.[22]

Near the town of Las Guasimas, walking along a narrow country road with thick bushes and prickly cactus on either side, conditions seemed ripe for an ambush. The troopers stayed alert. On the edge of town, Ham and his comrades suddenly heard "cuckoo" calls, only they couldn't pinpoint exactly where the calls were coming from. In the meantime, the trail they were on opened into an area with high grass on the right flank, underbrush and a barbed wire fence on the left.

Scanning the terrain, Ham and a few other Rough Riders spotted what appeared to be a dead Spaniard lying in the middle of the dirt road ahead. Moments later, Rough Rider Tom Isbell glimpsed a Spanish soldier through the brush. Without hesitating, he fired and "pinked him."[23] But in response, Spanish soldiers, hidden by the brush of the surrounding hills, delivered a torrent of Mauser bullets. Isbell got hit seven times, making him the first Rough Rider to be wounded in action (he somehow survived).[24]

At the sound of the gunfire, Culver sprawled on the ground and started firing away. He was more than just vulnerable; he was a sitting duck. Recognizing as much, Fish rushed forward to help him. Upon reaching him, Ham hit the ground next to Culver, positioning himself so as to protect him. Ham said ironically, "Old boy, you've got a good place here."[25]

The sun was blazing down as they lay there in the open road shooting back at the higher ground from which shots were coming. Within a matter of seconds, Fish felt a Spanish bullet rip through his chest. He turned to Culver and said, "Old boy, I'm wounded; I'm badly wounded."[26]

The bullet had entered the left side of Fish's body and traveled virtually straight through him, opening a deluge of internal bleeding. Upon exiting Fish's body, the bullet had struck Culver, too, just above his heart, lodging near his spine. Initially Culver thought his wound was lethal as well. He told Ham, "I'm killed." But really Ham had taken the brunt of the bullet's force.

As the firefight continued and Rough Riders from behind filled in, Fish managed to lift himself up onto his left elbow and say, "Give me your canteen, old boy." Culver did so. Smiling, Fish said, "You're all right, old boy."[27] Moments later he died. It happened that quickly.

Perhaps America's most eligible bachelor, a man with seemingly limitless opportunity, born into privilege, had just taken a bullet without hesitation for a poor and virtually unknown comrade from Muskogee while both fought for Cubans they had never met.

6

IN THE DAYS THAT FOLLOWED, reports of the battle and of Fish's death covered the front pages of newspapers across America. Fish was glorified and romanticized. The *Nebraska State Journal* ran an article highlighting Fish's "herculean" build, prestigious lineage, and exploits at Poughkeepsie as a member of Columbia's crew team.[1] The *New York Herald*'s Richard Harding Davis, whose coverage of Fish was carried by smaller papers like the *Times Democrat* of Lima, Ohio, noted that Fish died wearing a watch that read "God will give" and that bore the crests of his Grandfather Hamilton and his father Nicholas. Davis, considered the original superstar "yellow" reporter, added that Ham was given a "noble burial," alongside comrades who had also fallen on soil "they had died to set free."[2]

Meanwhile, a friend of Fish's wrote in the *Pittsburgh Dispatch*, "The young man [Ham] was idolized by the members of his distinguished family, and he was greatly admired in the conspicuous social set in which he moved."[3]

The Democratic *Galveston Daily News*, no fan of the eastern business elite, also praised Fish. The paper offered its version of a compliment by pointing out that, while Fish might have come from a distinguished lineage and considerable wealth and may very well have been a "blooming plutocrat," he had never held civil office.[4]

A lot of people held up Fish's life for its ability to not only reflect class unity in America but to strengthen it. In November 1898, the *Eau Claire Leader* carried a sermon by Rev. S. H. Doyle, who said, "Wealthy, aristocratic, educated, Hamilton Fish gave his life for his country just as willingly as the poorest and most ignorant volunteer, and this is but an illustration of what has been universally true. May it always be so!" Doyle also said, "The country seems to have a peculiar power of inspiring the intensest love and devotion of its citizens." And he credited the Spanish-American War with replacing all sectional division with unity.[5]

The *San Antonio Light* ran a poem commemorating Fish that read, in part:

> *Oh, cease the prate of the rich man's pride*
> *In the land where love abides;*
> *The plutocrat in a cowboy's hat,*
> *With his buckskinned brethren rides.*
>
> . . . .
> *And when it was o'er the son of the poor*
> *With the son of the rich man lay.*
> *Sons of the east and sons of the west*
> *Rode rough o'er the sons of Spain;*
> *And when it was done—at set of sun*
> *They found him among the slain—*
> *First in the van of the headlong charge*
> *First kissed by the lips of fame—*
> *His spirit freed by a daring deed—*
> *And a nimbus 'round his name.*[6]

On the morning after Ham's death, some 200 yards from the spot upon which he was killed, Theodore Roosevelt, Buckey O'Neill, and several other Rough Riders gathered atop a hill. (The day prior, the Rough Riders had ultimately forced the Spanish to pull back and reconfigure their position. Not stopping there, the American troops then moved into more open terrain so that they could see the enemy better. With the Rough Riders now on the assault, the Spanish ended up retreating further to a blockhouse. About that time, Brigadier General S.B.M. Young's regulars—the first, consisting of white troops, and the tenth, of African American troops—met up with the Rough Riders. Soon thereafter the Spanish were forced into a full-on retreat.)[7] Buzzards circled overhead. It was here that they would bury in an unmarked trench-like grave Ham Fish and six other comrades. O'Neill turned to Roosevelt and asked, "Colonel, isn't it Whitman who says of the vultures that 'they pluck the eyes of princes, and tear the flesh of kings'?"

Roosevelt was moved by the diversity of those they would bury that day. Of them, he would later write, "Indian and cowboy, miner, packer, and college athlete, the man of unknown ancestry from the lonely Western plains, and the man who carried on his watch the crest of the Stuyvesants and the Fishes."[8]

Presiding over the interment of this varied lot was the young and athletically built Rev. Henry W. Brown, in common overalls and a gray shirt. Only a little more than a month earlier, he'd resigned his post as the rector of an Episcopal church to become the Rough Riders' chaplain. This burial would be one of forty-four that he would carry out in a two-day period.[9] When he spoke the words "'Let us pray,'" each Rough Rider "removed his hat and went down on his knees in the mud."[10]

Several years earlier, in 1895, Columbia's seniors had been asked to provide a favorite literary quote for the yearbook. Fish chose this romantic, yet fatalistic line written by Nathaniel Hawthorne: "Mankind are earthen jugs with spirits in them."[11]

⭐ FISH'S BODY DIDN'T STAY in Cuba long. Rather than leaving his son to rest in an unmarked grave on a Cuban hill, Ham's father Nicholas made the arduous journey to Las Guasimas to bring his son home. On July 18 New York newspapers reported on the return of Ham Fish's body to the States. It was, naturally, a difficult time for Ham's father, Nicholas, and mother, Clemence Fish. When she had first heard vague reports of their son's death, she'd "hung pathetically to the hope that subsequent dispatches would bring word that her son had merely been wounded."[12] They hadn't. Instead, telegrams, condolences, and visitors streamed to their home the following day.

To cope, Mrs. Fish would escape to her bedroom every now and again. There she'd quietly read aloud an old Christmas wish list that Ham Fish had written as a young boy:

> *Dear Santa Claus:*
> *Please send to me one ape, two dogs, one giraffe and a small goat—*
> *all alive.*
> *Hamilton Fish*[13]

As sad as they were, the Fishes were also proud of their son. "Both his mother and myself felt that his experience as a soldier, should his life be spared, would have been of lasting benefit to him," Mr. Fish said. "Our son certainly never knew fear. So eager was he to reach the scene of action that when he ascertained that his own troop, in which he had held the rank of Sergeant, was not to go with the first transports, he resigned his rank and offered himself as a private in another troop, which had been ordered aboard the transport *Yucatan*." Clearly moved by his son's sacrifice, he added, "Hamilton died fighting like a man. He looked very much like his great-grandfather, Col. Nicholas Fish, who entered the Army in the Revolutionary War at the age of seventeen."[14]

In the Cuban town of Siboney, then, Nicholas Fish and undertaker J. C. Burton met ten armed guards, their team of six mules, and their big army wagon for the several-miles-long trip upon knotty roads, the roughest the undertaker Burton had ever known, to reach Ham's body.

Having made it to his son's resting place, Nicholas and his helpers dug for some time before coming upon Ham's body and the bodies of those who had been buried with him. They'd been wrapped in a blanket over which "heavy and large fan palms" had been placed. On top of the fan palms, several "good-sized" saplings had been put down, followed by yet more palms and soil.[15] The Rough Riders had taken care in putting their comrades to rest.

Nicholas returned to New York with Ham's body in mid-July, aboard the aptly named *Solace*.[16] The ensuing funeral took place at St. Mark's Protestant Episcopal Church, which still stands in the Bowery section of Manhattan, on Tenth Street and Second Avenue, on the site of the original Stuyvesant family chapel dating back to 1660.[17]

On the day of the funeral, in anticipation of and beginning quite early in the morning, hundreds of people amassed outside the entrance to St. Mark's. By the time the funeral started, thousands had discovered that they could not fit into the already packed church. They had to resort to observing through the gaps in St. Mark's iron fence or watch the proceedings from across the street.

Among those inside were about a dozen Rough Riders, including Ed Culver, who carried in his body the bullet that killed Ham, and fellow Troop L member Joseph Kline. The *New York Times* noted in its coverage that, given the soldiers' compromised physical condition, what with the bad rations, difficult travel, and rampant sickness, and given their celebrated reputation, they "received much sympathetic attention from the feminine portion of the crowd in the streets."[18]

The service, by all accounts, was solemn yet elegant. After it, the Fish family, their friends, and the soldiers from Squadron A who were tasked with transporting Fish's body went to Grand Central Station to board a train bound for Garrison, New York, some fifty miles upstate along the Hudson, where the Fish family owned land that it called the "Garrisons-on-the-Hudson." There Ham's body was lowered into its final resting place. The soldiers of Squadron A shot volleys into the air, and then taps was played.[19]

★ WE CAN ONLY GUESS what Ham Fish would have thought about the geopolitical dominoes that came in the aftermath of the Spanish-American War, about the Platt Amendment, the Philippines, and the rest. And we can only speculate about what he might have gone on to do in life had he survived the war.

What we do know is that Ham Fish lived at a time in American history when things were rapidly changing: America was assuming its role as the world's superpower, science and reason were continuing their assault on superstition, and technological advances were reshaping not just the American economy but daily life, chipping away at genteel traditions. Concurrently, newfangled takes on manhood were emerging.

Ham Fish's life reflects all of this. He was adventurous, independent, and rebellious, yet Victorian. He was eager to achieve great things and to make himself known in the world, a lot like America was, and yet he was eager to show that he was no more privileged than any other man. No matter how one felt about the world wrought by the Spanish-American War, all could agree that the courage of a man like Ham Fish—to act in the name of freedom—was striking.

TWO

Hobart "Hobey" Baker

7

IN NOVEMBER 1916, Hobey Baker and pilot Raynal Bolling, flying in a Curtiss "Jenny" airplane, were two of the first Americans to fly to a football game. The pair flew in formation with eleven other planes, part of a squadron of the New York National Guard. They flew from Long Island to Princeton to watch Hobey's Princeton Tigers play the Yale Bulldogs, routinely one of college football's biggest games of the year. The *New York Times* claimed the flight formation was the largest to ever take to American skies. As kickoff neared, the planes roared toward the stadium, performing airborne dips, spirals, and "loop-de-loops" above the crowd. Thrilled, the spectators repeatedly rose in their seats to cheer as Hobey and his flying mates originated the idea of the sporting event "flyby."

When the aviators walked to their grandstand seats in Old Nassau's 61,000-seat Palmer Stadium, they received hearty congratulations.[1] After all, the airplane itself had only been outfitted with wheels five years prior, and commercial flight was still over a decade away—and even then in limited capacity. For some spectators, these were the first planes they had seen in their lives.

For Hobey Baker, the flight to Princeton, the school at which he'd starred four years earlier in football and hockey, was yet another wondrous feat in an already remarkable life. As a punt returner and running back at Princeton from 1910 to 1913, Hobey Baker was one of the nation's most celebrated gridiron men. During his time at Old Nassau, he was also considered the nation's best hockey player. To this day, college hockey's equivalent of the Heisman Trophy is called the Hobey Baker Award, and Princeton University's ice rink is named after him. Baker would likely have been among the country's best track-and-field athletes, too, if not for Princeton's rule limiting students to two varsity sports.[2]

To boot, he was known to treat his opponents respectfully, to seek them out to acknowledge their play, and to rarely draw penalties. And he was quite modest. He rarely granted interviews because he didn't want to bring too much attention to himself, and he nearly quit an amateur hockey outfit that he played on after college because he thought the press paid too much attention to him at the expense of others.[3] These attributes were celebrated not only by his friends and teammates but by pressmen. The *Washington Post*'s J. V. Fitzgerald wrote of Hobey's humility, "From one who has known Baker many years, you can take it this was no pose with him."[4]

Hobey Baker in his Princeton uniform, holding a football; Princeton football, 1910–14. John D. Davies Collection on Hobey Baker, box 5, Princeton University Archives, Department of Rare Books and Special Collections, Princeton University Library.

To many, Hobey Baker embodied all that was good about the seemingly waning Victorian ethos: he was hardworking, honorable, morally upright, and immensely talented. Novelist and Princeton alum F. Scott Fitzgerald, whose time at Princeton overlapped with Baker's, admired the star. While the two did not share a close friendship, Fitzgerald once described Baker as "an ideal worthy of everything in my enthusiastic admiration, yet consummated and expressed in a human being who stood within ten feet of me."[5] Over the decades, cultural critics, authors, and journalists have built upon this idea of Hobey Baker representing a bygone era, of symbolizing the gentleman-athlete, of being clean-living, upright, modest, Victorian.

Upon closer inspection, however, this characterization of Baker has kept history from more fully knowing one of America's great heroes. The real Hobey Baker was more complicated than the almost inhuman idealizations of him that have reigned.

Even F. Scott Fitzgerald, an admirer, seems to have recognized that Baker was a more complex figure than the image suggested. In Fitzgerald's *This Side of Paradise* the name of the main character, Amory Blaine, was taken directly from Hobey (Amory was Hobey's middle name). In the novel, Amory has a problematic relationship with his mother, serves in World War I, and falls for a wealthy young woman who operates within an elite, superficial social scene into which he is drawn. Ultimately, Amory fails to win this woman's hand. She opts instead for a well-to-do man, leaving Amory to famously lament, "I know myself, but that is all." The parallels between the lives of Amory Blaine and Fitzgerald are well documented; the parallels to Hobey's life, less so. But Hobey also had a strained relationship with his mother, served in World War I, worried about money, and fell for an elite aristocrat who left him for an older, more established man.

A secondary character from *This Side of Paradise*, Allenby, the "football captain, slim and defiant" who was revered by his classmates, is clearly drawn from Baker. Furthermore, Fitzgerald likely had Baker at least partly in mind with the lead character in *The Great Gatsby*. In this novel, during training for World War I, Jay Gatsby falls for Daisy Buchanan, a flighty member of New York's "old aristocracy," only to lose her to a wealthy man. To win her back, Gatsby becomes drawn into the superficial world of the elite set, consumed by impressing Daisy with wealth and stature. At book's end, he dies tragically young. Fitzgerald likely saw the similarities with Hobey Baker.

Other quick examples of the disconnect between Hobey and his image: rather than drink rarely and only in moderation, he liked a good party every now and again, and if the conditions were right, he'd "get tight" on whiskey or champagne. Hangovers weren't a foreign concept to him. He liked women, too. While stationed in England during the Great

War, he wrote the following to his friend Percy Pyne: "Am at present making violent love to an English girl whom I met at Lady's Temple and who seems to be enjoying it as much as I am. You see, I have nothing to do but wait, which is expensive, but amusing."[6]

Hobey could be gentlemanly and refined. In many ways, he adhered to a traditional code of honor and love of country associated with the Victorian era. Yet he also enjoyed a good game of poker or a night of dancing, singing, and drinking. He was a man of his times socially, economically, and technologically, particularly as a fan of fast cars and airplanes. A lot like that of Hamilton Fish, Hobey's life represents the continuity and change that has run through America since the country's inception.

Delving deeper into what animated him, who he was, and how he behaved doesn't take away from Baker's stunning accomplishments. It gives us a better understanding of him and his times, of someone whose life, more than a hundred years later, still resonates.

8

BORN IN 1892, Hobey grew up in a Philadelphia suburb, where he lived what appeared to be an idyllic life. His father had starred in football at Princeton. His mother was a striking beauty. And Hobey was close to his brother, Alfred Thornton, who was one year older. But marital problems plagued the Baker household.

Those problems picked up in 1903 and ended in divorce in 1907. Meanwhile, Hobey's mother, Mary, gained a reputation for being a socialite. One New York paper characterized her as "beautiful but frivolous" and reported that she had kept the "Quaker city gossips in turmoil for many years before she and Alfred were finally separated for all times by the divorce courts."[1] Compounding matters, financial strain struck during the economic panic of 1907, when Hobey's father's upholstery business sputtered.

Partially prompted by their marital rancor, Hobey's parents decided to send their boys to the esteemed St. Paul's School in Concord, New Hampshire, some 370 miles away. Considered a kind of "training ground" for the "boys of an American aristocracy"—the Vanderbilts, Morgans, and Mellons had sent their boys there—St. Paul's had a first-rate reputation. (Even Ham Fish had attended St. Paul's in his youth.) It was the kind of place that would have been too expensive for the Bakers except that a cousin of Hobey's father, James Conover, was the schoolmaster there.

The Conovers, in addition to making it financially feasible, gave Hobey and Thornton a sense of family while at St. Paul's—a great help, since Hobey was only eleven at the time. James Conover's wife, Mary, became a kind of surrogate mother to them at a time when their parents, their mother in particular, might have seemed to have abandoned them.

The brothers found strength in each other at St. Paul's. Hobey idolized

Thornton, and Thornton saw greatness in Hobey long before the rest of America did. The brothers' bond was so deep that, upon graduating St. Paul's, Thornton became aware that their father could afford to send only one of them to college; he stayed home to learn the family business so that Hobey could shine on Princeton's playing fields like their father had. It was a moving display of selflessness that Hobey never forgot.[2] (As it happened, Thornton went on to do quite well for himself as an oilman and adventurer.[3])

Hobey's affection for Thornton is clear in letters he wrote during World War I. Whether writing to his father or Thornton's wife, Marie, Hobey frets about his brother's health and worries about him working too hard. Certainly, he wished Thornton could see how bold his little brother was in the air.

Still, even though they had each other, as youngsters at St. Paul's the situation had to be difficult for the boys. Hobey wrote a letter to his mother during his first year at St. Paul's that suggests the sense of abandonment that he must have felt. "I am twelve years old now," he wrote. "And I forgot all about my own birthday until I suddenly remembered that the 15th had passed."[4] No one had thought to tell him that he was twelve.

In another letter to his mother, Hobey wrote, "I wish you or father would send us some money because we have not a cent and when we want to get stamps we have to go and get money from Mr. Brinly." Later in the letter, he asked his mom, "Won't you please write more because I simply love to hear from you?"[5]

Early on at St. Paul's, Hobey showed a love for athletics, hockey in particular. During his first year there, he ice-skated for most of Thanksgiving Day: in the morning and then again after chapel, an activity he pursued alone until it got too dark to see the puck. Finally, he came in for a late supper to watch a "show." In a letter to his mother, he declared it a "slick Thanksgiving." Perhaps being out on the ice helped him escape his longings for home.[6]

As time passed, he became known for honing his game on St. Paul's "lower pond" for hours on end, working on manipulating the puck without looking down, an uncommon tactic at the time.[7] His wizardry with the stick complemented his blazing speed; later, he'd become known as "the fastest thing on ice," a title that even revered Canadian professionals came to accept.[8] In time, he helped turn St. Paul's hockey team into a juggernaut, good enough to beat the nation's best colleges. During the 1908–9 season he led St. Paul's to a 5-3 win over Harvard, outskating Harvard's speedy captain, Clarence Pell, in the process.[9] The following year—Hobey went to St. Paul's for an extra year so his father could save enough money to send him to college—the team won 4-0 versus Princeton, the college game's eventual champion that season.[10]

Hobey excelled in other sports while at St. Paul's, from football and baseball to cross-country and swimming. In college this continued. As a freshman, Hobey helped Princeton beat Yale's freshman football team with a dropkick fake that he turned into a touchdown dash.[11] The following season, now eligible to play varsity, he was one of only two sophomores to start on the squad. Despite carrying a mere 160 pounds (if that) on his five-foot-ten frame, he helped the Tigers win the 1911 national championship. Newspapers championed his speed and his ability to work his legs like "piston rods."[12]

The pivotal game that season occurred in New Haven, Connecticut, versus favored Yale. Some 35,000 fans came out to watch the affair. Though the playing field conditions were poor and the scoring low, the drama was high. Grappling for every inch, Princeton ultimately won the game 6-3, and Hobey finished the contest with sixty-three yards on punt returns, a Tiger record.[13]

More than the yardage, people marveled at Hobey's ability to take punishment. He returned thirteen punts on that day, all without a helmet—fans loved to see his blond locks waving as he ran—and all under rules that were far less protective of punt returners than nowadays.

For several years, college football's very existence had been threatened by serious injuries and even playing field deaths. In 1909 alone there were eleven collegiate football fatalities, and in the East in particular, where the forward pass was generally eschewed, football looked like the old "grinding, pushing, and pulling game." That Hobey Baker could excel under these types of conditions at 160 pounds was remarkable.[14]

The next season, that of 1912, the *Oakland Tribune* put Baker's name on its front page in an article written by legendary scribe Damon Runyon, who credited Baker with powering Princeton to a win over Dartmouth. A dazzling Baker punt return impressed Runyon the most. With the slithering, eighty-yard return for a touchdown in mind, Runyon referred to Hobey as the "lusty lad . . . who rose to football fame today."[15]

Baker scored 92 points in 1912, a single-season Princeton record that stood until 1974.[16] The *Boston Herald* described Hobey as the "most feared open field runner now playing the game of football."[17] As a senior, he captained the Tiger football team and set a career scoring mark that lasted until 1964.

At Princeton, Hobey's hockey teams won intercollegiate championships in his sophomore and senior years, and to a man he was recognized as the country's best player. Although the sport didn't resonate as powerfully with the public as football, his exploits on the ice generated considerable coverage in the press.

In the classroom at Old Nassau, Hobey earned above-average marks, majoring in history and political science. Socially, he won the respect of his peers. They knew him to be kind-hearted and courteous, someone who didn't participate in taunting lowerclassmen.[18] As F. Scott Fitzgerald biographer Andrew Turnbull explained it, "Varsity football players were looked upon as demi-gods, and 'Hobey' Baker . . . loomed so high in the heavens that he was scarcely visible. But Baker had the common touch. Now and then he came down from Olympus to fraternize with the freshmen, and Fitzgerald actually spoke to him one day in October."[19]

Baker started classes at Princeton just after Woodrow Wilson, the future US president, had ended his eight-year run as the school's president. Wilson had tried hard to strengthen Princeton's academics and stamp out its stuffiness. When it came to its academic profile, at least, he had a strong measure of success. In addition to making admittance to Princeton more competitive, he implemented the now common practices of dividing universities into academic departments and focusing students' studies so that they would adopt a "major."[20] But in some ways Wilson left Princeton feeling defeated. His efforts to democratize Princeton's social setup clashed with those looking to maintain its elite, genteel traditions—exclusive social clubs and the like—which proponents thereof saw as important to training a Princeton man. Wilson largely lost this clash.

While social exclusivity and, to many people, snobbishness infused Princeton, this idea of Princeton as a training ground to conserve tradition was correlated to the development of Hobey Baker the man. Author David Brooks, looking back to Hobey's time, wrote that Princeton aimed to take "men from prominent families and toughen them up, teach them a sense of social obligation, based on the code of gentleman and noblesse oblige. In short, it aimed to instill in them a sense of chivalry."[21]

In 1991, *Sports Illustrated*'s Ron Fimrite credited Hobey Baker not only with helping to cultivate this gentlemanly attitude while at Princeton—modest, clean-cut, respectful, fair, not boastful—but with influencing American athletes for decades. This code, Fimrite argued, was embraced by subsequent American athletes like Lou Gehrig and Joe DiMaggio, Joe Louis and Rocky Marciano. By the 1990s, Fimrite lamented, this attitude seemed more and more anachronistic.[22]

9

WHILE HOBEY BAKER was part of Princeton's old-school genteel traditions, in many ways his life also pointed to the future. This was evident when geopolitical plates shifted in the summer of 1914, ultimately leading to World War I. At the time, in quintessential Baker fashion, Hobey was in Europe on a motorcycle trip, working as a celebrity correspondent for the *New York Times* covering international track meets and crew races.[1]

Those geopolitical plates quavered on 28 June 1914, when a nineteen-year-old Yugoslavian nationalist, Gavrilo Princip, shot and killed the heir to the Austro-Hungarian throne, Archduke Franz Ferdinand, and his wife, Sophie, Duchess of Hohenberg.

A month later, Austria-Hungary, upset that its post-assassination demands had not been fully met, declared war on Serbia. By early August 1914, soldiers from Britain, which was allied principally with Belgium, a country that Germany aimed to use as a highway to get to France, were in Africa engaging German soldiers. It happened that quickly, and it was that convoluted.

The United States wouldn't join the fray until April 1917, and Baker wouldn't see action as a fighter pilot until the spring of 1918. Before then, he took residence in Manhattan—when not touring Europe by motorcycle—where he initially went to work for Johnson and Higgins, a mammoth insurance firm, then as a junior executive with the House of Morgan. He found both positions rather uninspiring.

With J. P. Morgan, Hobey entered a two-year training program at a modest salary of twenty dollars a week, or "twenty percent less than a Ford factory worker could make on the Model T assembly line." While his long-term prospects seemed bright, he felt as if he were "caged in a corporate mailroom."[2]

It was during this time that Hobey became close friends with Percy Pyne, a fellow St. Paul's and Princeton graduate. In certain ways, Percy and Hobey were opposites. Hobey was athletic and rugged, while Percy was unathletic and a bit of a "dandy." Hobey didn't have much money; Percy was filthy rich.

In fact, Percy, who was ten years older than Hobey, seemed to personify the lavish, carefree life often associated with America's wealthy class at the time. To wit, he belonged to no less than thirty-seven clubs and was known for his extravagant parties. Though relatively young, he also served on several corporate boards and was already a Life Member of the Board of Trustees of Princeton University. As an indication of his social stature within the elite strata, he was dubbed the "No. 1 clubman of the metropolitan Smart Set."[3]

One example of this is the mid-January 1914 dinner and dance party Percy hosted (and Hobey Baker likely attended). For it, Percy rented out the entire second floor of Manhattan's Sherry's restaurant. Some of the most celebrated ladies of the era, such as Mrs. Stuyvesant Fish (Hamilton Fish's aunt) and Mrs. Cornelius Vanderbilt, attended, as did some of the era's most coveted bachelorettes, such as Janet Fish (Ham Fish's cousin) and the well-known socialite Mimi Scott (with whom, in several years, Hobey would have a torrid love affair in war-torn France). In covering the party, the *New York Times* noted that as the star-studded attendees arrived, the "popular bachelor" Percy, accompanied by his mother, guided them to dinner tables decorated with lilies of the valley and pink roses that had been shipped in from the Pynes's country estate in Princeton, New Jersey. A Neapolitan orchestra kept guests entertained during dinner and then, during coffee in the "salon" room, a cadre of men in Louis XIV livery carried in the Baroness von Rottenthal (considered one of the world's most "finished" interpretive dancers), seated in a sedan chair, to perform her famed Oriental dances. The press described the party as "one of the most brilliant entertainments of the winter."[4]

Make no mistake: Percy was a connected man. His family had a box at the Metropolitan Opera House not far from Mrs. Vanderbilt's and Mrs. John Jacob Astor's. As a director of the Sheepshead Bay Speedway, Percy watched the 1915 Vincent Astor Cup race with Mr. and Mrs. Vincent Astor.[5] It was Percy who would introduce Hobey to race-car driving, polo, and, ultimately, flying.

Naturally enough, Hobey's legendary Princeton status helped him get plugged into this elite lifestyle. He might not have had the money for it, but he had the cultural currency through his athletic prowess and image. At one point, he even moved in with Percy at the Pynes's Manhattan mansion at 263 Madison Avenue and had the use of his chauffeured automobiles.[6]

Hobey Baker biographers have tended to present Percy as the ultimate playboy who was content to live off his family wealth, as someone who pursued expensive hobbies and cultivated lavish tastes but did little else. One Baker biographer, for example, notes that during the World War I era, while some men were willing to volunteer for war service, one of Percy Pyne's "uninspiring" goals was to "establish a policy at one of his expensive clubs to make six-course meals available twenty-four hours a day."[7] The suggestion here is that Percy lacked Hobey's depth and that somehow Percy managed to lure the idealistic and naïve Hobey into his vapid but alluring lifestyle.

Indeed, in letters to Percy during the war, Hobey ribbed his friend for acclimating him to fine tastes, needling Percy for playing golf during the war with a mere lord and not the king of England himself. Yet Percy Pyne was stationed in Washington, DC, for much of the war, where he worked for the Council of National Defense. He also thought seriously about joining the regular army.[8] Additionally, the Pyne family was instrumental in getting a flight training school established for Princeton in the spring of 1917.

The portrayal of Percy as a superficial mollycoddle who lured Hobey into his circle is also misleading because it suggests that Hobey didn't control whom he spent time with. Hobey chose to be friends with Percy, and he thought highly of the Pyne family, just like he would choose to get engaged to the elite Mimi Scott while stationed in Europe during the war.

★ IN ADDITION TO WORKING at the House of Morgan and hobnobbing with the smart set after graduating Princeton, Hobey stayed active during the winter months by suiting up for the St. Nicholas hockey team, for which he played from 1914 to 1916.

Hobey's transition from Princeton to playing for St. Nick's was relatively easy. It didn't hurt that in college—and even in prep school—Hobey had played in the St. Nick's arena on 66th Street and Columbus

Hobey Baker diving. In a lot of ways this photo captures how the young man lived. John D. Davies Collection on Hobey Baker, box 5, Princeton University Archives, Department of Rare Books and Special Collections, Princeton University Library.

Avenue. This not only gave him familiarity with the rink but also meant that New Yorkers already had had chances to become fans of his. And they did. Indeed, the rink's marquees would often read "Hobey Baker Plays Here Tonight," which reportedly embarrassed Hobey to no end. Legend has it that he often refused to go on the ice to play until the sign came down. Regardless, it's been estimated that, on many nights, half of the crowd at St. Nick's games had come to see the famed Hobey Baker.[9]

Hobey made his mark with St. Nick's right away. During his first season, in December 1914, a victory over a vaunted Canadian team from Toronto prompted the *New York Times* headline "Baker's Stick Work Saves St. Nicholas." The paper credited him with putting St. Nick's squarely on the hockey map, as he had Princeton.[10]

Baker also generated coverage with St. Nick's for his gentlemanly approach to the game. In March 1916, *Our Paper* applauded Baker for not "losing his head or appealing to the referee for unclean playing," despite facing "direct attacks" on the ice time and again.[11]

By 1916, though, these attacks were taking their toll on Hobey's body, and the generally less sportsmanlike tone of the amateur circuit was turning him off.[12] He would continue to play for a while, but his enthusiasm for the game didn't remain as high as it had at Princeton. Plus, the boom in the popularity of hockey in Manhattan had started to wane a bit by 1916. Papers commented on the dwindling attendance figures compared to those during Hobey's first season with St. Nick's, even though Hobey continued to draw capacity crowds on the road, especially in Boston, whose B.A.A. team beat St. Nick's for the 1916 amateur title.[13]

This didn't mean that Hobey stopped dazzling fans. Lester Patrick, who played professional hockey in Canada in Hobey's time and who later coached the New York Rangers, considered Hobey the only amateur he'd ever seen who could have played in a professional hockey game and immediately starred.[14] The Montreal Canadiens tried to entice Baker to do just that, offering him $20,000 for three years of service. Hobey turned them down. Though it's not entirely clear, it's been speculated that a driver of Hobey's decision was the ungentlemanly label associated with a man of his stature playing a sport professionally—if true, this is rather ironic, considering Hobey didn't like his desk jobs and didn't have much money.[15]

With his interest in hockey waning and his enthusiasm for desk work limited, flying offered Hobey an exciting new outlet. Meanwhile, World War I was raging across Europe. By 1916, the *Lusitania* had also been sunk, and war was on Americans' mind. Many Ivy Leaguers were looking for ways to support the Allies, which were led by Great Britain and France. That June, Hobey joined the Civilian Aviation Corps at Staten Island, a fittingly courageous and modern move. It's said that he learned to handle the Curtiss "military tractor in a matter of days." Within a year, he'd be a pilot in the US military stationed in Europe.

10

INTERESTINGLY, in the Civilian Aviation Corps, Hobey Baker served under Gen. Leonard Wood, the same man that Hamilton Fish first served under with the Rough Riders. In a mere eighteen years, General Wood had gone from training cavalrymen like Fish to overseeing the training of pilots like Hobey Baker, who hurtled through the sky in "aeroplanes" with machine guns mounted on top.[1]

In many ways, comparing 1898 America to that of 1916 is startling. In addition to the invention of the airplane, there's the emergence of the automobile, Hollywood, a radio that could receive signals from different stations, and the publication of Einstein's theory of relativity.

The year 1916, when Hobey joined the Civilian Aviation Corps, was also a presidential election year. Woodrow Wilson, the former Princeton president, ran for reelection as the candidate who had kept America out of war, while charging that the Republican nominee, Charles Evan Hughes, would get America into war.

By this time, World War I had already claimed millions of lives in Europe. The Germans were trying to "bleed France white" at Verdun, a ghastly battle that lasted nearly the entire year and led to some 750,000 casualties. At the Battle of the Somme that same year, British, French, and other allies fought the Germans for several months, resulting in over one million casualties. The length of the trenches, often rat-infested and pestilent, was astounding: strung together in a line, they could have circled the earth. On the Eastern Front, Russia's unexpected success in the brutal, months-long Brusilov Offensive, largely against Austria-Hungarian and German troops, came at a heavy cost—over two million casualties among the belligerents, a half a million of them Russians.

Hobey's sympathies lay with the English and French. In many ways this made sense. Hobey was surrounded by people who sympathized with the Allies: influential Princeton families, like the Pynes, and his employer, J. P. Morgan Jr. In 1915, in fact, J. P. "Jack" Morgan Jr. (who had also attended St. Paul's School), having organized a syndicate of banks, floated a loan to France and Britain in 1915 worth $500 million (over $10 billion in today's dollars). And for most of the war the House of Morgan served as the purchasing agent for both England and France.

Further indicating the firm's support, a Paris partner of J. P. Morgan used his position to seek taxis and buses and other privately owned autos, as well as young American men with an adventurous bent, to transport wounded soldiers from the battlefields to Parisian hospitals. Thousands of Americans applied for the positions. Those who were successful became members of the French Foreign Legion and, later, members of the US military.[2]

In addition to the Pynes and Morgans, many other Ivy Leaguers supported the Allied cause. Consider fellow Princeton football legend Johnny Poe, who played for the Tigers in the 1890s and was a cousin of Edgar Allan Poe. As many other Americans did, he figured out how to get to Europe to fight for the British three years before the United States became involved in the war. He volunteered for the kilt-wearing Black Watch, a largely Scottish battalion that the Germans referred to as the "Ladies from Hell," on account of the kilts and their tenacity. It was with the Black Watch that Poe took a bullet to the stomach and died in battle. His story was surely not lost on Hobey Baker.[3]

Supporting the Allied cause as well was Yale graduate and famed musician Cole Porter, with whom Hobey Baker and Mimi Scott, the socialite to whom Hobey would become engaged during the war, would socialize in Paris during the war. Porter came to Paris during the war because he thought it would be an exciting adventure and because so many of his good friends and classmates had volunteered.[4]

Germany, of course, often gave those Americans who were inclined to support the Allies reasons to do so. A full year before Hobey's June 1916 decision to join the aviation corps, Germany had sunk the *Lusitania*, a British commercial vessel, killing 128 Americans. Later, other vessels were attacked. This enraged US citizens, even ones who weren't looking for war. At times, Germany argued that any belligerent vessels in the Atlantic were fair game, but Americans thought its citizens should be able to travel the seas freely.

Then in March 1917 the American public became aware of the Zimmerman telegram, a diplomatic message in which Germany proposed an alliance with Mexico to make war on the United States if America joined the war. In return Germany would help Mexico gain back land that it had lost to the United States in the mid-nineteenth century, basically Texas, Arizona, and New Mexico. This further enraged Americans. In time even the reluctant Wilson could not keep America on the sidelines any longer. In April 1917, his request for an official war declaration arrived, and Congress obliged.

WITHIN TWO MONTHS of Congress's war declaration, Hobey Baker became one of America's first pilots to head to Europe. It was a perilous time for the Allies. It's been estimated that at the time the United States joined the war, Great Britain's military had been down to six weeks of food supply, while France's soldiers, having endured horrendous casualty rates from suicide-like attacks ordered by its own generals, were near mutiny.

The horror and inhuman conditions on the ground also made the idea of winning glory on the battlefield look senseless. In the sky, though, this new realm of warfare, things were different. The fighter pilot, blazing through the skies, gave people a new and exciting way for individual war heroes to emerge.

In the Royal Air Force, men like Capt. Albert Ball were celebrated in the popular press for their "high-scoring"—shooting down large numbers of German planes. As the World War I aero-historian Peter Hart has noted, these men gave Britons hope that individual valor could be achieved despite the industrialization of war. Their public images approximated that of "knights of the air."[5]

In his biography of famed Eddie Rickenbacker, an ace pilot with whom Baker trained for a time, the historian W. David Lewis stated that such men would find themselves "making triumphal appearances on state occasions, enjoying audiences with kings and queens, driving expensive cars" and receiving merry attention from women.[6]

These men and the planes they flew seemed to have mysterious superpowers. A popular book at the time, *An Airman's Outings*, which Hobey Baker read while training in England, captures this. The author, a British wartime pilot, wrote that on leave back home a pilot might very well be asked by a regular citizen, "Can an aeroplane stand still in the air?" One pilot was told by a charming lady that she assumed the pilots only had cold food while in France.

"Oh no," the pilot said. "It's much the same as yours, only plainer and tougher."

"Then you do come down for meals," the lady concluded.[7]

11

IT WAS IN LATE JULY 1917 that Hobey Baker boarded a steamer bound for Europe. Days later, it reached the "danger zone" in the Atlantic, an area within which Germans U-boats were known to attack, which made Hobey a little nervous.[1] But on August 10 he arrived in Liverpool, and within a matter of days he was in Paris, where, as one of the first American pilots to arrive, he hoped he'd immediately get trained on a "fast machine" and then sent to the front. Instead, he soon learned that he'd been tasked with "office work." "It almost sets me crazy," he wrote home, "especially since I walk around here and people look at me and wonder why I am not at the front."[2]

Initially, he found living in Paris "perfectly horrible, it is so expensive, and of course no exercise or anything to do outside of office hours for one who does not speak the language." A room, a bath, and a French breakfast cost eleven francs, which was no trifle, and all too often the opportunity arose to go out to a restaurant with fellow soldiers, where the food was good but the cost was high, thanks to wartime inflation. "It is very hard to eat any meal under seven francs," Baker wrote. Were he flying, his salary would have been $225.00 per month. Instead, he took in $166.67, plus $36.00 for quarters. He missed simple things, like white bread and sugar, both of which were hard to come by in war-ravaged France.[3]

By mid-September, Hobey became a commissioned officer stationed in Pau, in southern France, where he was put in command of some two hundred airplane mechanics. With the snow-capped Pyrenees to the south, the town provided a magnificent backdrop that seemed to lift Hobey's spirits.

In Pau, however, the flight training was dangerous. Not known for caution, even Hobey complained of the tight spirals at slow speeds that they were asked to practice. (He still used a Nieuport plane, which,

Hobey Baker in uniform, serving during World War I. John D. Davies Collection on Hobey Baker, box 5, Princeton University Archives, Department of Rare Books and Special Collections, Princeton University Library.

though nimble, was susceptible to rollovers.) Two men injured themselves on rough landings after this exercise. Hobey passed his acrobatics training, nonetheless, and remained eager to get to the front. He even hatched a plan to join a French escadrille rather than wait, although in the end this plan did not materialize.[4]

By November 1917, Hobey had completed the French-run flight certification process. Next he was sent back to England for further training at an Instructors' School in Gosport.[5] It was during this time that Hobey wrote his note to Percy about the English gal he had met at Lady's Temple.

In Gosport, Hobey sensed that he was becoming a better pilot, and his letters make it clear how passionate he was about learning. When an Englishman in command of a testing squadron came to speak to the trainees, Hobey mentioned how appealing it sounded to work in a testing squadron in which officers test all new and experimental planes. Dangerous work, to be sure, but just the type of thing that appealed to him.[6]

In letters home, Hobey also expressed his appreciation for gifts people sent him for Christmas 1917, noting that his father had deposited twenty-five dollars in his bank account; his aunt Laura had sent him a muffler, and brother Thornton and sister-in-law Marie added a leather vest, sweater, and pictures. Percy shipped him yet another haul of coveted cigarettes, which pilots bummed off Hobey to no end. Percy also had 1,300 francs ($250) deposited into Hobey's Farmers' Loan bank account, for which he was quite grateful. He planned to use at least part of the money to buy a fur-lined flying cap, flying shoes, and fur-lined gloves. As cold as it was on the ground, thousands of feet up in the air it was much colder. Aware of phony reports that he had died in battle, Hobey encouraged his friends and family not to believe what they read in the paper, joking that he felt like cabling, "The news of my death was exaggerated."[7]

Early in 1918, Hobey trained in Arcachon, France. There he had the opportunity to do air exercises with the famed ace Eddie Rickenbacker, who would win the Medal of Honor and earn credit for taking down twenty-six German planes (a pilot earned the "ace" distinction for five), a record that stood until World War II. "It is some job to keep him off your tail and to get on his," Hobey wrote of Rickenbacker.

Upon finishing training at Arcachon, still not sent to the front, Hobey and a group of other pilots were ordered back to Paris and then England, where they were to instruct new arrivals. Ironically, Hobey was paying the price for completing his training so quickly. As one of a small number of Americans qualified to teach pilots, it was deemed that this was how he could best be put to use.

One thing that eased his disappointment with not being at the front was Mimi Scott. It was during this time, in Paris, that Hobey Baker began his wartime romance with her. She was in the City of Light for a short break from her nursing duties closer to the front. It's not clear exactly how they connected, perhaps at one of Cole Porter's legendary Parisian parties—both hung with Porter during the war and both ran in the same Ivy League circles.[8] What is clear is that two of America's "most eligible" began a love affair in what many consider the world's most romantic city.

Like Mimi, Miss Scott's mother, Jeanne de Gauville, was known as a transfixing beauty. She was also born into great wealth, as her father, Mimi's grandfather, was a French nobleman known widely in America. Upon marrying, Mimi's mother became Mrs. George Scott and together they shared one of the marquee properties on Newport's uber high-end Bellevue Avenue. She died, however, when Mimi was a just a baby. Mimi was raised, then, in homes teeming with servants, among them two French maids, said to be at her beck and call.[9]

As a young adult, Mimi became a celebrated society figure.[10] From the time she was introduced to New York society, in late 1913, until she began training to serve as a nurse in World War I, she was considered one of the country's most photographed debutantes.[11] The *Washington Post*'s Eugene Mossman once wrote that she had "scores of suitors who longed to marry her, and that she was a great heiress and beauty goes without saying."[12]

Indicative of her standing, in 1913 the *New York Times* ran a story about a ball to formally introduce Mimi to New York society. Some 500 people attended, among them virtually all of the prominent people who summered in Newport. The list of guests included surnames like Vanderbilt and Belmont, Gould and Fish.[13] In September 1915, a newspaper in faraway Oklahoma ran a picture of her attending an equine exhibition in Newport, Rhode Island, accompanied with a short blurb: "Miss Mimi Scott in Vertical Stripes and Miss Sands in Horizontal Stripes," which highlighted how stripes had become a fashion trend.[14]

People speculated about her love life. The *Washington Post* ran a story in June 1914 that mentioned Mimi Scott's return to Newport after a trip to Europe and noted that she was indeed *not* engaged. Rumors while away had suggested otherwise. She was apparently amused to find congratulatory letters and flowers upon returning home.[15]

Ironically, though, Mimi Scott came of age at almost the exact point at which the glittering, Gilded Age–infused lives of America's elite was ending. The young ladies in Scott's clique represented the final flickers of a societal flame that had shone brightly for several decades, one of refinement and elegance, but also one known for hierarchy and superficiality.

By the 1920s, societal privilege lost ground as a cynical popular press ran rampant tales of "excess and moral turpitude," fermenting a popular sense of anger with the Gilded Age's lavishness.[16]

Related to this, Mimi herself has been characterized as a vapid, big spender who left Hobey for an older man with more money. That one-sided view seems inadequate in light of the facts, however. Even before heading to Europe to serve in the war, Mimi had shown a willingness to step out of the confinements of traditional gentility. She was a crack tennis player, could handle a horse (she even hunted), and word in Newport had it that she swam as well as Eleanor Sears—a champion long-distance swimmer out of Boston.[17]

She also had a contemplative side. As an idealistic fifteen-year-old, she was intrigued by life in a convent as well as the notion of missionary work in Africa. Mimi's bold, adventurous personality was influenced by her father, George Isham Scott. With her mother having passed away when she was young, she looked up to her father and felt close to him, embraced his hobbies, and took on parts of his personality. A lot like Hobey, Mimi's father raced cars and was enamored with flight. He belonged to the Automobile Club of America.[18] It's easy to see how Hobey would have appealed to Mimi, and vice versa.

Mimi's father died suddenly in 1915, leaving her parentless. At that point, she reportedly removed herself from New York and Newport's glittering social life, opting instead to volunteer in New York City for several hours a day at Belgian and French charities, making bandages, surgical dressings, and layettes for children caught in the throes of war.[19] She also, it was reported, took on the role of special representative of the Aero Club of America to help see to it that the Militia of Rhode Island developed an aviation section, something that had been a goal of her late father.[20]

In 1917, the gaiety of another elite Newport summer season approached, but Mimi opted instead to work at the uptown Women's Hospital in New York. Rather than frolic amid luxury, that spring and summer she put in ten-hour days, seven days a week, washing and tending to the sick. She would be so tired by day's end, a newspaper story maintained, that she'd routinely nod off at dinner. Her goal, with the United States having declared war, was to get "fitted" so that she could care for wounded soldiers in Europe, and that left virtually no time for a social life.[21] In November 1917, she shipped to Paris.[22]

By January 1918, Mimi Scott was in Cugny, France, working with a small group of nurses, one of whom, Nora Saltonstall, described their crew as "a funny crowd—Society of N.Y., cranky French ladies, various odd individuals and V.A.D.s [Voluntary Aid Detachments] all mixed up together." Nora, as it happened, roomed with and worked under Mimi in Cugny. They'd spend months together by war's end, and she grew rather fond of Mimi, describing her as "funny but a bit raucous." Nora got a kick out of Mimi's societal ways, such as how she transported a massive amount of luggage every time they moved to a new location, including a set of fancy tea cups and an elegant kettle. The nurses ribbed Mimi about the tea set, but also came to appreciate how it helped them take a mental break—even if just for a few minutes—from their daily grind, as if they were escaping to an elite life of leisure.[23]

In Cugny, Mimi was put in charge of supplies and sterilization. It was demanding work, and the number of wounded who needed to be taken care of could be overwhelming. "I have seen enough wounds to hate them, and I don't see how people who have been in it for 3½ years can bear up to it all, just one long unending hashing up of people," Mimi's friend Nora wrote.[24]

There was little time to think about it too much, though, because there was so much work to be done. The situation hit home especially hard when a curly-haired young girl, wounded by a bomb, was brought in. The young girl's mother had died in an ambulance on the way to the hospital, and the child's story brought tears to the eyes of all the doctors, nurses, and orderlies. Hoping to bring a little comfort to this young girl's life, Mimi found a chemise to cut into a nightgown for her.

Heartbreak was everywhere. As was fear, not the least of which arose from the continuous threat of errant bombs.[25]

During a stretch of ten days' leave in late January 1918, the period during which the romance between Hobey and Mimi first bloomed, she attended a wedding reception for Ethel Harriman and Henry Russell at the Paris Ritz. Cole Porter, the Ivy Leaguer from Indiana who had already enjoyed success on Broadway and had come to Paris in the summer of 1917 with the idea that he'd try to help the war effort in some way, was in attendance, too. And with the "expat crème de la crème gathered round," Cole Porter and Mimi Scott, who was "just brash enough, once the champagne had taken effect, to pull off Porter's racier numbers," sang an impromptu duet.[26]

Near the end of this leave, Mimi and Hobey started seeing each other. Their time together gave Hobey a "decided and heavenly thrill."[27] Soon, they were writing regularly. Five months would pass until they would see each other again, but their connection deepened. In a letter to Percy, Hobey admitted to entertaining thoughts of marriage. "Whet in 'ell I would marry her on I don't know," he wrote.[28]

12

MEANWHILE, DELAY AFTER DELAY continued to keep Hobey from the front. He complained to Percy that old age or a Parisian taxi were more likely to kill him than any war action; he thought there was a decent chance that the waves of American troops now arriving in Europe could end the war before he had an opportunity to take out a German fighter plane.[1] Like Hamilton Fish, he didn't just want the United States to win; he wanted to be a part of the victory.

Despite it all, he tried to stay positive. The walks he took with friend and fellow aviator Seth Low, both stationed now in the Champagne district, not too far from the front, brought the rolling fields and patches of green pines and hills into plain view. He appreciated the beautiful countryside. At night, though, if the wind was coming at them from the trenches, they could hear the boom of the guns that were causing such human and earthen destruction.[2]

Hobey tried to cheer himself up by putting pictures of his beloved family on his scanty barracks table: photos of his dad at home and of Thornton, Marie, and their children.[3] He made lieutenant in March 1918 and was finally assigned an actual plane that month. He also read another false report that he'd shot down a German Boche, which prompted him to write to the offending newspaper, demanding a retraction.

Finally, in April, Hobey was sent to the front, near the town of Fismes, as a member of the 103rd Aero Squadron. The 103rd, otherwise known as the Lafayette Squadron, was made up of many former members of the Lafayette Escadrille and the Lafayette Flying Corps—in other words, soldiers who had signed up to fight for the French before the United States joined the war. With the 103rd, Hobey flew the SPAD VIII and XIII. These French-designed biplanes were known to climb and dive well and had solid gun platforms.[4]

Hobey was excited about the appointment to the 103rd, seeing it as one step closer to taking down German planes at the front. In letters home, when writing about fellow airmen, he would often reference how many planes a particular man had to his credit, like a sports fan might talk about home runs hit or goals scored. He did not seem consumed by the fact that this really was an issue of life and death. Even when it came to writing about himself, he would oftentimes express the matter-of-fact equivalent of "It'll either be him or me." And he prepared his father for the prospect that he would not return from the front, in plain and simple terms.

As it happened, his first days on the front were quite dicey. Having finished a patrol, for example, he made a "beautiful" landing only to suddenly realize that a fellow pilot, Paul Baer—credited at that time with taking down three Boche planes and known to be "wild as a hawk"—had landed his plane on the other side of the runway. The two were headed straight for each other. Thinking quickly, Hobey turned his motors on to pick up power and turned his plane sharply. He avoided a collision with Baer but, in the process, touched a wing to the ground and broke five ribs.[5]

Shortly thereafter, Hobey went up on a patrol with the well-regarded pilot Charlie Biddle and realized quickly that it would take him a while to get his "vision of the air," the ability to see planes in the sky before it was too late. It might seem counterintuitive, but locating planes in the air— before they were on top of you—took some learning. On this day Biddle, a fellow Princeton alum, spotted several planes that Hobey hadn't perceived at all. "It is for this reason so many pilots are killed when first they go to the front," Hobey wrote. Compounding matters, it was difficult to tell whether a plane was friend or foe. Only in the last fifteen seconds or so—if you were able to spot the plane in your peripheral vision to begin with—could you determine a plane's nationality. And even then, depending on the plane's angle, it could be tough to tell.[6]

Hobey also learned early on that flying at the front gave pilots a unique perspective of the war. One moment you could be looking down at the snakelike trenches, the next at earthen craters created by the explosions of artillery shells near a town like Leon. One moment you might see several fires in Rheims, the next green fields and patches of natural-looking forest. All the while thoughts of vulnerability were never far away.

"Yes, I was scared up there today," Hobey wrote. "But [I] concluded that there couldn't be a nicer way to die, quick, sure and certain."[7] On one flight, he viewed a ground attack in the region of Loches. And "even from this height," Hobey wrote, "you could see the yellow gas clouds over the trenches."[8]

In one week with the Lafayette, Hobey's squadron lost four planes from battle, at least temporarily. Hobey's plane was shot up, and he shot up German planes.[9] He briefly thought he had taken down his first German plane. In a letter home his excitement at the prospect leapt off the page. "Two of them have been confirmed and I am _wild_ with _joy_," he wrote his father, adding, "I am so excited I can hardly write." Later in the letter, he wrote, "It was the biggest thrill I ever had in my life and I am still all excited over it just as I used to be after a big game."[10] But ultimately, with the Lafayette, he was never given formal credit for a takedown; getting this was harder than it might seem. Takedown credit required not only the pilot's report but also confirmation from another source, such as boots on the ground or soldiers stationed in an observation balloon.

The general strain of life on the front—Hobey's squadron lost three men in a three-week stretch in May—motivated Hobey to think about his future, namely Mimi Scott. She was at present stationed in a forward hospital in Compiegne. "I hear from her all the time and wish I could see her again somehow or other," Hobey wrote home. "I wish she did not have so much money and I more." He followed this lament with a statement that revealed his lack of confidence in his ability to earn good money in the business world: "I am at present saving out of my pay, but what will I do if I live through this war? I am worth about a franc a week to Thornton. I don't see why I did not get some of his brains since we are both your children."[11]

Here was a Princeton football legend, whose name was known nation-wide and who knew more about how to fly a plane and fix one than almost any other American in the world, worrying that he didn't have enough money to win the hand of the woman he loved or enough brains to figure out how to make it in the world. He took solace, though, in his bravery at the war front, writing to Percy, "I wish you could see how bold I am. Just like Thornton."[12]

As summer neared, news arrived that the French town of Fismes had fallen to the Germans. "It begins to look as though we had entered the war too late after all," he wrote home, now worried the Germans would win. And reports had the Germans attacking Soissons, which was close to Compiegne, where Mimi was stationed. He tried to get telegrams through to Mimi to see how she was faring, but the hospital personnel and patients had been forced to retreat from Compiegne on account of heavy shells, some of which were filled with gas. He wouldn't hear from her again until mid-June.

"It certainly is a real war," Hobey wrote. He wanted to see more signs of American help. "Ye Gods, if they would only stop talking at home and do something. Liberty motors, beautiful camps, intense enthusiasm, yet we over here haven't seen anything to back up the talk with."[13]

★ FINALLY, IN EARLY JULY 1918, Hobey got to see Mimi again in Paris. Pushing aside the strain of war, they took advantage of a stretch of shared leave by seeing each other nearly "all of the time," which lifted Hobey's spirits mightily.

"Seeing Mimi Scott in Paris was the most wonderful thing that has happened to me in a long while," he wrote. "You can imagine what it was after three months at the front with steady flying, and she is so absolutely nice to be with, and for those three days, we just did everything together. To sit in a restaurant and eat a good meal, to take a hot bath, to sleep between sheets seemed very good after living in tents with no floors. Mimi had a much harder time than I, so all those things were good to her too."[14]

Baker's leave came at a time during which he was switching from the 103rd to the 13th Aero Squadron. The man behind this move was the experienced and tough-minded Charlie Biddle. He had "Oscar, the Devil's Own Grim Reaper," the 13th's tagline, painted on his SPAD XIII, after all. Hobey was hesitant to leave the 103rd, but he'd worked with Biddle before and had confidence in him. In time, under Biddle, Hobey would be put in command of one of the squadron's three "flights."[15]

The formal transfer to Biddle's 13th occurred on 13 July 1918 and involved the issuance of yet another plane for Hobey. He saw action quickly. With the help of two other pilots, Hobey likely took down the squadron's first German plane. This wasn't technically confirmed, however—one observation post confirmed that the plane in question had crashed, but another post did not.[16]

For Hobey, helping Biddle get the 13th up and running was taxing but invigorating. The fellows put in long hours and operated under considerable stress, and Hobey's physical appearance reflected this. Hair loss progressed further up his scalp, and he felt like he looked as if he'd aged many years. No matter; battlefront news from the north, from Rheims and elsewhere, buoyed the pilots' spirits. It seemed as if the tide had now turned in the Allies' favor.[17]

Hobey managed three days of leave in early August. As it approached, he tried to figure out how he was going to see Mimi, but it seemed unlikely. Unbeknownst to him, she was orchestrating a surprise. Maj. Bill Thaw ordered an unsuspecting Hobey to go into town with him, and there he found Mimi waiting. They went to Paris by car, then to Bill Thaw's sister's house for some rest and relaxation. "It was absolutely ideal," Hobey wrote to his father.[18]

By late August, Hobey had been formally put in command of one of Biddle's squadrons, but it lacked the requisite number of pilots and other personnel. As if that wasn't bad enough, his partial squadron would be relocated to a new camp and would have to wait a month before heading to the front. "You can imagine how I feel about it," Hobey wrote, "but I am in the Army now and there is nothing to do except make the best of it here."[19]

At least relocating meant that Hobey needed to return to Paris to retrieve his "baggage," giving him an opportunity to perhaps see Mimi again.[20] Set to arrive on a Saturday night, he sent Mimi a telegram ahead of time but heard nothing back. A lovesick Hobey spent the night in Paris feeling lost. He ate dinner alone in his room before going to the theater, which he left early in favor of bed.[21] The next day looked to be more of the same; he lolled around, went to lunch, and generally pined for Mimi.

That evening, he telephoned her Parisian address, 23 Rue de Lille, but received no answer yet again. Prodded by friends, he decided to tag along to a get-together and late dinner. He returned to his Meurice Hotel and learned that Mimi had left a note asking him—no matter what time he received her message—to come see her at once. So he rushed across the River Seine.

He found Mimi looking a bit pale and worn from her difficult work at the front. This endeared her to him even more.[22] They reveled in each other's love, and before night's end they were engaged. Hobey hadn't planned it this way, hadn't even gotten a ring yet. But it was what he knew he wanted, and he made it happen.

"Don't quite understand how I put it across, but I did and she is so much what I have always wanted that I feel all sort of safe and happy," Hobey wrote to his father. "She is a very decided sort of person with lots of brains, not beautiful, but oh, I don't know, just so sweet and big and real."[23]

13

BACK AT CAMP a few days after the engagement, Hobey wrote to his friend Percy that no firm date had been set for the wedding, but that it would probably occur after the war. He asked Percy to arrange a $500 credit to his Farmer's Loan account so he could buy Mimi a ring; in the event that his stateside account didn't have enough money in it, he said, Percy could sell Hobey's Anglo-French 5 percent bond, adding, "I have one I believe."[1]

In the meantime, Hobey immersed himself in the job of getting a squadron up and running. It wasn't easy, especially since he faced all kinds of delays, as Charlie Biddle noted:

> Hobe[y] is still in the rear and has not even got his pilots and machines yet, and there seemed to be no immediate prospect of his getting them when I last heard from him. It is too bad, for Hobe[y] is one of the very best, a very skillful pilot, and has all the nerve in the world and is a thorough gentleman. He is one of the fairest, most straightforward fellows I know and should make an excellent squadron commander, but he struck rum luck from the start.[2]

As Hobey's men finally started to trickle in—mechanics and support personnel first, then the pilots—he put in long hours organizing flight schedules, doing maintenance work, and dealing with disciplinary issues, which arose more often than he'd have liked in the early going. In fact, he had to change out sergeants to bring about the level of order he wanted.

Biddle sent news to Hobey that his old squadron had taken down eight German planes in three days but had lost two men whom Hobey had known well.[3] The high casualty rates and the need for men was such that

Hobey was soon told that some of his pilots—which he'd patiently waited for, for so long—would be transferred to the front. "One boy told me his squadron had lost forty men in five flying days," he soberly wrote home.[4]

But by late September, Hobey was still not at the front, nor had he heard from Mimi since their engagement. "I have tried writing her several times, but I don't believe any of them ever reached her," he wrote to Percy. "It is a horrible feeling to be so utterly away and detached from everyone you love, and at times I get very depressed and blue, but if I could only see Mimi more often it would change everything."[5]

A couple of days later, he sat down to write a letter to his father, who had requested a picture of Mimi Scott. Hobey's dad also wanted to know more about Mimi and her family.

"I really know little of her family and it has never entered my head how little I did know until you asked me. Evidently her Aunt, Miss Scott, is the one she loves most," Hobey wrote, noting that both Mimi's parents had passed away. "I never thought she was beautiful, or even especially pretty, before I got to know her, and now it is the combination of all inside and out I am looking at and this is, Oh! So very wonderful."[6]

Within days, in mid-October, with his squadron still training vigorously and awaiting orders to the front, Hobey gained leave. He went to Paris to see Mimi, who'd managed leave as well. They hadn't seen each other since their engagement over a month prior, although in the most recent note she'd sent to Hobey she'd expressed her desire to get married right away. But then in Paris, Mimi unexpectedly broke Hobey's heart: she no longer wanted to marry him. She tried to explain, but he came away unsure and rattled.

After the breakup Hobey stayed in Paris for only a short while, feeling lost and heartbroken. "I think she is in love with another man," Hobey wrote his father in a painful letter. "I believe she honestly believed she loved me until the right one came along. I am certainly good when it comes to girls." Not yet ready to delve more deeply into the breakup, he added, "Some day, Father, I want to have a long talk with you about Mimi."[7] Rather than wallow in Paris, Hobey left the capital four days before his leave was up, eager to forget matters by rejoining his squadron and plowing into his work.[8]

Mimi seems to have rebounded from the breakup with relative ease. Soon afterward—perhaps beforehand—she became involved with Harvard graduate Philander Cable, a US attaché at the American Embassy in Paris.

Adding to the intrigue is a rather peculiar article that ran in the *Washington Post* shortly before Mimi broke up with Hobey. This full-page article covered Hobey and Mimi's wartime romance, and on the same day it ran in the *Post*, the *Philadelphia Inquirer* printed a virtually identical piece as a front-page exposé in its Sunday magazine.

Among a number of curious elements in the article, the author, Eugene Mossman, who claimed to have interviewed Mimi Scott (but not the media-shy Baker) for it, states that the pair's love affair started in June 1918 (from Hobey's letters, we know that it started months earlier). Not only that, according to Mossman, this June romance got its start in rather dramatic fashion: Mimi was standing in the doorway of a French refugee hospital, looking out to the horizon when she noticed an unusually low-flying fighter plane coming toward her. As the plane neared, she saw that the pilot was peering downward into the nearby woods. Puzzled, she continued to watch as the plane circled above, getting ever lower, before landing cleanly in a meadow across from where she stood. With his helmet in hand and a rush in his step, out jumped the pilot. He hurried over to Mimi and said, "There's three kids lying in a heap in that woods over there. I don't know whether they're dead or alive, but something ought to be done. Can you take 'em in here? I'll go and get 'em."[9]

Without a chance to respond, Mimi watched as the man turned and dashed to the side of the hospital. Moments later, she heard the nurses' lone Ford automobile start rumbling. She watched as the man drove it off through the fields and disappeared into the woods.

Her mind raced, wondering who this mysterious man was and how three children had ended up in the woods across from the refugee hospital. Soon, the article maintained, she saw the Ford rumble back toward her and come to a stop. The doors opened and three starving, desperate-looking young girls tumbled out. They'd been surviving on their own in the wilderness for two days.

Mimi Scott and the other nurses promptly fed and washed the children and found them a comfortable place to rest. With the children settled, Mimi then stepped back outside to see the pilot. By then, no longer hidden by his goggles and helmet, his sandy blond hair and blue-gray eyes seemed oddly familiar to her. She tried to recall who he was, but before she could place him, the man spoke up. "It's a long time since I saw you last, Miss Scott. And this place is not much like Princeton, is it?"[10]

"Why, you are Hobey Baker, and we all had lunch together after the game! How long, long ago that seems! And now you are fighting over here."

And there, this odd, yet seemingly detailed article reported, the two beautiful, eligible, American volunteers stood: Hobart Amory Blaine Baker, perhaps America's greatest athlete, fresh off of rescuing three children in a war zone, and Mimi Scott, a gorgeous Newport heiress on hand to take the children in.[11] It was a "meet cute" the likes of which Hollywood might've rejected for a lack of believability.[12] And it turns out it wasn't true.

Given the reputations of the *Washington Post* and the *Philadelphia Inquirer* and the detailed nature of the article about Hobey and Mimi's meet-cute, it's hard to figure why and by whom this story came to be. Did Mimi conjure it in a misguided effort to bring attention to herself? If so, did she realize her mistake and decide to break up with Hobey rather than face up to it? Did Mossman make it up? If so, to what end? It's an odd chapter at the end of what, up to October 1918, seemed like a wartime romance that would enjoy a storybook ending.

14

IRONICALLY, AT THIS LOW POINT in his personal life and with the war weeks away from ending, Hobey was sent to the front. And he encountered dramatic action on the first official patrol of his new squadron when he and some of his other pilots moved in on a German biplane, only to realize that German Fokkers were on their tails. "I was scared to death, for they [the new pilots flying under Hobey's command] did not see them [the Fokkers]; but I dived and the others followed me and we got away O.K.," he recalled.[1]

More heated action occurred days later when Hobey, out on patrol with two inexperienced pilots, dove on a group of Fokkers beneath them. Hobey's guns hit the Fokker that he'd locked in on, sending the plane into a downward spin and giving Baker official confirmation for an individual takedown—an uncommon achievement, since most takedowns involved several planes firing on the enemy and therefore shared credit. This marked Hobey's only individual credit of the war.

Just as he took this plane down, however, a German plane with an altitude advantage dove in on him, forcing him to pull up. Compounding matters, a batch of ten Fokkers arrived for support, prompting Hobey, over German lines now, to take his men on a screaming retreat back to camp. "It is the first time I have ever been chased in by Boche," an annoyed Hobey wrote. "But it couldn't be helped unless I wanted to commit suicide for myself and the two pilots I had with me."[2]

During these final weeks of intense fighting, Hobey's letters to his father picked up. "I find I am writing more to you now that I don't write to Mimi. This time in the evening always seems empty," he stated. It didn't help that, given how slow the mail was, he was still receiving letters from family and friends congratulating him on the engagement. "It is damned unpleasant, to say the least," he admitted.[3]

As November arrived, the war only days from ending, Hobey and his men continued to face fierce opposition.[4] During this stretch he took down another German biplane, giving him his third and final credit for the war.

⭐ WITH THE ARMISTICE OF NOVEMBER 11, 1918, the Great War ended, and Hobey's furious days of flying, organizing pilots, keeping mechanics on task, and doing all the other jobs that came with handling a squadron came to a screeching halt.

"Today I just loafed around and really did nothing," he noted on Armistice Day. "Of course I am glad it is over, but I would not have minded a few more weeks to get this squadron at the height of its efficiency." It pleased Hobey, though, that his squadron—of the five created at the same time—was the one that had managed to fully form and operate at the front. Plus, despite the war's intense final weeks, his squadron had lost no men.[5]

Throughout France, the news of peace brought raucous celebrations. Hobey and some buddies went to the nearby town of Nancy to join the revelry. They went by truck and saw the city "all dressed up, the streets crowded, everyone cheering and kissing each other." They had dinner at a quaint restaurant in which the locals sang French national songs and generally celebrated, and where the alcohol flowed and everyone "got tight."[6]

That night, he wrote, "I wish I had some influence so I could be relieved of this command and get home."[7] To that end, Hobey also wrote to Percy, telling him that he was afraid he'd spend another year in the army before he could get home "unless you with all your influential friends can do something for me." The end of the war, he admitted to Percy, had made him think of home much more. "You can't imagine how dull life is now that the war is over and we haven't the excitement of flying on the lines."[8]

On November 21, Hobey wrote to his father again. As he'd suspected, Mimi had fallen for another man. He'd received a letter from her in which she told him she planned to marry Philander Cable in the coming months. (She would divorce Cable in 1929 on "grounds of indifference and his formal refusal to live with her."[9] In 1937 Mimi married William Paul Lennon. They divorced in 1942. Oddly enough, in *The*

Autobiography of Malcolm X, it is claimed that in 1944, Malcolm Little, an eighteen-year-old servant of Lennon's at the time who would later become known as Malcom X, was paid to disrobe Lennon, "place him on a bed, sprinkle him with talcum powder, and massage him until he reached his climax." Mimi Scott appears to have lived out her later years of life quietly in Naples, Florida.)[10]

For whatever reason, from this point in late November 1918, there are no more letters from Hobey. It's likely that his final days looked a lot like his first week or so after the Armistice: not much work other than occasional flying and plane maintenance and a lot of pining for home. Finally, in December, he received papers to head back to America.

Before leaving, he decided to take one last ride. His pilot friends warned him that it was bad luck, but Hobey didn't go much for superstition. At the hangar a mechanic brought out a recently repaired SPAD that Hobey chose to fly rather than his own. Pilot etiquette considered it good form to test out a recently repaired machine. As squadron leader, Hobey figured he should be the one to test it.

Under heavy rain, he raced the SPAD down the runway and took to the air. A quarter mile or so into his flight, at little more than 500 feet in the air, the SPAD's new carburetor gave out. Capt. Edwin H. Cooper, who witnessed the crash, recalled, "Instead of running straight away to land he started to turn back toward the field. The wing slipped, the machine crashed and he was killed."[11] It was a daring maneuver to try to return the plane to the airfield rather than crash-land straightaway. To some, it was classic Hobey: attempt a risky maneuver to make a fantastic landing. To others, the entire scene suggested perhaps more than a crash. Were the loss of Mimi and the thought of returning home with his glory days behind him too much? Did Hobey Baker take his own life?

News of Hobey's death spread quickly in America. Journalists wrote about someone they clearly admired. The *Washington Post*'s J. V. Fitzgerald declared, "Hobey Baker is dead, but his athletic deeds, before he offered and gave his life to Uncle Sam, will live long in the memories of the thousands of Americans who follow the careers of the pick of our athletes." Fitzgerald credited Hobey with making hockey a popular sport in New York, with being the greatest all-around athlete any American institution of higher learning had ever turned out, and with convincing those who watched him, Canadians included, that Hobey Baker ranked among the greatest hockey players who ever lived. Fitzgerald celebrated Hobey's character. He "hated publicity," Fitzgerald said, pointing to there being no record of a public Baker interview and that the individual attention Baker received as a member of St. Nick's had made the star think seriously about quitting the team. "No more modest athlete than Baker ever lived," Fitzgerald concluded.[12]

Not only media lamented Hobey's passing; tributes from all kinds of folks occurred. A somewhat fitting example of this, given Baker's speed, came in September 1919, when a two-year-old horse named Hobey Baker bested the field at Havre de Grace.[13] According to Baker biographer Emil Salvini, a noteworthy number of Princeton alumni who had gone to school with Baker named children after him.

As noted, there was some, albeit limited, speculation about the nature of Hobey's death. A French paper suggested suicide as a possible motive, citing the breakup with Mimi. A column in a Wisconsin paper, "Sport Snap Shots" by Morris Miller, wondered if the demise of Mimi and Hobey's relationship had brought on a kind of recklessness in Baker.[14] What this analysis overlooks is that Baker was plenty reckless before the breakup.

As mentioned, Hobey had become an aviator not long after the airplane itself had been outfitted with wheels. It remained in 1918, even into World War II, an exceedingly dangerous endeavor. He liked fast cars. He'd motorcycled around Europe at an early stage in motorcycle development. Even his request for Mimi's hand in marriage—unplanned and offered late at night—was risky, seeing as they'd only seen each other in a few bursts for a few days at a time over the course of eight months, and that he didn't have much money.

Even in training, during high-speed simulations, Baker flew aggressively. Once, flying without his hat or goggles, he was momentarily blinded by machine-gun powder, causing him to fly straight into a balloon that had been intended for target practice. The balloon then wrapped precariously around his wing, leading to a tailspin landing that ended with the plane upside-down. The plane did not survive the crash, but Baker somehow emerged from the wreckage virtually unscathed.[15]

In short, if Baker acted "recklessly" after his breakup with Mimi, his behavior seems to have paled in comparison to that before it. As the end of the war neared, Hobey took solace in knowing that none in his squadron had perished and he himself had stayed alive. In late October, he ended a letter to a friend with "best of luck Wen and stay alive . . . [I have spent four months] working over the lines and while I don't figure among the leading aces I comfort myself with that thought."[16] As *Sports Illustrated's* Robert Cantwell put it in 1966, "Baker nowhere seems suicidal."[17]

There was, however, a sense of fatalism in him, as there was with Hamilton Fish. He had written a letter to his father, months before his death, after having flown beyond enemy lines for the first time with Biddle and having seen Biddle take down a German plane, in which Baker told his father that "there couldn't be a nicer way to die, quick, sure and certain."[18]

⭐ IN A WAY, BAKER'S DEATH symbolized the end of an era. Industrialization, corporatism, urbanization, and a more secular, materialistic popular culture had been chipping away at Victorianism for some time. But Hobey was not a remnant of the past; he was a man of his times, with a touch of the future.

In following decades, cultural critics lamented what they saw as the virtual extinction of the Hobey archetype, the Victorian noble. However, by the 1950s and 60s this archetype came under attack by some scholars and literary critics, who saw Hobey Baker as a gallant but unthoughtful embodiment of leisure-class values.[19] He was too Victorian, too patriotic. Neither portrayal gives us a clear picture, nor is either complete.

What is clear is that, time and again, Hobey Baker risked his life to fight for his country. That he dearly loved his family, his brother in particular. That he wanted to be known for his bravery, daring, and competence. That he wanted Mimi Scott to love him. And it's reasonable to assume that as a kid he wanted more reassurance that his mother loved him, too.

Ironically, in 1921 it was his mother, remarried by then, who, despite modest financial means, arranged to have Hobey's body moved from its burial place in Europe to a gravesite in the West Laurel Hill Cemetery in Bala Cynwyd, Pennsylvania. In February 1920, a memorial, covered widely in the press, had been held and a large number of Princeton students and Baker's friends and family had attended. At it the president of Princeton had paid tribute. As reported by the *Philadelphia Inquirer*, later at the 1921 burial, which included military honors, Hobey's brother Thornton attended, along with his mother, as did officers of the American

Expeditionary Force and many Princeton men. Rev. Floyd W. Tompkins, rector of the Holy Trinity P.E. Church, gave a short eulogy, describing Hobey Baker as a "fine sample of American manhood."[20]

While he lived, despite all his success, Hobey yearned to feel confident that he could make it, that he was good enough. It's surprising seeing how accomplished he was, how much people celebrated him once he arrived at Princeton and beyond. It makes one want to reach back in time, to 15 January 1904—the day that no one remembered to tell Hobey Baker that it was his birthday, that he was twelve years old—and let him know he's doing alright, pat him on the back, and tell him simply, "Happy Birthday, kid."

THREE

Nile Kinnick

15

ON 6 DECEMBER 1939, a five-foot-eight-inch, one-hundred-seventy-pound senior halfback with a good arm stepped to the podium to accept the Heisman Trophy. Early in the season, a more unlikely Heisman winner would have been hard to conjure, plagued as his junior year was by an injured ankle and playing, as he had, on a team that had won but a single game in each of the two previous seasons. Yet there the Iowa Hawkeyes' Nile Kinnick, class president and Phi Beta Kappa, stood—a small-town boy from esteemed Iowa bloodlines, staring into the bright lights of New York City's Downtown Athletic Club in front of some 800 dinner guests.

Kinnick had won a clear victory from the Heisman voters, a group made up of sportswriters and radio announcers. He tallied 651 Heisman points in beating out Tom Harmon, a tailback from Michigan who is considered one of the greatest college backs of all time.[1]

And in the end it was really no wonder Kinnick won. His 1939 season remains eye-popping. He was involved in sixteen of Iowa's nineteen touchdowns, throwing for eleven and rushing for five. To boot, he kicked the Hawkeyes' point-afters, using the drop-kick method. So all told, he was involved in 107 of the Hawkeyes' 130 total points. He played 402 of a possible 420 minutes—he played in the backfield on offense, the secondary on defense. In the defensive backfield, he recorded eight interceptions, a Hawkeye record still on the books. In 1939, he set fourteen school records, six of which still stand. And his team lost only a single game.

In addition to becoming Iowa's first and only Heisman Trophy winner, Kinnick was that year's only unanimous All-American in the Associated Press (AP) voting. He registered the largest margin of victory in the race for Big Ten MVP, and he won the Maxwell Award, similar to the

Nile Kinnick, number 24, playing halfback in the Iowa victory over Notre Dame on 11 November 1939. Before this, Iowa had not beaten Notre Dame since 1921. Nile Kinnick Papers, University of Iowa Libraries, Iowa City, Iowa.

Heisman, and the Walter Camp Memorial Trophy, given to the best back. He was nominated, along with Joe DiMaggio and Joe Louis, for AP Male Athlete of the Year. DiMaggio hit .381 in 1939 in leading the Yankees to their fourth straight World Series title. Joe Louis won all three of his heavyweight title defenses. Kinnick won AP Athlete of the Year.

It got pretty wild. One Iowa paper called for him to be nominated for president in 1956, the first year he'd be old enough to run. Readers of the *Cedar Rapids Gazette* nearly voted Kinnick Man of the Year. He finished second by one vote to Adolph Hitler, whom readers variably described as a "brutal, ambitious, autocrat," someone who was despised for his "sadistic persecutions," and yet someone who "made the world's wheels spin 'round most furiously." Josef Stalin finished behind Kinnick in third place.[2]

A big reason that Nile Kinnick received such attention in 1939 is that his team, dubbed the "Ironmen," truly rocked the college football landscape. Until then, Iowa football had been mired in a depression, just like the rest of the country, particularly farm states like Iowa itself. In 1933 the Iowa Hawkeyes scored one touchdown. In the last five games of 1938 it scored zero. In 1937 and '38 it won a single game.

Iowa hadn't even started the 1930s in the Big Ten. It'd been suspended for issues related to improper benefits for student-athletes. The

Nile Kinnick, number 24, scores the game-winning touchdown versus Notre Dame on 11 November 1939. Nile Kinnick Papers, University of Iowa Libraries, Iowa City, Iowa.

conference commissioner blamed alumni but determined that the Iowa athletic department lacked institutional control.[3] The suspension was lifted a month after it began—partly because Iowa moved to implement recommended changes and partly because a Carnegie Foundation study found that only Illinois and Chicago, among Big Ten schools, had "no charges or irregularities under investigation." Still, the uncertainty and negative press contributed to some rather lean years.[4]

But suddenly the 1939 team emerged from the leanest of times to enjoy unexpected greatness, and they did it with what seemed like sheer grit. The conditioning program of the team's new coach, Dr. Eddie Anderson, had trimmed the roster to the point that, at first glance, it looked like Iowa simply needed bodies, let alone talent. As it turned out, many players on the 1939 Iowa team played entire games, hence the nickname. Yet they kept winning, and people were inspired. People responded as if to say, *if this Iowa team can somehow get it done, maybe the whole state of Iowa can. What the heck, maybe the whole country can.*

"I can remember the desperation in my mom's face when it came time to buy coal," Kinnick teammate Al Couppee recalled of the Depression years. "The whole state was in a bad way. Farms were closing down, people were hungry. Then, out of a clear blue sky came this one little group of people with just the right chemistry—our team. There was an almost hysterical relief at having something at last to grab hold of, to believe in. And . . . we had Nile."[5] Teammates revered Nile.

How, people asked, could a program that had won two games in two years, that had in 1931 scored a grand total of seven points *all* season long, suddenly compete for a national title under a first-year head coach? As Couppee suggested, a good part of the answer was Nile Kinnick.

And, my, did Nile Kinnick fit as the leader of "Ironmen." His jaw seemed made of it. So too did his willpower and morality. With economic pain all too familiar and war raging in Europe, to a lot of folks he embodied all that was good and hopeful about America. The *New York Sun's* George Trevor wrote that the "square cut of Kinnick's jaw, the bulldog set of his mouth, and the look of eagles in his brown eyes, reveal the grim determination and fixity of purpose . . . Character is stamped in every line of Kinnick's alert, forthright face. Intelligence glows from his luminous eyes." The *Boston Post's* Bill Cunningham echoed such sentiment, offering assurance amid uncertain times, by writing, "The country is OK as long as it produces Nile Kinnicks. The football part is incidental."[6]

The Kinnick legend only grew when he stepped to the microphone upon receiving the Heisman. He opened his remarks by expressing how moving it was to win the award and giving credit to his first-year coach and his teammates back in Iowa City. He thanked the sportswriters and sportscasters that voted for him. Then he closed with, "I'd like to make a comment which, in my mind, is indicative perhaps of the greater significance of football and sports emphasis in general in this country, and that is, I thank God I was warring on the gridirons of the Midwest and not on the battlefields of Europe."

The previously silent yet attentive crowd erupted in applause at this. "I can speak confidently and positively," Kinnick continued, "that the players of this country would much more, much rather, struggle and fight to win the Heisman award than a Croix de Guerre [a French military decoration]. Thank you." The audience erupted again.[7]

The speech came at a time when the question of how the United States should respond to the problems in Europe generated heated debate. Ominous developments were indeed emanating from across the pond. Germany had taken back the Rhineland and Sudetenland, annexed Austria, and, only months earlier, invaded Poland, prompting France and Britain to declare war on the Nazis. Yet Germany had not commenced its full-on assault of Western Europe. And the surprise attack on Pearl Harbor, by Germany's ally Japan, was still two years off. A good number of Americans, then—with the horrors of World War I and its unsatisfactory peace in mind—were isolationists.

The audience at the Downtown Athletic Club, many of them undoubtedly eager to keep America out of another brutal war an ocean away, appreciated Kinnick's willingness to address the matter.

In turn, Kinnick has been portrayed as someone who was only drawn into World War II on account of Pearl Harbor. This, however, was not the case.[8] He volunteered for the navy months before Japan's December 1941 attack. In fact, his views from the time of his Heisman remarks to just several months later had shifted. And as events unfolded, they'd shift even more, soon turning him into an interventionist.

Just a day after Japan's attack on Pearl Harbor, Kinnick wrote in his diary, "How ridiculously short-sighted this sudden war has made the isolationists look." He wondered what ardent isolationists like the famed aviator Charles Lindbergh and Burton Wheeler, a US senator and leader of the anti-interventionist wing of the Democratic Party, now thought. And Kinnick lamented America's slow response to events that had been unfolding for years. "Oh, that this country and England had had the courage to forestall all this when Japan first went into Manchukuo [the name Japan gave to the puppet state it created after invading Manchuria in 1931] and Italy into Abyssinia."[9] (Abyssinia, a name used by Europeans for Ethiopia, was invaded by Italy in 1935.)

While the presentation of Kinnick as an isolationist has been bungled a bit, the media narrative—athletic wonder, academic whiz, morally upright—on balance really did fit the man. Yet even then it only covered the surface.

Through his diaries, correspondence, and actions, a much fuller view of Kinnick emerges. He was funny, deeply curious, intellectually active, and pragmatic, committed to his Christian Science faith, yearning to do meaningful things in the world, and eager to honor his famed Iowa bloodlines. Honing his political and social views on economics, war, education, and race relations, he devoured books and enjoyed movies. He loved his family, his country, and the Iowa Hawkeyes. He was committed to the war effort; indeed, he came to see it as a battle for Western civilization and its Christian underpinnings. He was, then, both traditional and forward-thinking. But the media, even with all the attention it gave Kinnick, did not delve too deeply into the man. The press showed reserve, mainly satisfied with highlighting things that most everyone could celebrate: Kinnick's courage, selflessness, athletic prowess, and love of country.

As noted, in *King Football,* college football historian Michael Oriard stated that while the 1920s have been known as the Golden Age of Sports, the 1930s "are more truly the Gold Age of Football." Radio and film, magazines and weeklies, celebrated the sport, which could be used as a kind of "shorthand to establish the heroic masculine character."[10] And Kinnick was perhaps the decade's most celebrated single-season gridiron star. Through how he was presented in the press, through his diary writings and letters, and through his actions, a view of America's hopes and dreams, its fears and uncertainties, its values and its times, and of the continuity and change rippling through America emerges.

16

NILE KINNICK CAME from an impressive line. His maternal grandfather, George Washington Clarke, had been the governor of Iowa. Many other Clarkes and Kinnicks were well educated and successful. Both families had roots in Adel, Iowa, a small town twelve miles northwest of Des Moines. Nile's parents met there and finished first and second in academic standing at Adel High School (his mother was the valedictorian).

Nile took pride in his lineage, wanted to represent it well. He strove, in particular, to emulate his Grandpa Clarke, for whom he had great respect as a man and a leader. After he was feted throughout much of the country on account of Iowa's 1939 season, he told his Grandmother Clarke, "*Nothing* you could say would make me feel happier than your statement that in many ways I remind you of Grandpa."[1]

Kinnick also held his parents, Nile Sr. and Frances, in high regard. He exchanged letters with them throughout his college years and his years of service in the navy. He looked to them for guidance, shared ideas, updated them on his dating life. They had a deep and abiding affection for each other.

In September 1942, for instance, while in Virginia for aircraft carrier flight training, Kinnick wrote to his parents about a recent visit home. "In your company all tension and worldly care disappeared," he wrote. "Love and affection and all that is good shone bright." He lauded them for their courage and faith as they prepared to send their two oldest boys—Nile, the oldest, and his middle brother Ben—off to battle and praised them for raising their boys, of which they had three, to not compromise with evil and to understand that the "way is through, not around."[2]

Though rarely ever mentioned in his era's press coverage of him,

Ben and "Belle", first of a series of four dogs.

Nile in his first business venture, 1926. morning delivery of The Des Moines Register.

Ben assumed the paper route the next year.

Photos from the University of Iowa's Nile Kinnick Collection give a glimpse into Nile's childhood. Shown here are Nile and his brother Ben, who would also die serving in World War II, growing up in Iowa.

Kinnick was raised in the Christian Science religion, and this was a significant part of his life. The religion, found by Mary Baker Eddy in 1879, holds as its philosophy that the physical world is a mere illusion; it is within the spiritual world that reality resides. Related to this, in general, Christian Science maintains that health problems result from mental error rather than physical issues and, therefore, modern medicine should be avoided. This has, of course, caused considerable controversy. In Kinnick's letters to his family, he uses terms that someone accustomed to Christian Science would know, such as "demonstration," historically used to convey the idea that the health of the body is not controlled by physical laws but by spiritual fact. Or "Mesmerism," akin to hypnotism, which Christian Science views as a troubling, perhaps evil, practice.[3]

Life in Adel was fulfilling for the Kinnicks. While Nile Sr. managed and worked farmland, Frances, who had studied music at Northwestern but gave up the idea of a career in music in favor of raising a family, tended to her boys. Both sides of the family, the Kinnicks and the Clarkes, would commonly gather for Sunday-evening dinners at Grandpa and Grandma Clarke's stately home. In many ways, Nile, athletic and bright, grew up living a version of a classic, midwestern rural upbringing.[4]

But Kinnick did come up during the Great Depression, and in the mid-1930s it took a toll on the family farm business to such an extent that his father would move the family to Omaha for a more secure, salaried job at the Federal Land Bank. Kinnick continued to thrive while finishing high school in Omaha. He maintained his A average and athletic prowess, earning All State recognition in football and basketball.[5] But when it came to college sports, Kinnick was considered a little small and, relative to many top collegiate backs, a bit slow, which is what made one of his college nicknames, "Cornbelt Comet," rather ironic. Ultimately, he wasn't recruited heavily. He had an interest in attending Minnesota, which had won college football national titles in 1934 and 1935, and even drove to the campus to see if the Gophers' coaches might have an interest in him. "They didn't, not at all," Kinnick's father recalled.[6]

Kinnick's high school coach from his Adel days took him to the University of Iowa and introduced him to Rollie Williams, the Hawkeyes' basketball coach, and to Ossie Solem, the football coach. Iowa football, hapless as it was, was receptive to the idea of bringing Kinnick on. And in the end Kinnick saw in Iowa an opportunity to help rebuild a program.[7]

He earned rave reviews on the frosh pigskin team and then again as a sophomore signal-caller in his first year of varsity. Bernie Bierman, Minnesota's revered head coach, perhaps rethinking his rejection of Kinnick, said he was "one of the finest young backs I have ever seen. He's exceptional as a kicker and out of the ordinary as a passer. He has plenty of speed and is very elusive in a broken field." Still, Iowa won just a single game in 1937.

Kinnick also played varsity hoops as a sophomore. He was known for his defense, but he could put it in the bucket, too. The Hawkeye cagers finished fifth in the Big Ten standings, with Kinnick the squad's second-leading scorer.[8] Before a basketball game at Indiana University that year, the Hoosier football team wrote a letter to its hoops squad that read:

> Dear Basketball Team:
>
> Last November we played Iowa and a young sophomore powerhouse, Nile Kinnick, turned out to be papa, mamma and sonny trouble. We understand this driving athlete heads a strong Iowa five which has a "date" with you Monday in the fieldhouse. Please don't forget to handcuff Mr. Trouble in that game for, although he's a guard, we hear opponents find him underneath their basket too, too often.
>
> Wishing you goals of luck,
> The Indiana football team

After a summer spent outdoors working for Doc Monilaw's famed midwestern summer camp, Nile returned to Iowa City for his junior year with high hopes. The Hawkeyes, however, opened the football season with a loss to UCLA, and an early-season ankle injury hampered Kinnick. After UCLA came a home loss to Wisconsin, leaving Kinnick frustrated. "We looked terrible—no punch on offense and no fight on defense," he wrote home.[9]

Compounding matters, against the Badgers Kinnick reinjured his ankle. It would prove to be a season-long problem. For Kinnick, it became a kind of religious test. He told his parents, "Please do not be disturbed, this is an opportunity for me to show definitely where I stand (vis-à-vis Christian Science) and show that stand is right in principle and efficacy. Let us know that error cannot strike at me thru Iowa football and vice versa."[10]

In his book, *The Ironmen*, author Scott M. Fisher claims that during this 1938 campaign Kinnick avoided treatment for his ankle and even eschewed the use of ankle straps on account of his religious views. Freshman Al Coupee, who played with Kinnick in the backfield the following season, said of the injury, "It's probable the ankle was fractured. You could see the pain in his face when he punted."[11] And in a 1987 *Sports Illustrated* article, author Ron Fimrite, who interviewed several players for the piece, wrote that no one knew for certain whether the ankle was broken because "as a practicing Christian Scientist, he [Kinnick] would not allow the injury to be examined or treated."[12] According to Fisher, "Although some of the men did not understand his reasoning, they respected his faith and dedication."[13]

Complicating matters, however, on this question of injury and treatment, in a 1939 letter to his mother, Kinnick mentioned that a separated shoulder he'd suffered was healing daily "taped the way it is."[14] This throws into question Fisher's claim that Kinnick didn't use treatment or ankle straps for religious purposes.

Still, the question of Kinnick's religion did arise in a meeting he had with his embattled football coach in 1938, Irl Tubbs, on the eve of a road game versus Chicago in October. Tubbs, only in his second season with the team, had breakfast with Nile and asked him directly if he was a Christian Scientist. Kinnick told him what the coach already likely knew, that he was. Coach Tubbs responded, according to Kinnick, by telling Nile that he could have as much time off as necessary and that it'd be all right if he needed to miss the upcoming game. Nile was grateful for the words but decided to play anyway. "I wish so fervently that we could get going for the coaches' sake—they are as fine a bunch as ever lived," Kinnick wrote in a letter to his mother. "The papers and wolves are after them hot and heavy—the rats."[15]

It's easy to assume that Coach Tubbs felt frustration if indeed his star player wasn't availing himself of medical care. At the same time, perhaps he marveled at Kinnick for playing in games on an injury that would have likely kept a lot of others out. Regardless, by all indications, Coach Tubbs and Kinnick maintained a good relationship, even if by the end of the year Kinnick felt that the situation was such that it was best for Coach Tubbs, who faced considerable heat from Iowa supporters, to move on.[16]

As it happened, the 1938 team registered its only win in the Windy City versus lowly Chicago. The morning afterward, Kinnick had breakfast with Mrs. Wieneck, a fellow Christian Science practitioner. He wrote to his mother that Mrs. Wieneck told him that her son Jacob struggled with a leg injury, too, "and he received an idea (angel) and would not let it go until it blessed him." She encouraged Nile to hang to his good "idea" as well. "That sounds good to me and I shall hang on," Nile wrote home.[17]

Mr. Kinnick wrote back, telling his son that he and his mother were impressed by his confidence in victory. He said it'd be infectious to those around him. "I do not refer alone to football wins," Kinnick Sr. wrote.

"They are of passing importance. I mean those steps which day-by-day are proving the Principle that you are building on."[18]

After another one-win season Kinnick took inventory of his life. He didn't like the way the football went, and his grade point average had dipped. He decided that his living situation at the fraternity to which he'd pledged needed changing, so he switched roommates. He decided against playing hoops, too, telling Coach Rollie Williams, "I came down here primarily to get an education."[19]

17

SHORTLY AFTER THE 1938 SEASON, Iowa hired a new football coach, Dr. Eddie Anderson. Hawkeye brass had wanted the Iowa native badly. In fact, at a secret meeting in Boston, Iowa University personnel had worked out the broad details of a deal with Dr. Anderson, who was coaching Holy Cross (in Worcester, Massachusetts) at the time, before his season ended.[1]

In Dr. Anderson, Iowa got a man with a remarkable biography. He'd starred at Notre Dame under Knute Rockne, earning All-American honors. After Notre Dame and a three-year coaching stint at a small college in Iowa, he entered medical school at Rush Medical College in Chicago, where he also coached at DePaul University and played in the NFL for the Chicago Cardinals.[2]

From there, he went to coach at Holy Cross, where he enjoyed striking success, amassing a 47-7-4 record over six seasons.. At Iowa, in addition to coaching, he would often spend mornings working in the urology department at the University of Iowa Hospital. And during World War II he would serve in the US Army Medical Corps. He was a versatile man.

Anderson was also Roman Catholic, which in the late 1930s could raise some eyebrows with certain folks. It seems to have done so with the Kinnicks. In a letter to his family shortly after Anderson's hiring, Kinnick wrote, "Aside from the R.C. [Roman Catholic] angle the situation seems to look pretty good." He added, "He has a lot of fire & enthusiasm & looks to be a very determined man."[3]

Several months before the start of Iowa's epic season, Kinnick felt compelled to justify playing for the Hawkeyes' new Roman Catholic coach. Having met him in person by then, Kinnick said, "I am sure that he was well impressed with me—as I was with him." He did not ignore their different backgrounds. "He and I will of course differ in opinions, beliefs and convictions," he acknowledged. "However, that we must clash personally can be metaphysically obviated." Kinnick added that both he and Coach Anderson knew that cooperation and mutual effort were important to their success. While religious convictions and philosophies might differ, even widely and bitterly, Kinnick maintained that "disassociation from people for such reasons is inexcusable; it is representative of bigotry and intolerance."[4]

In this same letter Kinnick declared to his family his intention to become the "roughest, toughest, all-around back yet to hit this conference." However, while Kinnick found a way to be confident heading into the 1939 season, the media did not see Iowa doing much. Resume aside, Dr. Anderson was, after all, taking over a reeling program.[5]

Unsurprisingly, heading into the 1939 pre-season, Big Ten polls had Iowa outside of the top seven. As for national player rankings, the *Saturday Evening Post*'s Francis Wallace didn't have Kinnick among the top twelve backs.[6]

While the media was discounting Iowa's chances of figuring prominently on the national football scene, it did have high hopes for the 1939 college football season in general. More forward passes and speedy play, it was predicted, would lead to exciting action. And with headgear mandatory for the first time, a rule enacted in part because of the eight fatal skull fractures in college football the previous season, the action would presumably be safer.[7]

In addition to Kinnick, Dr. Anderson, with his scheme and his emphasis on conditioning, proved crucial to Iowa's turnaround. Spring practice, which actually started in February, was so grueling that of the eighty-five players that came out, only about thirty-five remained by June. Player George "Red" Frye, a fan of Coach Anderson's, humorously recalled, "He's the only physician I've known who believed running was the cure for everything from a sprained ankle to a missed signal."[8]

Dr. Anderson actually took it relatively easy on his players, however, when the real season began. Fall practices involved less contact and more classroom lectures and drills.[9] Come game time, he wanted his team fresh and alert as well as fit.

Schematically, Dr. Anderson borrowed from his college coach, Knute Rockne. In his offense the quarterback didn't actually handle the ball much. He'd call plays and direct matters but was more likely to block would-be tacklers or receive a pass than throw one. The snap usually came to the left halfback, Kinnick's position, who would then hand it off, pass, or run. The complexity in the action came from the many variations and tweaks during the handoff, run, or pass options.[10] Commenting on the offense in a letter to his younger brother George during spring practice, Kinnick wrote, "You would like to see us practice our spins, fakes and shifts," and he described the system as "truly a beautiful thing to watch; a poetry of motion, once perfected."[11]

In late September 1939, Dr. Anderson had his Hawkeyes scrimmage for the first time. There were positives, particularly with Kinnick's play, the backfield in general, and the team's blocking. Dr. Anderson came away upbeat but worried about depth. Sensing how much they'd rely on the first string, he told a reporter, "They'll have to be iron men," marking the first mention of what would become an enduring nickname.[12]

The Hawkeyes opened the season with two wins, the first at home in front of a relatively sparse crowd, 41-0 over South Dakota. Kinnick ran for three touchdowns and threw for two. Forty-one points was an eye-catching total, considering Iowa had scored only forty-six during the entire previous season. Still, South Dakota wasn't a Big Ten foe. The next win, also at home, 32-29 over Indiana, caught people's attention. Iowa hadn't won its first home Big Ten game of the season since 1933. And the win over Indiana marked the team's first conference win of any sort over a team not named Chicago since 1935.

Early in the blistering affair, played in ninety-four-degree heat, Iowa got down 10-0. A seventy-three-yard Kinnick punt return shifted the momentum, yet with just minutes remaining in the game, Iowa still trailed 29-26, and it faced a fourth-and-long, fifteen yards from a touchdown. Looking back on the game years later, Indiana's standout lineman, Emil Uremovich, who would go on to play with the Detroit Lions, remembered what happened next.

"I heard Kinnick give some guy hell and said he was calling the play," Uremovich said. Rather than kick a field goal, Kinnick told his teammates, "Forget the tie, we're going all the way." Sure enough, Kinnick proceeded to throw a dramatic touchdown pass to Erwin Prasse, who made a fingertip snag for the win.[13] It was the duo's third TD hookup of the game, an Iowa record that stood until 2005. Kinnick also ran for a score.

The following week, the Hawkeyes endured their only loss of the season, to Michigan, which featured junior Tom Harmon, the man who would finish second in the Heisman voting to Kinnick. Kinnick threw a long touchdown pass for Iowa's only score, but the 27-7 loss was sobering. Kinnick was hard on himself, writing to his parents afterward, "It breaks my heart to have let him [Coach Anderson] down. He really is a fine fellow and a swell coach."[14]

Iowa responded with a 19-13 win at Wisconsin, a contest in which Kinnick again threw a game-winning, fourth-quarter touchdown, his third TD pass of the game. Fans could hardly believe it. Iowa hadn't won in Madison in a decade. Kinnick and four other Hawkeyes played all sixty minutes. Coach Anderson told the press he was coaching "Iron-men." The nickname began to spread across the land.[15]

Up next was Purdue, picked among the Big Ten favorites to start the year. Only once since 1923 had Iowa beaten the Boilermakers. And this game, like Iowa's previous two, was on the road. It's hard to fathom going by modern standards, but Iowa played more Big Ten road games than home in 1939, four to two. Teams worried about low gate receipts in Iowa City and at that time could manipulate the schedule accordingly.[16]

The Ironmen largely controlled the action versus the Boilermakers, but an untimely false start on a would-be touchdown pass and turnovers kept them from reaching the end zone. In fact, neither offense scored at all in this gnarly, physical affair.

The Hawkeye defense came up big, though. It yielded only seventy-five yards and registered two safeties. The game ended in Iowa's favor by the decidedly uncommon score of 4-0. No matter how it happened, back in Iowa City fans were thrilled to near disbelief. Iowa had just won its fourth Big Ten game. Thousands came out to greet the team upon its return to Iowa City, resulting in a spontaneous parade.

Excited as they were, fans knew that fourth-ranked Notre Dame and Minnesota, which had won the previous two Big Ten championships and the 1934, '35, and '36 national championships, loomed.

Some 50,000 people came out for the Notre Dame contest in Iowa City. But many of them, deep down, probably didn't think Iowa could win. Notre Dame, coached by Elmer Layden, had won six games in a row and had not lost to a Big Ten team since 1935.[17]

In the first half, Iowa only subbed one time, late in the second quarter, when Buzz Dean came in for an injured Ed McLain.[18] Near the end of that opening frame, the Hawkeyes found themselves with the ball near the Irish goal line. At halftime of their previous game, against Purdue, a frustrated Coach Anderson, who thought Kinnick should have gotten more touches near the goal line, had "introduced" his signal-caller Couppee to Kinnick. Now, near the goal versus the Irish, Couppee called a rare huddle. He wanted to run it to the right side of the line, but, surely with Anderson's instructions in mind, he wanted to give the ball to Kinnick. So he ordered the halfbacks to switch positions. Halfback Buzz Dean wasn't happy with the switch, and captain Erwin Prasse told the young signal-caller Couppee not "to screw things up like this." But Couppee made the call, and Kinnick scored on a short, bruising run.[19] The "Corn-belt Comet" connected on the point-after, too, giving Iowa a 7-0 lead that it would never relinquish.

As an indication of just how big the win was, the University of Iowa canceled classes for the entire student body the Monday after it. Across the state—really, the country—the "Ironmen" were the only thing people talked about. The win was extra special for Coach Anderson, who had, of course, played at Notre Dame, as had Iowa's backfield coach Frank Carideo and line coach Jim Harris.

Still, the mighty twentieth-ranked Minnesota Gophers loomed. The Hawkeyes had momentum heading into the game, for sure—they were ranked for the first time in school history, and a packed, boisterous crowd of some 50,000 came out to back them. But Minnesota boasted an imposing championship pedigree.

Things did not go well for Iowa the first three quarters. Kinnick threw two interceptions, and the offense simply couldn't score. At the start of the fourth, Minnesota led, 9-0.

Somehow, though, Kinnick yet again caught fire down the stretch. He threw two touchdowns in the fourth, the first a forty-eight-yarder. The second, a twenty-eight-yarder with just three minutes left in the game, put Iowa ahead for the first time, 13-9. To seal the matter, Kinnick then intercepted Minnesota. For the sixth game in a row, he played a full sixty minutes.[20] A Chicago paper, calling the game the most spectacular in modern Big Ten history, reported the score as Nile Kinnick 13, Minnesota 9. In the *Chicago Daily News*, James Kearns marveled at the postgame scene, during which the crowd poured onto the field by the thousands and Kinnick was carried about. "There's a golden helmet riding on a human sea across Iowa's football field in the twilight here," Kearns observed, adding that Kinnick had led a "frenzied little band of Iowa football players to a victory which was impossible. They couldn't win, but they did."[21]

The season ended with a bit of a whimper in the form of a 7-7 tie against a well-regarded Northwestern team on the road, Iowa's fourth Big Ten road game. The game was an odd, difficult affair for the Hawkeyes. Kinnick was sidelined with a separated shoulder in the third quarter, and Coach Eddie Anderson pulled signal-caller Couppee in the fourth. Some reports had Couppee being pulled for an injury. Fimrite, in his 1987 *Sports Illustrated* article on Kinnick, for which he interviewed Couppee, had it another way. He maintained that Coach Anderson pulled Couppee, who was frantically calling plays to break the tie, under the impression that a tie would still give Iowa the Big Ten title. He put in backup Gerald Ankeny and reportedly instructed him to "sit on the ball." After the game, according to Fimrite, Coach Anderson apologized for the error.[22]

Ohio State won its final conference game and therefore finished a half-game ahead of Iowa in the standings. Yet Iowa ended the season as the highest-rated Big Ten team in the AP poll, ninth, to Ohio State's fifteenth. Neither team played again because at this time the Big Ten did not allow member schools to play in bowl games. No matter; the Ironmen had just delivered a season for the ages, a season that, for decades to come, Iowa Hawkeyes fans would use as a barometer to measure all others.

18

ON 28 NOVEMBER 1939, three days after Iowa's final game, Kinnick learned of his Heisman win. The news put him in a kind of "daze." On 5 December 1939, he and Dr. Anderson left for New York City. Kinnick was to receive the Heisman, Dr. Anderson the *New York World-Telegram* Coach of the Year award.[1] That week also included the NFL draft, which took place in Milwaukee's Schroeder Hotel. The Chicago Cardinals wanted to choose Kinnick with the first overall pick, but when reports arose on Kinnick's trip east that he didn't want to play pro ball, the Cardinals chose George "Bad News" Cafego, a back out of Tennessee.

Kinnick went fourteenth overall, in the second round, to the Brooklyn Dodgers, whose brass had decided to take a chance on the Ironman in the hopes of somehow convincing him to play.[2]

Meanwhile, though Nile had sent out word that he didn't want to play pro ball, privately he vacillated. He didn't feel as if playing was the "right direction," but at the same time he didn't want to pass it by "if it seems to be the ultimate consummation of my endeavours in this field [football]." And he imagined the money he was being offered, $10,000 a year or $1,000 per game, would look pretty big in a few years. Trying to decide, he came at the question from a religious viewpoint. He wrote to his mother:

> It may be that matter is trying to put the "squeeze" on me—make me run away or depend on it to establish the structure. Or it may be that this physical demonstration is a little beyond us—which I hate to admit.[3]

Ultimately, he would decide there were more significant ways for him to develop and to make a positive, beneficial mark on the world.[4]

In early January 1940, Kinnick and Dr. Anderson took another trip east to receive yet more awards. Kinnick picked up the Maxwell Award, given to the best college football player as chosen by sportscasters, sportswriters, and coaches, in Philadelphia on January 9. And he was formally presented the Walter Camp Award, given to the nation's best back, in mid-January at the Washington, DC, Touchdown Club. He received this award alongside Louisiana State's Ken Kavanaugh, who was being recognized as the nation's best lineman. The two would serve together in the US Navy a few years later.[5] Upon receiving it, Kinnick delivered a statement that echoed his Heisman remarks. "I thank God I've been dodging tacklers and not bullets; that I've been throwing passes and not hand grenades."[6]

There was also the not-so-small matter of winning AP Athlete of the Year, beating out Joe DiMaggio and Joe Louis. With the accolades and fame came speculation about the "Cornbelt Comet's" love life. Not long after the Heisman ceremony, the *Sioux City Tribune*, apparently working off rumor, claimed that Kinnick was engaged to be married to Barbara "Bibba" Miller, an Iowa student he'd dated on occasion. That wasn't the case.

Reports that Kinnick had met a young, striking heiress, Virginia Eskridge, in New York on the night of the Captain of the All-Americas dinner in mid-January, were true. Miss Eskridge is reported to have said to Kinnick, upon encountering him, "Oh, you're from the school that has that famous All-American." Later that evening Kinnick and Coach Anderson went to the well-known Kit Kat Club, where a photographer snapped a shot of Kinnick, clad in a tux, smiling big, sitting next to Virginia Eskridge. She had a highball in hand, Kinnick a glass of milk. The *New York Journal-American*'s gossip columnist, Dorothy Kilgallen, ran with it, claiming Kinnick and Eskridge were "yum, yum."[7] It made for good press, but the two didn't date.

Kinnick, however, did actively date and liked being social. He enjoyed dancing, good music, dinner parties, and, though sometimes presented as a nondrinker, he drank on occasion. One young lady he began to date in the spring of 1940 was Celia Pears, a Vassar graduate and soon-to-be University of Chicago graduate student. She was three years older than Kinnick, but the two hit it off. In a letter to his parents, he wrote positively of his first date with Miss Pears. Once she began graduate school, he would take several trips to Chicago to see her. They dated before Kinnick reported for duty for the Navy Air Corps in early December 1941, and during the war the two wrote each other until a few days before he died.[8]

When the awards circuit finally wrapped in mid-January, Kinnick had a lot of school to catch up on, local speaking engagements to keep, and decisions about his future to make. He managed the school part some-how, keeping his stellar grades and ultimately earning two law school scholarships. Yet upon graduating from Iowa, in May 1940, he contin-ued to wrestle with what exactly to do with the rest of his life—attend law school, play pro football, go into sales, coach.

The shocking developments in Europe complicated matters further. In April 1940, as Kinnick wrestled over his future, the Nazis secretly sailed into major ports in Denmark and Norway. The Danes surrendered in two hours. Norway held out until June but went down, too. In May 1940, Hitler invaded Belgium, Luxembourg, and the Netherlands. Lux-embourg fell in a day, Holland in five, Belgium shortly thereafter. The lack of readiness seems incredible. In a letter to his mother, in which he kicked around what to do with his future, Kinnick wrote, "You know in reality our problems are rather small in comparison with the people across."[9]

Winston Churchill, who became the British prime minister during this frightful time and who would become an inspiration to Kinnick, soon delivered his famous "We shall fight them on the beaches" speech. Yet the direness of matters in Western Europe could hardly be overstated.

In his commencement remarks as class president at Iowa's Com-mencement Supper, in late May 1940, Kinnick touched on the problems in Europe but did not dwell on them. He'd prepared the remarks several weeks prior and admitted his concern that the "bloody holocaust raging in Europe with its possible repercussions in this country" could make his talk seem rife with "foolish hopes and mere fictions." He had come to more fully realize that events across the pond were too big for the United States to ignore.

In his speech he looked ahead to a world that his generation, with pos-itive mental courage, could make better. He didn't suggest it'd be easy. "By now we should realize that the battle is life itself," he told his fellow graduates. "And that our joy and happiness should lie as much in the struggle to overcome as in the fruition of a later day." He lauded the Iowa faculty for helping his class with mental discipline and inspiration, which to him were two fundamentals of education. And he urged his fellow classmates to add a third fundamental, that of mental courage—"courage of conviction, of morality, of idealism, courage of faith in a principle tangible proof of which is slow in appearing."[10]

IN THE SUMMER OF 1940, as Kinnick continued to ponder his future and war in Europe raged, a US presidential campaign took place, pitting FDR versus Wendell Willkie. Kinnick, a Republican, backed Willkie, even introduced the candidate at a rally in Iowa Falls.

The war question figured prominently in the campaign, but neither candidate called for direct US involvement. FDR had cited the Nazi menace as the motivating force behind his decision to run for an unprecedented third term, and as president he did do what he thought politically feasible to support the British. But he also knew the strength of the country's isolationist bent. Days before the election, he stated, "I have said this before, but I shall say it again and again: your boys are not going to be sent into any foreign wars."[11]

The isolationist sentiment in America came from across the political spectrum. Republicans like Robert Taft, an Ohio senator, Democrats like Joseph Kennedy, the US ambassador to Great Britain, and Progressives like Robert La Follette, a Wisconsin senator, wanted America on the sidelines. The "Fortress America" argument, the idea of protecting the United States and Canada while letting Europe figure out its own affairs, resonated.

FDR's opponent, Wendell Willkie, was a dark horse candidate with an uncommon background for a Republican nominee. The former lawyer and corporate executive had actually been a longtime Democrat. He switched his party allegiance in 1939 and, though he didn't run in the party's presidential primaries, positioned himself for the Republican nomination if the convention were to become deadlocked. It did. And in the end Willkie emerged with the nod.

While not an interventionist, he was not a strong isolationist like others in the field. He backed the United States' support for Britain and agreed with FDR's peacetime draft. As the election neared, Willkie's campaign planned a September trip to Iowa. It was determined that Kinnick could be of help. He was a national figure, after all, and his grandfather a former Republican governor.

From Kinnick's perspective, there was risk in dividing his fan base by stepping into the political fray. Dr. Erwin J. Gottsch, a man Kinnick did not know, wrote to Nile to warn him of this, urging him not to appear with Willkie at a political rally because neither candidate could help him and he stood to lose half his national popularity by choosing one over the other. Kinnick, unbowed, wrote back that any profession that interested him could expose him to criticism. "Perhaps I have made a mistake," he concluded. "If so it will not [be] the first and I shall recoup. However, I am doing what I think is the thing to do."[12]

On 27 September 1940, Nile drove to Webster City, Iowa, to catch a train upon which presidential candidate Willkie was riding. Soon thereafter he met the "Big Bear" in person and came away impressed.

Having been driven to the rally with candidate Willkie, next thing Kinnick knew, he was put in front of a mike to address the crowd. He introduced the governor of Iowa, expecting him to then take over and introduce Willkie. Instead the governor merely smiled and waved before sitting down again, and someone nudged Kinnick back to the mike to introduce the Republican nominee for president of the United States.

Kinnick said Willkie was a "friend of labor, a friend of business and a friend of the farmer; and he will translate that friendship into positive action when elected this fall." He came away happy with what he'd said by way of an introduction and impressed by Willkie's subsequent remarks. When Willkie finished speaking, Kinnick signed autographs for nearly an hour. Still, he wasn't under any illusions when it came to the election. He knew Willkie faced a steep climb. He wrote to his family afterward, "The cause of course isn't lost at present but it doesn't look too good."[13]

19

LATE THAT SUMMER OF 1940, Kinnick played in the seventh annual Chicago Charities College All-Star game, pitting college stars, coached by Iowa's Eddie Anderson, against the previous year's NFL champion Green Bay Packers, coached by Curly Lambeau. This kind of matchup simply wouldn't happen nowadays, but not only did it happen, the college all-stars had won three straight leading up to this contest.

The game, seen as a kind of kickoff for the upcoming football season, was wildly popular, with some 84,500 fans in Soldier Field to watch it. Newspapers across the nation ran stories about the game, and the staging for it was cutting-edge. For instance, the lights went out before the All-Stars' lineup was announced. A spotlight was then flashed on each starter as he was called to run onto the field, and the band played his college's fight song. It was an American spectacle.

The Packers won the "Aerial Duel" 45-28. But Kinnick, "the amazing little iron man," acquitted himself well, completing a fifty-seven-yard touchdown pass and a near-touchdown twenty-four-yarder, returning a punt nineteen yards, and connecting on three point-after attempts.[1] Despite his quality play, it was at this time that Kinnick decided once and for all to spurn pro football in favor of attending Iowa Law.

At law school Kinnick maintained an active pace. He studied hard, coached, read, dated, and served as halftime commentator at home football games. He'd finish third in his class that first year and continued to develop his interest in politics and leadership. He envisioned following a path similar to that of his revered Grandfather Clarke. His law school roommate, Bill Stuart, maintained, "I have no doubt in my mind that had he lived, he would have accomplished that like everything else he tried."[2]

In October 1940, at the beginning of his opening year of law school, Kinnick registered for the country's first peacetime draft. He'd become increasingly convinced that the United States needed to get involved in the war and was developing quite a fondness for Britain's Churchill.

As noted, by the summer of 1941, even though Pearl Harbor was still months off, Kinnick decided to volunteer for military service rather than wait on the draft. As his dad explained it, "Nile saw there was a job to do, and knew he was one of the young men qualified to do it."[3] So he traveled to Kansas City to volunteer for the Naval Air Corps Reserve.

It wasn't until early December, though, days prior to Japan's stealth attack on Pearl Harbor, that he received his active duty call-up. In the interim, knowing he would soon be called, he'd decided not to start his second year of law school. He did, however, live in Iowa City, where he continued to serve as an assistant football coach.

Upon being called up in December, Kinnick reported straightaway to Kansas City for training. And he commenced a wartime diary. He was fully aware of the stakes, but he considered it best to go "through, not around" problems. "Every man whom I've admired in history has willingly and courageously served in his country's armed forces in time of danger," he wrote. He considered it his duty and honor. He asked God for the courage and ability to conduct himself "in every situation that my country, my family and my friends will be proud of me."[4]

Kinnick had just arrived in Kansas City with the Naval Air Corps when news of the Japanese attack at Pearl Harbor broke. In his diary the night after the attack, he wrote that the global conflict was being "engineered in its grand strategy directly from Berlin."[5]

Months later, Kinnick would reflect back on a college theme paper he'd written at Iowa in which he'd expressed an isolationist view and said he was "tired of hearing of a nation's manifest destiny and of the often inevitability of war." He'd also declared in this paper that he'd "fight when I saw the tank coming up #6 highway [into Adel] and not before." After Pearl Harbor, as a member of the US Navy, he characterized the views he expressed in that college paper as "immature."[6]

Kinnick spent the ensuing weeks training in Kansas City. There he started dating Merle McKay, a young woman who had gone to Iowa for one year, in 1939. She'd caught Kinnick's eye then, but he hadn't asked her out in Iowa City, and he didn't want to miss his second chance.

"Hi, Merle, this is Nile Kinnick, Iowa U., remember?" she recalled him saying when he rang. She thought it quite funny for him to ask if she remembered who Nile Kinnick was. Of course she did.

They saw each other quite often over the next several weeks, and Kinnick became quite smitten. In his diary he raved about their first date, which included a visit with Merle and her family at the McKay home followed by sandwiches and milk with Merle in front of the McKay fireplace while Mrs. McKay took her boys out to dinner. "Not bad, not bad—a fine home, good radio music, a pretty girl, and a fireplace fire, what could be better . . . ?" he wrote in his diary.[7]

A week later, he went out to dinner with the McKays. Afterward, Merle had play practice—she worked at a small theater in Kansas City and during the day at a radio station—so Kinnick went to a Christian Science lecture with Mrs. McKay. He came away from date two just as impressed. "I wish to goodness I had called her sooner," he wrote. "Too bad she is so busy with her dramatic work and I with my flying."[8]

More dates followed, and Kinnick's fondness for Merle grew. Merle considered the courtship a "highlight of my life," yet it was also a confusing time, she'd recall—a time when people yearned for something to hold on to, a time of war bonds and victory gardens, rationing, blood donating, and blackouts. There was so much uncertainty, making it hard to build something that could seem enduring. Merle remembered her twelve-year-old brother idolizing Kinnick, and she recalled the twinkle in Nile's eye when the former gridiron star made some far-out comment. She told Kinnick biographer D. W. Stump that sometimes she and Kinnick would talk and talk, but that Nile had quiet moods, too. At times she would chide him, telling him "he was truly an Iron Man."[9]

In late February, Nile left Kansas City for more training in New Orleans. After a couple of weeks there, it was on to Florida for flight training and additional studies. Merle and Kinnick wrote, but it was hard to build something sustaining.

★ DURING THIS TIME, across the oceans, things were quite difficult for the Allies—particularly in the Pacific, where Kinnick's "flight" would ultimately be stationed. In the six months since Pearl Harbor, Japan rip-roared across the Pacific, taking Guam, Wake Island, Hong Kong, British Malaya, and more. In Europe matters looked quite bleak, too. The Germans pushed deep into Russia, and in North Africa the Nazi field marshal, Erwin "Desert Fox" Rommel, snaked his way toward the vital Suez Canal.

Writing in his diary in April 1942, Kinnick wondered, "When will the Allies take the offensive? Sometimes this war looks to be an interminable mess." The Philippines would fall the following month. India and Australia suddenly appeared vulnerable. In July, given the significant German advances in the Battle of the Caucasus (an area of land connecting Western and Eastern Europe between the Black and Caspian Seas), Kinnick said, "The war news is awfully dark these days."[10]

His diary during this period reveals a man thirsting for knowledge, keenly curious, and open to new ideas. From early April to July 1942, alone, he read voraciously. He started with Steinbeck's *The Moon Is Down*, the theme of which Kinnick felt "stirs the soul of any man, to wit, a free people cannot be permanently conquered."[11] Next he read a collection of poems by Rudyard Kipling. The protagonist, Oliver, in the next book he read, George Santayana's *The Last Puritan*, shared some similarities with Kinnick that one might not expect. Both served in war. Oliver, meanwhile, couldn't seem to find a true soul mate; Kinnick never felt like he quite had, either. Oliver dies in a car accident; Kinnick in a plane crash. And the book challenges idealism, which is something that Kinnick would question in his diary in the ensuing months—he was frustrated by politicians who, claiming to stick to some ideal, would not work with others on a pragmatic solution.

After *The Last Puritan*, Kinnick read Carl Sandburg's *Prairie Years*, a book on Abraham Lincoln, whom Kinnick admired. And then he thoroughly enjoyed Phillip Guedalla's biography of Winston Churchill. "He is the man in history who has completely caught my fancy and imagination," he wrote of Churchill. "I read his every speech and writing with absorbing interest. He is a man of thought, of action, of resolution, and the man of the hour in the world's greatest crisis."[12] On Independence Day, 1942, Kinnick finished Antoine de Saint-Exupery's *Wind, Sand, and Stars*."[13] From there it was on to Pringle's biography of Theodore Roosevelt and Steinbeck's *Grapes of Wrath*. Kinnick then started in on Tolstoy's *War and Peace*, a book that numbers well over 1,000 pages.[14] It was a torrid stretch of reading. He also found time for church and would go to a Christian Science reading room on occasion.

Kinnick enjoyed movies, too. He found the films *Night of January 16* and *Tortilla Flat* entertaining, but two movies that really captivated him were *Sergeant York* and *Mrs. Miniver.*

Sergeant York, an Academy Award–winning film, tells the story of a reluctant hero, Alvin York, who had a poor country upbringing in Tennessee and stretches of hell-raising as a young man, yet became one of America's most decorated World War I soldiers. Kinnick considered it the first "really good cinema entertainment" he'd seen in a long time. "I laughed & wept & thoroughly enjoyed it."[15]

Mrs. Miniver won the 1942 Academy Award for Best Picture. Set in a fictional village outside London, it tells the story of the war's impact on a somewhat ordinary British family, the Minivers, and their fellow villagers. Love is in the air, men are sent to war, the Germans attack the home front, tragedy strikes. It has all the makings of a dramatic war film, one that stands as an argument for the Allied cause and a testament to British resolve.

Similar to Kinnick's evolution from 1939 to 1941, as events unfolded in Europe, the script of *Mrs. Miniver* underwent changes. Preproduction on the film started in the fall of 1940, when the film's tone and tenor was much softer regarding the Allied cause and the urgency of the moment. In time, the script took on a much stronger, more overt pro-British viewpoint. The film ends with an iconic sermon delivered by the vicar at the local church to villagers who have suffered terrible loss and are still under siege. The vicar frames the battle they face as a struggle for freedom. He acknowledges the losses they've all endured and the resolve they all must show. "This is the People's War," he states. "It is our war. We are the fighters. Fight it then. Fight it with all that is in us. And may God defend the right." Kinnick wrote that the film "brought forth in me more heartfelt emotion than I have felt for a long time."[16]

In the months ahead, Kinnick would continue to stretch himself, to think deeply about big ideas: the best form of government, how to manage a complex, industrial economy, the need to address America's troubled race relations. He also developed an elastic view of the Constitution. The Constitution isn't a "dispensation from on high," he wrote, not something that people should be afraid to let grow and change.[17]

Still, politically Kinnick maintained his support for Willkie over FDR. He thought FDR relied too heavily on governmental intervention. FDR's willingness to intervene in markets, to grow governmental bureaucracy in a seemingly endless way, to pit social classes against each other, and his "flippant attitude toward the importance of private initiative and enterprise," among other things, in Kinnick's view, "undermined the moral fibre" of the country. Looking ahead to the 1944 presidential election, Kinnick expressed his hope that Willkie would run.[18]

Interestingly enough, then, he maintained both progressive and traditional views. He thought, for American democracy to succeed, it needed to maintain a moral basis, a common respect for the innate dignity of man, and a sense of justice, for American families to be close-knit and for local government to be efficient and robust. It started, for him, with a sound life at home, school, and church.[19] At the same time, he didn't think idealism should stand in the way of pragmatic policy.

Surely, given the time, Kinnick would have continued to develop intellectually. One can only speculate where that development would have taken him with regard to the big issues America would face. The way Kinnick's Iowa teammate Al Couppee saw it, Nile Kinnick's intellectual development, drive, and personality would've taken him to the White House.[20]

20

IN LATE SUMMER 1942, Kinnick received three weeks' leave. Still smitten by Merle McKay, he stopped in Kansas City before traveling to his parents' home in Omaha. Kinnick later visited Iowa City, too, the day before a home football game. On his first day back to campus, he met with Dr. Anderson and the coaching staff, went to practice, and visited the law school and his old fraternity. In the evening, he went on a date with Barbara "Bibba" Miller, the friend from his Iowa City days who, years earlier, had mistakenly been reported as affianced to Nile. Then Kinnick took supper with the "boys" at the Union. "It was just like old times," he wrote; "eager appetite, good food, lusty, happy companionship, the prospect of a game the next day; I enjoyed every minute of it."[1]

Next day, he did a halftime radio interview at the game. Word quickly spread among the crowd that Nile Kinnick was in attendance, and a "We want Kinnick" chant rose up. In the press box, he didn't hear the cheer at first. When told of it, he stepped to the door and heard it loud and clear. "We want Kinnick! We want Kinnick!" He acknowledged the crowd with a wave of the cap, much to its delight. "Such a fine, spontaneous gesture!" he later wrote.[2] Altogether it was a splendid visit back to the site of his glory days, a place he loved dearly.

Back on duty in the autumn of '42, Kinnick continued his training, maintained his intellectual curiosity, and hung out with his navy mates, playing cards, swimming, catching the occasional show.

Meanwhile, the war shifted in favor of the Allies. The Soviets managed a crucial victory over the Germans in Stalingrad, the site of fierce fighting and ghastly casualty rates. There an estimated two million people were either wounded, killed, or captured, making it one of the biggest and most gruesome battles in human history. In November, General Dwight D.

Eisenhower, backed by some 400,000 Allied soldiers, invaded North Africa. By May, he could claim full victory there.

Many people, the Soviet's Stalin foremost among them, had hoped to see the British and Americans follow their success in North Africa with a full-scale invasion of the Nazis from England, certainly by the summer of '43. Churchill, however, wanted more time. Rather than launch a massive invasion across the English Channel, he was able to get FDR to agree to attack the Germans through Italy. The massive D-Day Invasion of the beaches of Normandy would not occur, then, until June 1944. Still, by May 1943, the tide of war in Europe had changed markedly.

The same could be said of the Pacific. In May '42, in fact, at the Battle of the Coral Sea near Australia, Japan's months-long surge had been checked by the US Navy and Australia. More momentously, a month later at the Battle of Midway the Japanese lost four aircraft carriers and several destroyers over three days, decisive blows that left the US Navy with a clear advantage in that theater.

In time, US troops island-hopped their way across the Pacific, on and around places like Guadalcanal, Guam, and later Iwo Jima and Okinawa, but with jarring casualty rates.

These islands were the types of places that the men with whom Kinnick trained would end up, and he assumed he'd be with them. In a March '43 letter to his Uncle Chas, he wrote, "Note that Nimitz [Admiral] speaks of important naval action in the Pacific this summer. Very likely I'll get in on it." He further told his uncle he'd try to draw down on Japanese pilots "the way you use to knock those ducks."[3]

By March '43, Kinnick, stationed now in Rhode Island, was taking part in sophisticated carrier-related training exercises. On the afternoon of March 4, for instance, his squadron took part in a large training exercise with three other squadrons. "Donning our oxygen masks 20 fighters went up to 18,000 feet and escorted 24 dive bombers, 12 torpedo bombers on a simulated attack on a carrier," he wrote to his brother George. A small island off the coast served as the target. Kinnick was struck by the sight of "over fifty planes in concerted action."[4] He saw improvement in his performance and felt as if he could be sent off to fight without much notice any day.

His parents would send him books and supplies. Kinnick was grateful and wrote home to remind his dad that the critical periods of US and world history were of special interest, and that he wanted to learn more about the "British Empire and the evolution of the parliamentary system." He also asked his dad if he could send along his leather cribbage board, which Kinnick enjoyed playing with his flight mates.[5]

On a cool, rainy mid-March night in Providence, Rhode Island, Kinnick had just returned from Boston on short leave and was happy to be among his books and with pen in hand. He told his parents of his time in Boston, how on his first evening there he took in a bill at the RKO Theater. He found Jack Benny's *The Meanest Man in the World* to be funny enough, but said it was a Leon Errol short that left him feeling weak. "Gus [a nickname Nile Jr. had for his father] would have choked with repressed mirth and rolled into the aisle," he wrote. Beatrice Kay, backed by Bob Allen and his band, performed live, which he enjoyed, and then he dined at the Hotel Statler. "Some day," Kinnick concluded, "I want to take mother to dinner at such a place. We will chat, dance a waltz or two, linger over our desserts, and then go to the theater or the opera."[6]

The next day, still in Boston, Kinnick read in bed till 11 a.m. and then went to a bookstore. From there it was on to the renowned Dinty Moore's restaurant with an unassuming entryway at the end of a dirty alley but, inside, a "quiet, unhurried" atmosphere that suited him. He capped an excellent meal with a piece of apple pie before heading to an uproariously funny show, *Kiss and Tell*, at which the "audience almost expired en masse." Kinnick declared, "I love to laugh." He enclosed a *Time* article about farm life for his parents, and then he ended the letter, "without foreboding but as a matter of common sense," with a request regarding his will: "I desire that mother have the lady's wrist watch and father the *New York Sun* pocketwatch." The rest of his possessions he wanted put to use for the benefit of the Kinnick family at the discretion of his mother and father, with his younger brother George's education "being of prime importance."[7]

The letter was loving, thoughtful, lively, and engaging, one that you'd have to imagine would stir the heart of any parents who had sent their boy to war. Here was their son, aware of the risks at hand, enjoying laughter and good times, yet thinking of the future—of dancing with his mom and helping to send his youngest brother to school.

On the morning of 2 June 1943, the USS *Lexington*, to which Kinnick and his flight had been assigned, was in the Gulf of Paria, between

Trinidad and Venezuela. The water was placid, the sky blue, the sun bright as Kinnick and his fellow aviators readied for exercise flights off the carrier's deck. These men knew that they would likely soon find themselves in vicious fighting with the Japanese in the Pacific. Until then, they needed to prepare.

At about 8:30 a.m., Kinnick took off in his Grumman F4F-4 Wildcat and flew for over an hour without any problems. But then, while flying wing on Bill Reiter, a member of his four-man fighter team, his plane experienced a major oil leak. Reiter spotted the leak and alerted Kinnick, who called in the problem, businesslike and calm. Reiter then got behind his wing mate so that he could follow Kinnick back to the USS *Lexington*. Several miles before reaching the carrier, however, Kinnick realized that the severity of the leak would render his machine inoperable and he would have to make a water landing.

A water landing sounds daunting, and it was. On this occasion Kinnick seems to have executed the landing quite well. Reiter, watching from the sky, described it as a "perfect wheels-up landing in the water." However, aviation historian Eric Bergerud thinks the hazards of such a landing were quite significant and the idea of a "perfect belly flop" not realistic.[8]

Passing by in his plane above the spot where Kinnick landed, Reiter saw his wing mate clear of his Wildcat but "received no signals from him." In a letter written to Nile's parents shortly after the crash, Reiter explained that after circling a few times to mark the spot, he went to escort the rescue boat to the crash site. By the time he returned with the crash boat, however, he found no sign of Kinnick.[9] Altogether, from the time Kinnick put his plane in the water to the rescue boat's arrival to the scene, only about eight minutes had passed. The plane itself had sunk by then, but paint chippings and oil made it clear that they were at the right spot.[10]

The problem seems to have been the Grumman F4F-4 Wildcat, generally a celebrated craft. Though slower and less maneuverable than Japan's "Zero" plane, with its durability and with skilled pilots implementing the Thach Weave at low altitude, it had proven effective in battle. But it had only lap belts, no shoulder harnesses, and Wildcat seatbelts were known to "let go under sudden impact," which could lead to the pilot getting knocked out in a crash. "The only logical conclusion I can draw from the whole affair,' Reiter wrote to the Kinnicks, "is that Nile was rendered unconscious when the plane hit and was thrown clear."[11]

The Kinnicks had little opportunity to follow up with Reiter; on 5 September 1943, at Wake Island, he was killed in action. In the end, of the four members of Kinnick's flight team, only one would survive the war.[12]

Stories of Kinnick's death ran in newspapers across the country. He was praised for his hard work, clutch play, and competitive drive, as well as his kindness, modesty, smarts, and service. One reporter described him as an "intensely human symbol, a square-jawed lad with close-cropped blond hair and a friendly grin, who accepted adulation with a disarming naturalness." Papers ran quotes from Iowa's governor, the university president, and Kinnick's former coach, Dr. Eddie Anderson, who said that Nile was "loved by everyone who knew him; his kindness and consideration for others stamped him as a typically ideal American."[13]

KINNICK SPENT THE LAST WEEKS of his life largely at sea. His diary during this time was written in an increasingly less formal, almost staccato fashion. Yet it still reflected a man who was ruminating deeply on life, who took time to take in the splendor of nature. One night he wrote, "Moonbeams dancing on the water tonight in ever changing forms—a kaleidoscope of geometric pattern."[14] Several days before his death, he summed up his views on life, writing, "Christian Science, Yankee pragmatism, laughter are the tools with which I fashion my life."[15]

And, just days before his fateful crash, he waxed poetic about Iowa City and his beloved university in a letter, presumed to be his last, written to Celia Pears, the University of Chicago graduate student he had dated for several months before entering the navy and with whom he corresponded throughout his wartime service. Celia received the letter on the evening of 4 June 1943, shortly after reading in the paper of her dear friend's death.

In her last letter to him, she'd written about a recent visit to Iowa City. In his final letter to her, Kinnick told Celia that he was delighted to have read of her enthusiasm for Iowa City. "It is almost like home," he wrote. "I love the people, the campus, the trees, everything about it."

It's not hard to picture him sitting on a carrier on the vast and lonely sea, thinking of a woman he cared for and a place he loved. He closed by writing, "I hope you strolled off across the golf course just at twilight and felt the peace and quiet of an Iowa evening, just as I used to do."[16]

For Nile Kinnick's parents, unfortunately, their grief didn't end with the loss of their oldest son. Their middle son, Ben—a year younger than Nile and a Marine Corps pilot—went missing eighteen months later while flying over Kavieng Peninsula in the South Pacific.[17]

It was shortly after the war that someone put forth the idea of naming Iowa's football stadium after Nile Kinnick. Kinnick Sr. thought it best to demur. At the time, with the wounds of war so recent and deep, he didn't want to single out one lost son over another, or seem to take away from others who had lost their lives in World War II.

However, when the effort resurfaced decades later, the elder Kinnick thought the time was right, saying, "You know, if they would rename the stadium for him, it would be his greatest award."[18] Shortly thereafter, Iowa did just that. Kinnick Sr., whose wife had passed by then, attended the ceremony and was quite pleased.

Nile Kinnick and his brother Ben were, of course, not alone. Nearly a half million Americans lost their lives in World War II. Worldwide some fifty million soldiers and citizens perished, millions more from war-related illness and hunger.

Today there is a twenty-foot-tall bronze statue of Kinnick near the Hawkeyes' team entrance to Kinnick Stadium. It features Kinnick dressed as if he's heading to class, with books in his right hand and a football jersey slung over his left shoulder. His helmet sits by his feet.

Soon after its unveiling, a game-day tradition arose—on his way into the stadium, each Hawkeye player rubs Kinnick's helmet. Really, every Big Ten player encounters Kinnick on game day, as each Big Ten game begins with a coin toss featuring a special coin with Nile Kinnick's likeness on one side.

Times change; the world's problems shift. Yet Americans still love football and their country. The military and sports still maintain a special correlation. And the values the media celebrated in Kinnick during his day—hard work, scholarly pursuit, athletic greatness, sacrifice, and love of country—continue to resonate.

21

IT IS HARD TO PICK ONE fallen athlete to highlight from World War II. America lost nearly a half million soldiers in it, many of them athletes. Indeed, Kinnick wasn't the only player from Iowa's storied 1939 team to perish in World War II. Back Burdell "Oops" Gilleard, an orphan from New London, Iowa, died in November 1944 at the Battle of Leyte, the amphibious invasion of the Philippines. Assistant coach Bill Hofer suffered terrible wounds, also in the Pacific theater. Tackle Mike Enich took a sniper's bullet to the lung in Okinawa and survived. Unbelievably, every member of the 1939 Iowa football team, coaches and players alike, served during World War II.[1]

Outside of Iowa, there are men like Joe Routt. Considered one of the greatest linemen out of the Southwest in the 1930s, he played on the line at Texas A&M and twice earned All-American honors, in 1936 and '37. He and his wife Marilyn had two young daughters. He was killed in action in the Netherlands on 10 December 1944 and was awarded a Bronze Star and Purple Heart.[2] A major avenue north of Texas A&M's Kyle Field is named after Joe Routt.

Jack Chevigny played halfback at Notre Dame under Knute Rockne. He is credited in part with helping to cement the "Win one for the Gipper" legend when, after Rockne gave his iconic speech during halftime of a game versus Army, Chevigny scored a touchdown and declared, "That's one for the Gipper." Chevigny coached under Rockne and graduated from Notre Dame Law School before becoming the head coach of the NFL's Chicago Cardinals, in 1932, and the Texas Longhorns, from 1934 to 1936. He was killed in the battle of Iwo Jima at the age of thirty-nine.[3]

At this time, few combat roles were available to African Americans in the still-segregated US military. Yet through his exploits in World War II, Doris "Dorie" Miller of Waco, Texas, a former fullback at the all-black A. J. Moore High School, was awarded a Navy Cross and a Purple Heart. On the morning the Japanese attacked Pearl Harbor, he was serving on the battleship *West Virginia*. In the chaos of the attack, he presented himself for duty and ultimately took control of a Browning anti-aircraft machine gun, firing away at the Japanese overhead. That day he also gained credit for saving lives for moving injured sailors to safety.[4] Celebrated in the press, he was sent out by the US military to raise money for war bonds. In late 1943 Miller was deemed "presumed dead" after the ship he was serving on was struck by a Japanese torpedo. Reportedly six-foot-three and 200 pounds at the age of seventeen, it's not hard to imagine a man like Dorie Miller starring in an SWC or SEC backfield. Unfortunately, such fields would not integrate until the mid- to late 1960s. This is of course but a small sampling of the tremendous sacrifices made in World War II.

FOUR

James Robert "Bob" Kalsu

22

IN MAY 1970, on a typically beautiful day in Hawaii, Jan Kalsu, a gorgeous, twenty-two-year-old brunette, several months pregnant, sat in her room at the Illaki Hotel, blowing bubbles to her year-and-a-half-old daughter Jill. Her husband, Bob Kalsu, slept on the bed.[1] Their hotel sat next to the beach, near Kahanamoku Lagoon, a dream vacation spot for travelers from around the world. The scene, then—wife blowing bubbles for daughter, husband taking what would appear to be a lazy nap nearby—could have easily looked like something out of a travel magazine.

But then out in the courtyard below, someone set off a round of small firecrackers. Bob Kalsu, a hulk of a man, at six-three and 255 pounds, awoke with a start at the sound. His wife recalled he "tore out of that bed frantic, looking for cover, terror and fear on his face." Jan, still sitting next to their daughter, holding a bubble wand in hand, watched in shock, wondering to herself, *What's happening?* She realized that her husband had not told her everything about his time serving in the Vietnam War.[2]

She knew, of course, that the situation there was difficult. When she and Jill had arrived in Hawaii for her husband's Rest & Relaxation (R&R), she'd been taken to a room with other soldiers' wives to meet with an army chaplain. Like Jan, most of the wives were quite young—the average age of a US soldier in Vietnam was twenty-two, compared to World War II's twenty-six. The chaplain told these women that their husbands had "been to an earthly version of hell, and please do not bring any problems that are going on at home to them."[3] Bob's letters, however, hadn't made it seem that bad.

After meeting with the chaplain, the wives had watched as buses full of soldiers began to roll in. Jan waited eagerly with Jill for Bob to emerge. The first two or three buses emptied with no sign of him. When his bus

Bob Kalsu with daughter Jill. Courtesy Jan Kalsu.

finally arrived, he stepped off, spotted his family, and started for them like a "galloping buffalo." He enfolded his pregnant wife and daughter in his arms, clearly moved to be back with them. But Bob's size and enthusiasm scared young Jill, who started crying. Bob started to well up, too, thinking his tiny daughter, whom he hadn't seen in many months, had forgotten him.

Happily, as Jan recalled, Jill's memory of her father was soon renewed and the two quickly became an "item together" in Hawaii. With a portable camera, the young family took videos of their time there—of Bob burying Jill's feet in the sand, of him swinging his daughter over the ocean water. That time, though, was too short. Soon they would have to say goodbye again—Bob bound for Southeast Asia, pregnant Jan and daughter Jill headed back to Oklahoma.[4]

Jan and Jill's plane left first. Bob ran alongside the trolley that whisked Jan and Jill to their plane, holding his wife's hand as long as he could. "Please be careful," she said to Bob.

"No, Jan, you be careful—you're having our baby," he said before their grip broke.

To Jan, deeply religious, that baby was a special gift amid a trying time. Months earlier, before her husband had left for Vietnam, she had gone up to the tabernacle at Oklahoma City's St. James Catholic Church, the same church in which she and Bob had wed, to pray. With combat duty looming for her husband, she was in a frightened and emotional state. She recalled asking, "Jesus, if you feel like you need Bob more than I need him, then please give us a son to carry out his name."

Weeks after this prayer, not long after she'd dropped her husband at the airport to head to Vietnam, she'd gone to her doctor, who confirmed her suspicions. She was pregnant, their baby due 21 July 1970. "My heart rushed with the thought of the prayer before the tabernacle," Jan recalled. "Of course, I was scared in the meantime, wondering what God had in mind."[5]

As fate had it, on her due date—21 July 1970—her husband would die fighting in the Vietnam War, perishing in the last major military engagement between the United States and the North Vietnamese army. Two days later, back in Oklahoma, the son Jan had prayed for would be born.

When a soldier is killed in combat, the US Army tasks one of its own with going in person to the fallen soldier's next of kin to inform them of their loss. As such, two days after Bob Kalsu's death a soldier arrived at Jan's parents' home, where she and her family lived while Bob served. Jan's parents, siblings, and Bob's parents were inside the home when the soldier knocked. Upon seeing a uniformed man at the door, they knew right away. Jan wasn't home, so the soldier couldn't say why he was visiting, but they knew. When Jan's little brother Patrick, who idolized Bob, realized matters, he rolled in anguish. The soldier was told that Jan could be found at the hospital, where she'd given birth to a baby boy that very day. The soldier left for the hospital, and Jan's family quickly got a hold of her doctor, Dr. Maguire, to ask him to get to Jan's room.

Dr. Maguire had seen Jan earlier in the day on morning rounds. When he came into her double room a second time, she was surprised to see him. "Oh, hi, Doctor, what are you doing?" she wondered. He asked the husband and wife sharing the double room with Jan if they could go outside, and then he took a seat near the head of Jan's bed. He put his arm around her and said, "There is going to be a soldier that is going to come in to talk to you."

"Bob's been killed, hasn't he?" Jan asked. And then she went into "automatic," explaining to Dr. Maguire in detail how she thought Bob would like her to raise their children.[6]

"And this poor soldier came in," Jan recalled, "and, God love him, he was crying after he found out I had just had a child. But he had his orders, and he said, 'I'm sorry to inform you, but your husband has been killed.'"[7]

At that time, women often stayed in the hospital a week after child-birth; this time, however, Jan looked at her doctor and said, "I want to go home." She did just that. But first she made sure she had the baby's name changed to that of her husband, James Robert Kalsu.[8]

⭐ JAMES "BOB" KALSU died fighting a war that could hardly have been more dissimilar than World War II, both in how it came about and how the country reacted to it, especially at the time of his death. And he is the only active professional American athlete to die fighting the Vietnam War.

In 1968, he'd completed a stellar rookie campaign with the Buffalo Bills. A year before that, as an offensive tackle at Oklahoma, he had capped his All-American senior season with an Orange Bowl victory over Tennessee. It was after his rookie year with the Bills that Kalsu's military call-up arrived, a result of his Reserve Officers' Training Corps (ROTC) obligation, which was compulsory for all male freshmen and sophomores at the time at a land-grant university like Oklahoma, but which Kalsu continued with through his five years there.

Most of the draft-eligible pro athletes in the 1960s found their way to guard or reserve duty, where they could stay stateside and still play pro-fessionally. Only six football players and a bowler, among all the nation's professional athletes, served in the war. This situation caused some con-troversy. In January 1967, *Sporting News* reported that 311 of the 360 pro-fessional athletes in the guard or reserves had joined after becoming pro athletes. Secretary of Defense Robert McNamara soon issued an order "that guard and reserve vacancies henceforth would be filled on a first-come, first-served basis."[9]

By 1968, then, the year of Kalsu's call-up, between the draft, which gave deferments to college students, and the way spots in the reserves and guard were slotted, the dynamic had changed. Yet the prospect of reserve or guard duty was still an option. Kalsu's teammate and friend, John Frantz, urged him to get the Bills' brass to help him land a spot in the reserves. But Kalsu didn't try. "I gave 'em my word. I'm gonna do it," he told Frantz.[10] He'd told his wife Jan the equivalent well before, saying, "Jan, I'm no different than anybody else."[11]

Like so many lesser-known young American men, Kalsu became a casualty of the Vietnam War. Yet even in his case there was very little media coverage of his death. Here was a likely future NFL star, a former All-American at Oklahoma, with a beautiful wife, daughter, and new baby boy, killed serving his country. But unlike with Hamilton Fish, Hobey Baker, or Nile Kinnick before him, or Patrick Tillman after him, few newsmen reported it. In the days, weeks, and months afterward, no articles appeared about him in national newspapers or in *Newsweek*, *Time*, or the *Saturday Evening Post*. *Sports Illustrated* didn't write an article about him until thirty years after he was killed. It's as if America wanted to forget an unpopular war, and highlighting Bob Kalsu's sacrifice would make it hard to do that.

23

ON 1 JANUARY 1968, just two and a half years before their tearful goodbye in Hawaii, Jan watched on national television as her fiancé and his Oklahoma Sooners teammates, ranked third in the country, played the second-ranked Tennessee Volunteers at the Orange Bowl in Miami, Florida.

Jan had hoped to be in the crowd at that Orange Bowl. Newly engaged, the two had realized that if they scheduled their wedding date just before the Orange Bowl in Miami, they could save money, which was in short supply, by using the trip to Florida as their honeymoon. Of course, Oklahoma had to win an invitation to the Orange Bowl by clinching a Big Eight title first. In November, playing at home in Norman, the Sooners did just that when they beat Kansas. Jan watched that clinching game from the sixty-sixth row and when the clock ran out, she recalled, she "tore down those steps, through that gate, and ran onto the field." She jumped into Bob's arms and he twirled her about.[1]

But, alas, Oklahoma head coach Chuck Fairbanks, with whom Jan maintained a friendship until he passed in 2013, caught word of the plan and put the kibosh on it. "You're not getting married; your mind is going to be on this game," he told Bob Kalsu. So instead of going to Florida, Jan stayed home and wrote announcements for their 27 January 1968 wedding date.[2]

That year's Orange Bowl ranked as one of the season's biggest games. For years, under the direction of Earnie Seiler, the Orange Bowl had been booming, with its marquee matchups, its dazzling game-day parade, and pregame and halftime shows attracting fans and sponsors. By the late sixties, the amount the Orange Bowl paid out to its participating teams approached a whopping $1 million.[3] For this New Year's Day matchup, Oklahoma and Tennessee took the field with 9-1 records, their only losses coming early in the season. NBC used the contest as its feature tilt for the New Year's Day bowl coverage.

Other than the old-school graphics and sponsors (like Salem cigarettes), the broadcast shares a lot of similarities with what's seen nowadays. The pregame coverage, aired in color, featured highlights of players, shots of the over 76,000 attendees in the crowd, and footage of the general pomp and circumstance that comes with a huge college football game, then and now. Before kickoff, NBC showed a massive band, fronted by a choir, marching onto the field playing "My Country, 'Tis of Thee," then fanning out to make a vector-shaped image in the colors of the American flag. Shortly thereafter, at the back of an end zone, as the choir sang and the band now played "This Is My Country," a massive, sixty-foot-tall Statue of Liberty ringed in lights rose high into the sky, as if levitating on its own. Below it an American flag, ringed in lights as well, rose up. As both the Statue of Liberty and the American flag reached their apex, coming into full view of the huge crowd, the choir sang:

I only know I swell with pride and deep within my breast
I thrill to see Old Glory paint the breeze.

The fans roared with approval. Next, the band played "The Star-Spangled Banner."

It had all the makings of what would become recognized as a classic American presentation of a major New Year's Day bowl game. Yet, at the time, elements of the presentation were still relatively new. Not until World War II, for instance, did the practice of playing the national anthem before sporting events even begin. And not until the 1960s did the patriot-filled pageantry now commonly seen at big football games really take off—it took off at the Orange Bowl thanks to the efforts of Earnie Seiler, who directed the game from 1935 to 1987. College football historian Michael Oriard wrote that at the Orange Bowl in the sixties, Seiler "seized the moment of war, civil rights protest, and countercultural discord to drench football spectacle in superpatriotism."[4]

Viewed in this light, the 1968 Orange Bowl broadcast occurred at a rather ironic time, aired as it was on the first day of one of the most tumultuous years in American history. By the end of 1968, the number of American servicemen participating in the Vietnam War would exceed half a million, a result of President Lyndon B. Johnson's tripling of US troops in the area since 1965. Over 30,000 of those servicemen would be killed in 1968, making it the deadliest year of the entire war. Also killed that year, by assassins on US soil, were Martin Luther King Jr. and Robert Kennedy. Race riots roiled America after King's death. Clashes between antiwar protesters and police marred the 1968 Democratic National Convention in Chicago. The antiwar movement seethed at the convention because Vice President Hubert Humphrey, viewed as representing President Johnson's take on the war, emerged as the Democratic presidential nominee even though some 80 percent of the primary voters had supported one of the party's antiwar candidates, including Eugene McCarthy and, prior to his assassination, Robert Kennedy.

Still, NBC's coverage of the 1968 Orange Bowl on New Year's Day was patriotic and festive, full of excitement and possibility, not just for the game. Americans had reason to value their country—as exemplified here by two great universities, backed by youthful bands and dancers, fans and athletes, all with seemingly so much in front them, few more so than Bob Kalsu.

The senior All-American had led his team from a three-win season as a sophomore starter to among the nation's most elite teams as a senior. He was the team captain, did well in school, and had recently gotten engaged to his college sweetheart. "He did everything the way you're supposed to," Sooners defensive end James Riley told *Sports Illustrated* thirty years after Kalsu's death. "He didn't cut classes. He never gave anybody a minute's trouble."[5] The NBC cameras focused on him as he ran onto the Orange Bowl field to be announced as one of the starters. He appeared tall, strong, and strikingly handsome. "Number 77, a senior, offensive tackle, from Dell City, Oklahoma, in Business Education, Bob Kalsu," the stadium announcer bellowed to millions of viewers across the land.[6] The camera seemed to make Kalsu a little shy, and yet his face expressed confidence and optimism. He looked like someone Hollywood might cast as Superman.

Kalsu made it clear early in the game that he aimed to play like Superman, too. On the Sooners' first offensive play from scrimmage, they ran directly off Kalsu, who cleared a huge hole for Ron Shotts. That opening play set the tone for what would become a colossal Orange Bowl victory for Oklahoma. The win gave them a final record of 10-1 and a good argument to be considered the national champions. In an era that relied on AP polls, however, that distinction technically went to a one-loss USC team, which beat Indiana in the Rose Bowl, 14-3.

⭐ RATHER THAN JUST BEFORE THE ORANGE BOWL, Jan and Bob wed a few weeks after it. They'd met in mid-October 1966 on a blind date set up by Ron Winfrey. The route to that date was a little circuitous. Jan, who went to Central State College in Edmond—about forty miles from the University of Oklahoma—was out having a Coke with her friend Debbie when they heard a disc jockey on the radio say that the Oklahoma Sooners football team, which had just beaten Texas, would soon land at the Will Rogers Airport. The disc jockey asked listeners to show support for the Sooners by coming out to the airport to welcome the team home. On a whim, Jan and her friend decided to go.

Upon reaching Will Rogers Airport, they joined the crowd and cheered along as the players stepped off the plane. Then Jan saw someone she recognized, a childhood friend, Ron Shotts. She found him and said, "Ron, I didn't know you play for OU. . . . Wow, there are some good-lookin' guys here."[7] He told Jan he'd fix her up with a date if she'd like, and two weeks later Ron called to set up a date with his roommate, Bob Kalsu. She agreed. On that first date together, the actual date of which Jan can easily recall—15 October 1966—she and Bob immediately connected.

They both cherished their Catholic faith. They both liked the idea of a big family. Bob, an only child, thought they looked fun. Jan, the third of nine Darrow children, already knew they were. The pair's values and senses of humor aligned, too. When she was dropped off at her parents' home after their first date, Jan recalled, "I flopped on the bed next to my baby sister, who was nine years younger than me, and woke her up and said, 'I think I just met the man I'm going to marry.'"[8]

She didn't immediately get tied down to one man, however. As a student at an all-girls high school, she didn't have much experience with dating. So, although Bob was ready to "go steady" pretty quickly, she continued to date for a while. This created some tricky situations. At

Bob and Jan on their wedding day.
Courtesy Jan Kalsu.

her freshman dorm, for instance, there was a curfew at which time the phones would shut off. She remembers more than once walking back to the dorm after being dropped off from a date with someone other than Bob and hearing her roommates tell her through an open window, "Get in here quick, Jan, Bob's calling." She'd rush in and pick up the phone and Bob would ask her what she'd been up to. Then the phone would go dead on account of curfew. "Early the next morning I'd get a call," Jan remembered.[9]

Bob stuck with it. In time, Jan, who actually felt like Bob was the one all along, made it "official" when she accepted his "drop." In the 1960s in Oklahoma, a "drop" was a special piece of necklace jewelry, monogrammed with initials, which a man would give to his lady to symbolize that they were going steady.

Bob and Jan went steady from then on. She got a kick out of seeing this massive man come to campus to visit her. By the summer of '67, they were engaged.[10] They were focused on each other, the upcoming football season, and finishing college. The rest would work itself out. As such, Bob's ROTC commitment wasn't something they talked about much. At the time, Jan didn't really even know what the post-college ROTC fulfillment entailed.[11] And it wouldn't have mattered anyway. She'd found the man of her dreams and was eager to start a new life with him.

That man had been born on 13 April 1945 in Oklahoma City. He was the first and only child of Frank and Leah Kalsu, residents of Del City, a relatively affluent suburb just outside Oklahoma City.

Bryan Kalsu, a cousin to Bob, remembered the Kalsu family as a "very loving, loyal, disciplined Catholic family." Bob's mom ran a tight ship, didn't complain, yet was "one of those ladies that if you went to her house, she went to the kitchen and brought you something to eat or drink." Bob's dad, Frank, whose brother had starred in basketball at Oklahoma State and who had tried to make it on the hardwood with the Cowboys himself, believed in a hard day's work, discipline, and the importance of family and faith.[12] Raised during the Depression in a rural part of Oklahoma, he was a sheet-metal worker at Oklahoma City's Tinker Air Force Base, which was built on the eve of US involvement in World War II and a key reason a lot of families settled in that area during and after the war.

24

AS IT HAPPENED, within a few weeks of Bob Kalsu's birth, America celebrated Victory in Europe, the unconditional surrender of Germany in World War II. Three months later Japan surrendered as well. Western democracy had prevailed. But so, too, had communism, leading to the subsequent decades-long Cold War. Before Bob was even born, then, the elements that would interact to bring him and hundreds of thousands of other US troops to Vietnam had begun to swirl.

Though it's a relatively small Asian country, struggle has beaten a path through Vietnam for millennia. For centuries, off and on, that struggle pitted native Vietnamese against invading Chinese. During the seventeenth, eighteenth, and nineteenth centuries, in fits and starts, the struggle featured France. The French ultimately subdued Vietnam for much of this period, taking, in the view of many natives, Vietnamese culture and wealth and its right to self-determination.

During World War II, Japan took over Vietnam. After the war, with Japan defeated, Vietnam declared its independence; France, however, had other plans. It aimed to recolonize Vietnam.

FDR had aided Vietnamese efforts to beat back the Japanese, and, recognizing the follies of colonialism, had expressed support for Vietnamese independence. Post–World War II, though, America viewed matters through the lens of the Cold War. In short, Truman, who became president after FDR's April 1945 death and who would win reelection in '48, wanted the support of France in his effort to keep communism in check. America wanted France, and France wanted Vietnam. In turn, by the late 1940s the United States bore much of the cost of France's Vietnamese colonization efforts.

The focus of America's Cold War lens sharpened in 1949 when

China's civil war ended in victory for the communists, a major development. That same year, Russia detonated a nuclear device while America had to confront Stalin's Berlin Blockade in East Germany. American leaders were consumed by fear of the desire by Mao and Stalin, along with communist allies like Vietnam's rebel leader Ho Chi Minh, to take over the world in an international communist conspiracy.

Still, by the mid-1950s, with Dwight Eisenhower now president, the United States chose not to provide ground military support in Southeast Asia to the French as their effort to recolonize Vietnam crumbled. In May 1954, the French lost the brutal Battle of Dien Bien Phu and surrendered soon after.

With France's departure, Vietnam ultimately split in two—the South propped up by and allied with the West, the North led by communist Ho Chi Minh and allied with the Soviet Union and China. Complicating matters, in South Vietnam a guerilla-style rebellion eventually coalesced into the Viet Cong, supported by the North.

For a young Bob Kalsu, the developments in Vietnam were surely one of the last things on his mind. He was eleven in 1956, when North Vietnam and South Vietnam formally split, and surely more interested in listening to Elvis Presley records, running over to the Del City ball field to meet up with his friends on his Little League baseball team, or watching the Oklahoma Sooners win yet another football game. In the mid-1950s, after all, the Sooners won a still-standing record of forty-seven straight games under their legendary coach, Bud Wilkinson, the man who several years later would recruit Bob Kalsu to Norman out of Del City High School.[1]

Motivated and coached by his father, young Kalsu excelled at sports and grew like a weed. He also loved to compete. "He played every kind of ball imaginable," his mother Leah told *Sports Illustrated* in 2001. "He was even on a bowling team. He loved to play cards—canasta, hearts. We'd play Chinese checkers head-to-head. We played jacks when he was seven or eight. He played jacks until he was in *high school*. He'd never quit when he lost. He'd say, 'Mom, let's play another.'"[2]

In 1959, Kalsu matriculated at Del City High School. There he would play basketball and baseball as well as football, in which, in addition to playing on the offensive line, he punted and kicked. As an upperclassman, Kalsu even found time to join a buddy, Jack Fried, in writing reports on local football action in the school paper, the *Eagle Eye*.

He might have loved golf best, though. He turned himself into a four or five handicap partly from arising early enough on Sundays for 7:00 a.m. Mass at St. Paul's Church to make an 8:30 a.m. tee time with his beloved Uncle Mitt, occasionally shooting fifty-four holes in a day.[3]

During Kalsu's years at Del City High, Presidents Eisenhower and Kennedy were committed to supporting the anticommunist South Vietnamese government—authoritarian, nepotistic, and corrupt as it might have been—against North Vietnam and Ho Chi Minh, who wanted to unify the country under communist rule. Both presidents gradually ramped up the US military presence in South Vietnam, Kennedy in particular. In 1963, Kalsu's senior year of high school, President Kennedy deployed over 16,000 "advisors" to South Vietnam. Still, issues between North and South Vietnam didn't register strongly in the collective American mind. When Kalsu chose ROTC at Oklahoma, his wife said, "I'm sure when he took ROTC he didn't think of Vietnam or anything like that." Yet, as noted, when he got called up, he accepted it.[4]

It might not have registered strongly in the American mind, but inside the White House the situation in Southeast Asia was quite worrisome. By 1964, just months after Kennedy's assassination, President Lyndon B. Johnson and his advisors wrestled with how to proceed there. Uncertainty regarding exact US objectives abounded, along with confidence in their attainability.

A major issue entailed South Vietnam's shockingly unstable government. From 1963 to 1965 alone, several coups took place. As LBJ searched for solutions, his secretary of defense, Robert McNamara, admitted privately, "The frank answer is we don't know what's going on out there." In May 1964, having mulled matters further, LBJ told his aide McGeorge Bundy, "I don't think it's worth fighting for. . . . It's just the biggest damned mess I ever saw."[5] By that time Bob Kalsu was a freshman at Oklahoma. In the end, LBJ, who shortly after becoming president had told the US ambassador to Vietnam, "I am not going to be the President who saw Southeast Asia go the way China went," applied a strong Cold War mentality to the region. With a congressional resolution in the wake of the controversial Gulf of Tonkin incident giving him the leeway, LBJ significantly broadened the war effort in August 1964. Over the next several years, he and Secretary of Defense McNamara would send hundreds of thousands of US troops to Southeast Asia and spend hundreds of billions of dollars, doubling, even tripling, down on the effort to keep South Vietnam from communist control.

Forty years after admitting ignorance about Vietnam to his boss in the Oval Office, McNamara released his memoirs, hoping in part to warn future leaders. He wrote that he and fellow policymakers, viewing matters from their own experience, had envisioned South Vietnam as hungry and determined to "fight for freedom and democracy." In actuality, he and other US leaders "totally misjudged political forces in the country . . . underestimated the power of nationalism to motivate a people . . . failed to recognize the limits of modern, high-technology military equipment" and more.[6]

25

IN 1963, during Kalsu's freshman year, Oklahoma ended the season in the top ten. After it, the Sooners' legendary coach, Bud Wilkinson, retired. Freshman still weren't eligible under NCAA rules, so Kalsu didn't play varsity, and the following season he was redshirted. Still, he and his buddies enjoyed college life. James Riley and V. Larry Alford, who came to Oklahoma as part of the same class as Kalsu, remembered their friend similarly—as fun-loving, hard-working, mature, and principled.

Riley lived across the hall from Kalsu sophomore year and several years later, in 1968, would line up against him as a defensive lineman for the Dolphins. Riley characterized their dorm life as "continued nonsense," meaning card games and youthful energy. Yet Kalsu, Riley said, handled himself with a level of control and kindness that set him apart. He didn't overdo it on the social scene and nearly always maintained an upbeat disposition. "As nice a person as I've ever known," Alford said, emphasizing that he doesn't say that in the least bit lightly. It's simply the way it was.[1]

Kalsu's sophomore year proved a tough one for Sooners football. The team finished an uncharacteristic 3-7, and head coach Gomer Jones, who had taken over in 1964, resigned at season's end (although he did stay on as Oklahoma's athletic director). By all accounts, Kalsu maintained a good attitude but still found the season to be dispiriting. When a good friend from Del City, Steve Coleman, who was three years younger and who Kalsu had adopted as a kind of surrogate brother, was being recruited to play football at Oklahoma, Kalsu told him he might want to look around. Coleman ended up at Vanderbilt. Ironically, a couple years later Tennessee would whip Coleman's Vanderbilt team in its last game of the regular season before falling to Kalsu's Sooners in the 1968 Orange Bowl.[2] Coleman watched on television, marveling at the turnaround his "big brother" had helped engineer at Oklahoma.

Oklahoma's new coach for the 1966 season, Kalsu's junior year, was James Mackenzie. He'd spent the previous seven seasons at Arkansas, six of which had ended with the Razorbacks among the nation's top ten teams. As Steve Coleman remembered it, teams like Arkansas and Alabama were winning by playing guys who were mobile, hostile, and agile. With this in mind, Coach Mackenzie actually had Kalsu cut weight, to less than 220 pounds, helping to turn him into a dominant offensive lineman who was indeed mobile, hostile, and agile.[3]

The Sooners improved to 6-4 in Mackenzie's first year, but their new coach, just thirty-seven years old, died suddenly from a heart attack that spring. His assistant, Chuck Fairbanks, took over the Sooner program. In his first year as a college head coach, he led Oklahoma to one of the most magical seasons in its storied history.

Kalsu's teammates elected him captain at the start of that 1967 season, and during it he emerged as one of the best Oklahoma linemen of all time. The Sooners got off to an auspicious start on the first play of their first game, versus Washington State in Norman, Oklahoma. Offensive guards Eddie Lancaster and Byron Bigby teamed up to drive a Cougar lineman down the field, opening a path for running back Steve Owens, who peeled off a twelve-yard carry. Before Lancaster could get up after the

Bob Kalsu as a lineman at Oklahoma. Courtesy Jan Kalsu.

play, he found Kalsu standing over him and Bigby yelling, "Good God, awright! Look at this! Look at what you did!"[4]

Fans, players, and scouts would say much the same about Kalsu throughout the rest of the season. Kansas State head coach Vince Gibson had watched film on the Sooners. He told Coach Fairbanks on the field prior to their game, "Kalsu is the best blocking lineman I've ever seen." Upon cataloguing all its game film from 1967, Coach Fairbanks and the Oklahoma staff determined that "our average gain on all plays going over Kalsu, including short yardage and goal line plays, is 6.2 net yards rushing. . . . This is what we coaches grade as . . . near perfection."[5]

All the while, of course, Kalsu was courting Jan. And it wasn't just her that he liked being around; he enjoyed her whole family. Even before the season, in the summer of 1967, he'd become like a tenth child at the Darrows's seven-bedroom home on Country Club Drive. Jan's siblings quickly learned that Bob, imposing as he might appear physically, was more like a gentle, big-hearted giant, one who loved to play games, carry out practical jokes, and eat—whole meals, it seemed, in a few chomps. He struggled mightily, though, in the Darrow kitchen as a burgeoning pastry chef.[6] Of course, that didn't really matter to Jan or the rest of the Darrows. Her family could tell what both Jan and Bob knew. They were madly in love.

⭐ AFTER THE MAGICAL SEASON AND WEDDING, the newlyweds finally did get to go on a honeymoon in late January 1968. During it Bob Kalsu was chosen in the eighth round of the 1968 NFL/ AFL draft by the Buffalo Bills. (After the merger of the NFL and AFL in 1966, the two leagues alternated picks in what was dubbed the "common draft" until the leagues fully merged in 1970.) The Dallas Cowboys and Denver Broncos had scouted Kalsu during his senior year but seemed concerned about his ROTC commitment, which had made Jan think a bit about the commitment's potential repercussions.[7]

Interestingly, at first, Bob didn't hear from the team that actually drafted him. The newlyweds learned about the draft upon returning from their honeymoon, when Jan's sister Diane started singing to them, "Buffalo Bob, won't you come out tonight?" They hadn't a clue what she was getting at until she finished, "Haven't you heard ? You've been drafted by the Buffalo Bills."[8]

With Kalsu's Orange Bowl win, marriage, and getting drafted by the Bills, January 1968 seems to have been a great month. Little did he know the impact of the Tet Offensive on the Vietnam War, which was launched on the day before the Buffalo Bills selected Kalsu in the draft and would be a factor in his future. The Tet Offensive counted as the largest military campaign up to that point of what had become the years-long Vietnam War. It included over 80,000 troops attacking more than one hundred South Vietnamese cities and towns.

Oddly enough, in the immediate weeks after it, it became clear that on the actual battlefield the Tet Offensive had failed. North Vietnamese casualty rates soared while they lost much of the gains they made in their initial wave. In the arena of public opinion, however, the offensive delivered a mighty blow in the United States. Americans who had been told in late '67 by Gen. William Westmoreland that there was a "light at the end of the tunnel," who had been made to believe by President Johnson and his advisors that the United States was winning, seemed stunned that North Vietnam could carry out such a wide-scale attack on South Vietnam this many years into the war. From 1965 to 1967, the media had generally supported the war effort. But after the Tet Offensive, CBS anchorman Walter Cronkite, viewed as a national voice of reason, captured the frustration and confusion when, learning of the attack, he asked, "What the hell is going on? I thought we were winning the war."[9]

In late February 1968, a month after the Tet Offensive, Cronkite went to Vietnam. Upon returning, he declared on air that the only rational way out of the war "will be to negotiate, not as victors, but as honorable people who lived up to their pledge to defend democracy, and did the best they could."[10] After seeing a clip of Cronkite's comments, President Johnson purportedly said, "If I've lost Cronkite, I've lost Middle America."[11]

Whether President Johnson said this exactly or not, it pretty well summed things up. After the Tet Offensive, media coverage of the war turned more negative.[12] Television, in particular, impacted public opinion significantly. In 1950 only five million households had a television. By 1960, estimates put that number at over fifty million. Unlike in World War II, during the Vietnam War reporters routinely received accreditation to embed with soldiers without any censorship. Though this practice lessened as America's displeasure with the war increased, this meant that the brutality of war could arrive in graphic form in American living rooms each night on the evening news. Morale sank at home, just as it was sinking with many soldiers abroad.

It's impossible to measure the exact impact of television, but it was certainly rising, and fast. In 1964, for instance, the percentage of people who got their news from newspapers slightly led those who got it from television. By 1968 the television viewers enjoyed a clear advantage. Even more striking, by 1972, a survey conducted by the Roper Organization for the Television Information Office found that 48 percent of respondents picked television as the medium they would be inclined to believe, given conflicting accounts, compared with just 21 percent who picked the newspaper.[13]

In short, the Tet Offensive, although technically ending in tactical military defeat for the North Vietnamese, changed the media's presentation of the war, shifted many Americans' views on the war, lessened the political will to fight it, and thereby impacted the conditions that Bob Kalsu and his fellow soldiers in the 101st Airborne faced two years later at Fire Support Base Ripcord.[14]

26

IN JULY 1968, Kalsu left home to try to make the Buffalo Bills' roster, with no guarantees. At that time, a player could learn at training camp that he'd been cut by opening his locker and finding no uniform. "So I think everyone was scared to open their lockers," Jan recalled.[1] Worried as he might've been, Kalsu equipped himself well.

In August, Jan got to watch her man play live against the Houston Oilers in a preseason game in Texas. Soon after, they learned that he'd made the squad. She joined him in Buffalo but returned to Oklahoma as the time to have their daughter neared. Happily for Jan, the Bills were on television a lot that year, so she could watch from afar.

The Bills, however, struggled mightily, finishing with a 1-12-1 record. Still, Kalsu earned recognition as the Bills' Offensive Rookie of the Year, beating out the likes of wide receiver Haven Moses, the Bill's first-round pick that year and a future NFL Pro Bowler. Veteran Buffalo left guard Billy Shaw, a future Hall of Famer, saw a bright future for Kalsu, bright enough that he worried Kalsu could take his job. "He had real good feet, and he was strong, good on sweeps," Shaw told *Sports Illustrated* decades later. Kalsu, at the urging of the Bills, had increased his weight up to 250 pounds on a steady diet of potatoes and chicken, and yet showed that he could still be quite effective.[2]

The season ended with a loss at the Houston Oilers on 7 December 1968. Kalsu then returned to Oklahoma to be with Jan and Jill. Not long afterward he received word of his call-up to active duty with the US Army.

The news arrived at an ugly time in the war. The United States seemed half-in, half-out. Richard Nixon had won the recent presidential election, telling the American people that he aimed to deliver "peace with honor" by implementing a new approach in Southeast Asia. This new approach in time became known as "Vietnamization," which called on the South Vietnamese to bear more of the fighting burden.

In late 1969, Nixon ended the draft, yet it would take years for the United States to leave South Vietnam. In the interim the geographic scope of the conflict expanded at times into Laos and Cambodia, and the fighting, up through the July 1970 battle at Ripcord, in spots remained fierce and deadly.

As noted, paths existed for pro athletes to avoid dangerous duty. At the end of the Korean War, this practice of athletes, helped by their teams, joining reserve units to fulfill military obligations, picked up. "Yeah, a lot of us [teams] did it," recalled Emil "Buzzie" Bavasi, a longtime baseball executive. "I helped guys get into reserve units. I got Drysdale and Koufax in in the late '50s and we were still doing it when Vietnam started."[3]

The reserve or guard routes many athletes were taking also seemed to have "tightened up" at least a bit in the interim. When the Pittsburgh Steelers' Rocky Bleier's 1A classification letter arrived in August 1968, he assumed the Steelers would get him in the guard. In fact, Steelers head coach Bill Austin had pulled Rocky aside and said, "Now, listen, we think you're good enough to make this team, and we'll take care of this obligation for you." Rocky checked on matters in October, however, and was told, "Ah, we're having a little difficulty, the General retired, the Congressman had been defeated, we're still working on it." He never ended up in the reserve or guard, but instead shipped out to Vietnam and on 20 August 1969 suffered a gunshot wound to his left thigh and shrapnel wounds to his lower right leg, losing part of his right foot. Incredibly, after many surgeries, months of rehab, and having been waived by the Steelers on two occasions, he became a starter, a four-time Super Bowl champ, and one of the franchise's all-time leading rushers.[4]

Kalsu never even tried the reserve or guard route. As mentioned, teammates encouraged him to. Bills center John Frantz told his buddy, "Bob, it's hell over there. You've got a wife, a child." Kalsu shook his head and said, "I'm committed."[5]

James Riley, the defensive lineman who played at Oklahoma with Kalsu and then later against him in the NFL, said methods were known among NFL players for either staying out of the regular army altogether or getting stationed so as to avoid active duty. Most actively looked to stay out, but Bob accepted things as they came. "I think that's the way Bob was," Riley said. "He was going to serve his country." Riley doesn't blame others for trying to stay out of the convoluted war. At the same time, he respects Kalsu's approach.[6]

Only later did Jan Kalsu really understand this route that athletes took to the reserves. Her Bob simply came from a different cut of cloth, she concluded. Kalsu's mom, according to Jan, did try to keep her son out of harm's way by reaching out to one of Oklahoma's US senators. Bob told her, "No, I signed my commitment and I'm going to follow through."[7]

⭐ BEFORE SHIPPING TO VIETNAM, Kalsu and his family went to Oklahoma's Fort Sill for training. There the family tried to live as normally as it could. Committed Catholics, they took comfort in connecting with the local Catholic church. Jan remembered how Bob loved to carry their daughter in the communion line. "People would say it looked like he was holding a football, he would carry her in such a way to show her off." And they felt grateful for their priest. When he said the Consecration, Jan said, "You could feel the presence of God. Bob and I would hold hands during the Consecration and be in awe of what was happening."[8]

About eight months into his training at Fort Sill, in September 1969, Kalsu received his orders to head to Vietnam. He arrived home from the base that day visibly shaken, sweating through his green uniform.

They had a month together before he would leave. Low on funds anyway, and with Bob wanting Jan and Jill to have support while he was gone, they decided to move into Jan's parents' home in Oklahoma City. Bob stayed with them until it

Bob Kalsu serving in Vietnam. Courtesy Jan Kalsu.

was time to go. He traded in their little GTO, which lacked power steering, in favor of a car he thought Jan could handle better. They tried to enjoy their time together.

As the date of his departure neared, while washing clothes in her parents' laundry room, Jan asked Bob about her worst fear: "What if you die over there? What am I to do?"

"I want you to go on with your life. I want you to marry again," Bob told her.

Jan refused, in tears. "I don't want to marry again. I couldn't."

The day before he left for the war, Bob and Jan and their extended family held a first birthday party for Jill. During the party, Jan realized that the door to her and Bob's bedroom was locked, something unusual in the family. Concerned, she used her nail to turn the lock, an old trick she knew from having grown up there. Stepping into the room, she heard a popular song from that time, "Jean," playing on the record player. And she saw Bob dancing, holding their one-year-old daughter, who was resting her head on his shoulder as tears streamed down her father's face. Realizing that she'd embarrassed him, Jan immediately regretted opening the door and infringing upon this special time between father and daughter.[9]

Kalsu would soon be serving as an artillery officer in the Vietnam War, with the US Army's 101st Airborne, nicknamed the "Screaming Eagles," possessors of one of the most decorated histories of any division in American history. From its D-Day landings in Normandy to its performance at the Battle of the Bulge in Belgium to the present, it has been at the forefront of the US Army's capabilities. And during his time serving, he would write many letters home. He wrote mainly of his love for Jan and their family and looked ahead to reuniting with them. He didn't get into much detail regarding the war. Jan knew he served on fire support bases as an artillery man but not too much more. Bob wanted it that way. He didn't want people overly worrying about him. It's not that he didn't realize the dangers he faced. He did.

In all the stories about Bob Kalsu, his ability to put his focus on human connection comes through—whether it was as the big man on campus his senior year at Del City High School, taking freshman Steve Coleman under his wing, organizing his classmates to vote a girl homecoming queen who didn't rank as one of the popular ones, becoming a part of the lives of Jan's big Darrow family, or coming outside one night, rather than sleep in a bunker below, to talk to an enlisted man who was pulling guard duty on Fire Support Base Ripcord. Bob sat and talked with the man, asking him about his family, life back home. He knew he was in one of the most dangerous places on earth and that he could be sleeping in a bunker down below. He wanted the young man to feel a little better about things, worry less about what they all faced as he kept guard.

Decades after the war, when Jan Kalsu mustered the courage to go with her two children to a reunion of soldiers who served at Ripcord, it was stories like this that most moved her.[10]

27

THE BATTLE FOR FIRE SUPPORT BASE RIPCORD ranks among the most frustrating engagements of the entire brutal, muddled, and increasingly unpopular conflict. Fought by Kalsu's 101st Airborne, the last remaining full-strength division in theater, the Ripcord battle lasted a little over three weeks, from 1 July to 23 July 1970. It marked the last major engagement between the US military and the North Vietnamese army. And, as noted, two days after Bob Kalsu died fighting to defend Ripcord, the US Army abandoned it.

In March 1970, several weeks prior to the North Vietnamese army's surprise July 1 attack on Ripcord, the US Army had started to rebuild the base, with the idea that it could be used to disrupt enemy supply lines and as a starting point for offensive action into the mountains across the valley, where the North Vietnamese army had bases.

Abandoned earlier in the war, the Ripcord base sat atop a mountain on the eastern edge of the A Shau Valley, which was some twenty miles long and counted as valuable real estate during the entire war. This valley runs between two mile-high mountain ranges in South Vietnam, not far from the demilitarized zone that separated North from South. At points, the valley comes within just a couple of miles of Laos. As such, many offshoots of the hundreds-of-miles-long Ho Chi Minh Trail, which ran largely down Laos and Cambodia and functioned as a pathway for the North Vietnamese and Vietcong to move men and arms, connected with it, giving enemy soldiers access to South Vietnam.

In short, whichever side controlled the mountainous terrain overlooking the valley had access to an important artery into and out of South Vietnam. In turn, whoever controlled Fire Support Base Ripcord, a light-colored crest among jungle-grown mountains overlooking the valley, could use it to block this artery from the enemy.[1]

Up until the Battle of Hamburger Hill—which involved a deadly battle for a heavily fortified hill of seemingly little strategic value that the United States would soon abandon, eliciting criticism at home—Nixon's troop withdrawals had focused on North Vietnam. He responded to the backlash wrought by Hamburger Hill, however, by making marked drawdowns of troops in South Vietnam. In 1968, US troops in theater totaled over half a million. By 1970, that number dropped to some 334,600. Similar to the earlier Tet Offensive, the fallout of Hamburger Hill didn't end there. According to *Ripcord* author Keith Nolan, Hamburger Hill "would reshape the conduct of the entire ground war in Vietnam," making it less likely that troops pinned at a place like Ripcord in July 1970— as happened to Bob Kalsu and his comrades—would be reinforced with more troops.[2]

Now, by the spring of 1970, with major troop reductions occurring and soldiers' morale sinking, it is understandable to find the idea of the United States trying to gain a foothold in the dangerous A Shau Valley via Ripcord, and then going on the offensive, a little confusing. As unrealistic as it might have been by this date, the Nixon administration wanted to inflict damage on North Vietnam so that an independent South Vietnam could survive after the United States left.

This is why, much to the chagrin of an increasingly confused and war-weary American public, in April 1970, as Kalsu's 101st was rebuilding Ripcord, Nixon appeared on television to announce that US and South Vietnamese troops planned a no-longer-than-sixty-day "incursion" into neighboring Cambodia to disrupt part of North Vietnam's supply trail. (Nixon also wanted to send a message because he was upset that the North had not accepted his peace overtures.)

Fed up, the American public responded with fury that Nixon would expand the boundaries of the war while seeming to draw down. Protests erupted on college campuses. At Kent State a rowdy 4 May 1970 protest against the "incursion" into Cambodia turned deadly when members of the Ohio National Guard shot and killed four students. Two of the students killed weren't even protesters. They were just walking to class. In response, more protests across the nation took place, closing down hundreds of colleges and high schools for a short period. And then, eleven days after the Kent State killings, a similar episode left two students dead at Jackson State University in Mississippi, one of them a high school senior. Public opinion against the war dropped further while confidence in the US government plummeted. Meanwhile, back in South Vietnam, the 101st continued to reconstitute Fire Support Base Ripcord.

Complicating matters, in hindsight, some historians have argued that while the media and college students, now subject to the draft, turned increasingly negative, the US military was actually performing much more effectively by the spring of 1970 than in earlier years. Lewis Sorley, for one, argues that matters in Vietnam changed significantly after the Tet Offensive when Gen. Creighton Abrams replaced the United States' commanding general, William C. Westmoreland. Westmoreland had implemented a "search and destroy" strategy—find the enemy and destroy them; get casualty rates high enough to break the enemy's will to fight. Westmoreland did not give much attention to increasing the capabilities of the South Vietnamese army, even less to developing a coordinated plan to empower and partner with the rural South Vietnamese population, which the North terrorized, coerced, and used for covert operations.

Abrams, on the other hand, Sorley argues, implemented a "clear and hold" approach. Abrams unified combat operations, pacification of the countryside, and the building up of South Vietnam's military capabilities into one mission, the goal being security for the South Vietnamese. In many ways, Sorley maintains, Abrams's plan yielded results. Sorley characterizes America's forays into Cambodia and Laos as militarily effective efforts to limit North Vietnam's ability to fight. He notes that in the South, former tenant farmers gained title to land by the hundreds of thousands. He also highlights South Vietnam's ability, aided by US air support, to turn back the North's massive 1972 Easter Offensive as an example of the enhanced abilities of the South Vietnamese army under Abrams. Unfortunately, he argues, the prospect of using these successes to develop a lasting peace for South Vietnam was squandered by a Congress that had lost interest in the war and an American public that had turned against it.[3] It is hard to align this assessment, though, with what went down at Ripcord in the spring and summer of 1970.

As the US Army, through air assaults and ultimately a ground attack, secured the ridge upon which it rebuilt Ripcord, the North Vietnamese army quietly kept tabs, biding its time to strike back, to hit the US Army in advance of any planned US assaults. Indeed, well beforehand, the North Vietnamese had turned the area surrounding Ripcord into "an invisible fortress, the most elaborate and well-defended enemy staging and supply area in all of South Vietnam."[4] The United States just didn't know it.

⭐ DURING THIS DANGEROUS PERIOD, during which the 101st rebuilt Ripcord, Kalsu's unique ability to connect showed up in the form of an unlikely friendship with a fellow soldier, David Johnson, a poor, black enlisted cannoneer from Arkansas. At first glance, the two might not appear to have much in common. As Capt. James D. Harris put it, "Kalsu and Johnson had nothing in common except their size and their hearts."[5] Those hearts, however, actually meant they shared a lot more in common. Similar to Kalsu, Johnson didn't have to serve in active, frontline duty like he did. He'd been footing the bill to attend Philander Smith College in Little Rock, Arkansas, when he chose not to put in for another deferment. Years after his death, his sister, Audrey Wrightsell, told *Sports Illustrated* that her brother had said, "I'm tired of this. I'm gonna serve my time."[6]

Kalsu and Johnson also both liked to compete. They played cards, and they challenged each other physically. Even during the tumultuous three weeks in which the North Vietnamese surrounded Ripcord and pummeled it with mortar, Kalsu and Johnson tested each other. After a helicopter would drop ammunition at the base, for instance, they'd carry the big rounds from the base's helipad to its Howitzer artillery guns. Each Howitzer round weighed ninety-seven pounds. Most guys would carry two at a time, one over each shoulder. But Kalsu and Johnson liked to carry three, the third laid across the back of their necks and supported by the massive rounds on their shoulders. They'd go back and forth from the helipad to drop points in a contest to see who would "say uncle" first.[7] Both were well liked by their fellow troops, too. Looking back at the Ripcord battle, a soldier remembered of Kalsu and Johnson, "They were together all the time."[8]

Other soldiers developed a fondness for Kalsu. Just the fact that he was an officer carrying ammo impressed the men. "Kalsu used to help us haul ammunition," an enlisted man remembered. "For an officer that was unheard of. A lot of the section chiefs [enlisted] didn't even hump ammo." Another GI recalled of Kalsu, at a time when tensions between the officers and enlisted men were quite high, "He was one of the few officers completely at ease with the enlisted men, and they with him."[9] Mike Renner, who served under Kalsu on Ripcord in the 101st's 2nd Battalion, 11th Artillery, said, "He had a lot of respect. I liked him. There's a lot of officers I didn't like, but Lieutenant Kalsu was a different guy." During the North Vietnamese army's July siege at Ripcord, Renner remembered how at times it seemed like mortar rounds and rockets were coming in everywhere. He'd taken some shrapnel to the hand. Kalsu came to look in on him, see how he was doing. "Lieutenant Kalsu told me I could get off the hill if I wanted to. And I noticed that he had had a bandage on his left shoulder, where he had been nicked by shrapnel. And I thought, if he's staying, then I'm staying."[10]

★ THE FULL-ON NORTH VIETNAMESE SIEGE of Ripcord began on 1 July 1970, catching the Americans off-guard. In the ensuing days, seemingly every tactic the US Army carried out to regain the advantage met an effective counter from the North Vietnamese.

It soon became clear that, to regain the upper hand, division headquarters would have to pile on significant numbers of troops. By this point in the war, though, the army desperately wanted to avoid another Hamburger Hill. Division headquarters, then, did not respond with numbers as they would likely have done earlier in the war.[11]

Even in taking surrounding territory that otherwise put Ripcord in the line of fire, the US Army showed hesitation. On day twelve of the siege, for example, one battalion did secure a strategic hill near Ripcord. Upon doing so, it faced assaults from the North Vietnamese army for five nights straight, all of which the battalion repelled. But when it was airlifted out to recuperate, fresh troops were not dropped in to replace them. As a result, the North Vietnamese army immediately retook the hill.[12]

As an indication of just how little the US Army knew about the enemy, twenty days into North Vietnam's siege of Ripcord, a US company was dropped on a ridge near Ripcord only to find itself engaged in battle with North Vietnamese troops who had emerged from "yet another hidden bunker complex." That same day a soldier discovered, along a narrow trail a mere mile and a half from Ripcord, an active North Vietnamese communications land line. The North Vietnamese army seemed to be everywhere and ready for every American move.[13]

The incoming North Vietnamese mortar attacks took a major toll. When US choppers would fly in, barely slowing down to drop their supplies, the troops on the base would scurry for cover. Incoming choppers meant incoming fire. "We felt helpless, at the mercy of the enemy," Lieutenant Edwards recalled. "Sustained incoming has to be one of the worst tortures ever inflicted on a soldier." Down below in the bunkers, the heat, the deluge of tear gas, and the impact of the high explosives raining down made fresh air seemingly nonexistent.[14]

On July 21, Lt. Fred H. Edwards wrote of the dire situation in his diary. Howitzer guns intended to replace the firepower lost when a downed US helicopter had landed on a munitions stash and blown off part of the mountain had not arrived as planned because of the risk of the choppers being shot down while flying in. Meanwhile, the number of dead and wounded rose. With no supplies arriving and the hill "all but wiped out," Edwards guessed that the North would soon attack by ground. "Really feel low," he wrote.[15]

Desperation, resignation, a kind of mental uncoiling occurred as troops realized they were, for the most part, alone on that hill. Some troops became sort of paralyzed, unwilling to emerge from their bunkers. Some, saying the equivalent of "flip it," took bets on whether they could "survive walking from one bunker to the next amid the incoming, whistling, hands in their pockets."[16]

Kalsu wrote to his wife two days before being killed. He and his fellow soldiers had endured nearly three weeks of North Vietnam's siege. Yet from the letter you wouldn't have guessed the danger that he and his fellow soldiers faced:

Dearest Janny Belle—

How're things with my beautiful, sexy, lovable wife. I love & miss you so very much and can't wait till I'm back home in your arms and we're back in our own apartment living a normal life. The time can't pass fast enough for me until I'm back home with all my loved ones and especially you Jan and Jilly and Baby K [Bob's name for his soon-to-be-born baby]. I love and need you so very much.

The wind has quit blowing so hard up here. It calmed down so much it's hard to believe it. Enemy activity remains active in our area. Hopefully it will cease in the near future.

> *I'm just fine as can be. Feeling real good just waiting to hear the word
> again that I'm a papa. It shouldn't be much longer until I get word of our
> arrival . . .*
>
> *I love you, xxx-ooo*
> *Bob*[17]

Just like when, that night during the Ripcord siege, Bob went outside to
talk about family and home to an enlisted man on night watch, in his
letter to Jan he didn't focus on the danger he faced or the political and
strategic quagmire Vietnam had become.

Instead of dwelling on such things, he had a way of connecting with
people in more personal ways. When it came to politics, he seems to
have kept matters pretty straightforward. His father was of Czechoslo-
vakian heritage and had raised his son to appreciate the opportunities
America presented, the role it had played in World War II, a war Bob's
father would have liked to have served in had a medical issue not kept
him out. So when Bob decided to continue with his ROTC commitment,
he'd agreed to serve if called. It was hard and he missed his family dearly,
but he kept his focus on the men around him and on reuniting with his
family.

As night began to fall on 21 July 1970, an American Chinook had just
sped past the base, dropping ammunition on the battery helipad. The
North Vietnamese responded with a barrage of 82 mm rounds meant
for ammunition carriers like Kalsu and his friend from Arkansas, David
Johnson. Kalsu had stepped outside of his bunker, probably to avoid
the oppressive heat and tear gas down below and in preparation to haul
ammo. He and fellow soldier Nick Fotias were talking about the contents
of a letter that Jan had penned to her beloved husband. Kalsu told Fotias
that his wife expected a baby that very day. "I remember the joy on his
face as he read the letter to me," Fotias recalled years later. "He said, 'My
wife's having our baby today.'" Not long after, *boom.* One of the 82 mm
rounds launched by the North Vietnamese landed some five feet from
where they stood. Temporarily knocked out, Fotias came to at the bottom
of the bunker's stairs with someone on top of him. When Fotias rolled
the man off him, he realized that a shrapnel-induced wound to the head
had killed Bob Kalsu.[18]

Kalsu's good buddy David Johnson also lost his life in the deluge, as did Specialist Fourth Class Roberto C. Flores of Bravo Two, a Texan with a wife and baby at home.

Two days later, in possession of evidence that the North Vietnamese planned to storm the beleaguered fort and with the situation deteriorating further, the remaining soldiers at Ripcord were airlifted out under heavy fire. Shortly thereafter, the army sent in American B-52s to carpet-bomb the area and render the fort useless.

The US Army, looking to avoid the same negative attention brought on a year earlier with Hamburger Hill, had kept the media largely away from Ripcord and now tried to explain the evacuation as a redeployment. News accounts did call it a retreat, but there was little follow-up.

In actuality, Ripcord ended in a major win for the North Vietnamese. This crucial gateway of a valley for the Ho Chi Minh Trail remained accessible to them. And this battle, as the last major engagement between the North Vietnamese and US troops, represented in many respects the end of matters in the Vietnam War.[19]

With the US drawdown continuing apace, however, what looked inevitable was that the North Vietnamese army would, in time, successfully invade the South and "reunify" the country under communist rule. In 1975, that's exactly what happened.

So while the mortar round that killed Bob Kalsu was likely made in the Soviet Union, an indication of how the conflict was a kind of Cold War proxy battle between the United States on one side and the Soviet Union and China on the other, the strategic goal of the Vietnam War—a free and stable South Vietnam—by this time was not likely to be realized.

Perhaps if the US Army had brought in more and more troops and implemented a systematic plan to root out the North Vietnamese soldiers—who, one would imagine, would have retreated back into the hills—the US Army could have controlled the valley for a period. But by July 1970, with a marked decrease in troop levels already being carried out and with the war having dragged on for years, the amount of manpower and resources it would have taken to defend the base actually made the point some Americans were trying to express. South Vietnam's viability was too uncertain, the cause too far away, the fight not America's. They'd had enough.

28

AFTER LEARNING OF her husband's death in the hospital and going home with her new baby, Jan understandably struggled to digest what had just happened. A regret she has is not going to see Bob's body once it finally arrived back in Oklahoma City. It took a week or longer for that to happen. When it did, she recalls, her dad asked if she wanted him to take her to see Bob's body, "and I couldn't do it," she says. Bob's parents couldn't, either. His Uncle Mitt, the one Bob loved playing golf with growing up, went instead.[1]

The funeral took place soon after, at the Czech National Cemetery. Family and friends, former coaches, and teammates from around the country gathered at the gravesite. Teammate Byron Bigby remembers, "I looked around and there was not a dry eye." Barry Switzer, a young assistant at Oklahoma when Kalsu played there in 1967 and future Super Bowl champion NFL coach, remembers a poignant scene that he happened to witness after the funeral. Kalsu's father had gotten his wife and Jan back to the car and everyone else had left the gravesite. Switzer was walking back to his car when he stopped to look back. Then he saw Frank Kalsu lie down on his son's casket.[2]

⭐ IN THE MONTHS AFTER HER HUSBAND'S DEATH, the Catholic faith Jan shared with Bob sustained her, as did the love and support she received from Bob's parents. "We did so much crying and hugging and leaning into each other," Jan recalls. "We were always sharing it, keeping it open."

Still, she struggled to move forward. "I was so devastated by my husband's death, there were times I couldn't even cope," she says. Sometimes, in the weeks after Bob's funeral, she'd go into her bedroom, throw

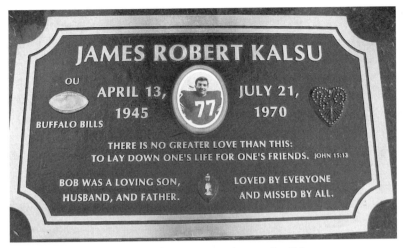

Commemorative stone at Bob Kalsu's gravesite. Courtesy Jan Kalsu.

herself across the bed, and sob. Her two-year-old daughter Jill would bring her mother Kleenex, sometimes even shut the door to her bedroom to give her privacy. "Here, Mommy, I take care of baby," Jan recalls her daughter saying. "And, honest to God," Jan says, "she'd sit right by him and watch him." Jan might cry for ten minutes before regaining her composure, "get my act together, and brace myself."[3]

In the years after Bob's death, Jan felt guilty about the anger she felt over her loss, almost like it was un-American. As years passed, however, she came to feel more comfortable about it. "A lot of upper men in the government have a lot to answer for," she told Laura Palmer in the 1987 book *Shrapnel in the Heart*.[4]

Kalsu's parents struggled with their country's Vietnam War decisions, too. "My son didn't die for his country but because of it," Bob's mom Leah said, years after her son's death.[5]

⭐ UNLIKE WITH HAMILTON FISH, Hobey Baker, or Nile Kinnick, there was very little coverage in the press on Bob Kalsu's death. Here was the Buffalo Bills' Offensive Rookie of the Year, a former All-American at Oklahoma, the only active professional athlete killed in Vietnam, and yet few wrote of him. Even the Kalsu family didn't get full details on the battle that led to Bob's death until years later.

It's not, of course, as if the NFL didn't figure prominently at the time.

Nearly 80,000 would attend the 1970 season's Super Bowl V, which took place at the Orange Bowl, the same stadium in which Bob Kalsu had helped power the Oklahoma Sooners to victory a few years earlier. Super Bowl V drew nearly fifty million viewers for an eye-popping Nielsen Rating of a hair under forty. Sure, Kalsu played on the offensive line, a position known for getting less attention than marquee spots. But there may have been more to the lack of attention than that. It was as if the media and the rest of America wanted to forget the war, and covering men like Bob made it that much harder.

Not until about the turn of the millennium did Kalsu's story truly emerge in the mainstream press. In 1999, NFL Films produced a documentary-style video about him, which included gut-wrenching interviews with Jan and Kalsu's now-grown son, Bob.

In August 2001, *Sports Illustrated*'s William Nack wrote about Kalsu in a now-celebrated article that was chosen in 2014 as one of the top 60 in *Sports Illustrated*'s history. In it, Kalsu's son Bob says that, if he had a chance to talk with his father, he would embrace him and tell him he loves him. And he'd ask, not in a derogatory or mean way, "Did you fully contemplate the consequences of your decision? I feel like I lost out, and I wish you had not made the decision to go."[6]

Yet that very article also brought a better understanding of matters for the Kalsu family. Kalsu's son, an aviation lawyer and father of two by 2001, in particular felt as if a weight had been lifted when he read Nack's story. Up until then, he'd borne a burden of guilt—thinking, as had become a kind of family assumption, that his father had died while running to meet an incoming helicopter, eager to hear news of his baby's birth. The Nack story allowed him to realize that simply wasn't true.

As Bob has continued to grow his family and develop his outlook on life, he now thinks more of his dad than himself. "For me, it's kind of changed a little bit," he told a reporter in 2016 at a ceremony to name the Del City post office after his father. "As I've gotten older and had my own kids, I'm kind of sad for my dad. He hasn't gotten to see his kids grow up, and his grandkids, and what he's missed out on as well."[7]

If you visit Del City on the right fall night, you can catch a Del City High School football game at Kalsu Stadium. At Fort Campbell in Kentucky, a company bears Kalsu's name. In 2000, Kalsu joined the Buffalo Bills Wall of Fame; each year, the Oklahoma Sooners give out the

Bob Kalsu Award to a player or players who show his type of leadership and example. For Jan, Bob's legacy lives on more intimately than this, though. It lives through the smile of one of the nine grandchildren that he never got to meet, through the way his children love those grandchildren and love their mom.

Jan also thinks of Bob when America goes to war. She worries about what families might go through. And she hopes that America's leaders understand the weight of war and make sound strategic decisions whenever sending troops off. Perhaps the story of Bob Kalsu, a man devoted to his country, to his fellow soldiers, and to his family, can give future leaders pause.

FIVE

Patrick "Pat" Tillman

29

FOR YEARS AFTER HIS 2004 DEATH, Pat Tillman, the only NFL player to perish in combat since Bob Kalsu, remained in the headlines. As noted in the introduction, in March 2007 a fifth military investigation into his demise released its findings, setting off yet another surge of Tillman coverage. Readers of msn.com could see a front-page picture of Tillman and click on a story about him. ESPN.com featured him.

A link in that ESPN.com feature sent visitors to audio of Pat's mother, Mary Tillman, who had been a guest on ESPN's *Dan Patrick Show* days earlier. For years, she'd tenaciously stayed after the military to dig into the details surrounding her son's death and to investigate why the Tillman family had initially been told that Taliban fighters had killed Pat rather than friendly fire.

Other ESPN links allowed people to read a PDF file of the inspector general's report about Tillman's death, access a story about an Army Ranger who said the account of Pat's death was "doctored," and listen to audio of John McCain commenting on the military's "mistakes" in the Tillman investigation. ESPN.com subscribers could read a three-part series about Tillman with the titles "An Un-American Tragedy," "Playing with Friendly Fire," and "Death of an American Ideal."[1] The coverage signified that Tillman's story still resonated and that technological advancements gave Americans easy access to an array of information.

And Tillman's story has registered with Americans regardless of party. Indeed, some of the more outspoken pundits on both sides of the political spectrum have found things in Pat Tillman to highlight. In December 2004, six months after he died, right-wing political pundit Ann Coulter wrote that Pat Tillman "was an American original: virtuous, pure and masculine like only an American male can be." She lauded him not just for serving and doing his part to liberate 28 million Afghans, but for dying for his country. She argued, "There is not another country in the world—certainly not in continental Europe—that could have produced a Pat Tillman."[2]

Ten months later, in October 2005, the leftist Dave Zirin wrote an op-ed in *The Nation* that charged the "Pentagon spinmeisters" with creating an inaccurate G.I. Joe image of Tillman after he died in Afghanistan. Zirin mocked Coulter's manly description of Tillman and even asserted that "in death he [Tillman] was far more useful to the armchair warrior than he had ever been in life," because alive, Tillman had turned down Pentagon overtures "to be its recruitment poster child" [Tillman gave no interviews as a US soldier]. A dead Tillman, according to Zirin, would allow Pentagon brass to promote their agenda. The Pentagon's narrative broke down, however, Zirin argued, when details surrounding his death emerged and journalists started to probe the situation more deeply. In place of the Pentagon narrative emerged a portrait of a deep-thinking, fiercely independent man who thought the Iraq war was "f***ing illegal." Pointing out that for several weeks the military hid details of Pat's death from the Tillman family, Zirin asserted that the fallen star had joined "WMD and al-Qaeda connections on the heap of lies used to sell the Iraq war." This would not sit well with the "Bush-Coulter gang," he concluded.[3]

Yet simply looking at the Tillman phenomenon as a reflection of America's political divide does not capture its essence. Tillman has struck a common chord among a wide swath of Americans—left, right, and in between.

For one, Americans in the new millennium seemed drawn not only to Tillman's volunteerism, humility, and physical acumen, but to his liberalism—not collectivist liberalism, but the more traditional liberalism of Thomas Jefferson and John Stuart Mill. This traditional liberalism, while not socially unaware or nationally indifferent, puts an emphasis on individual freedom.

One of Pat's favorite authors, it turns out, was Ralph Waldo Emerson, an American writer and leader of the nineteenth century's Transcendentalist movement, which championed individualism and encouraged adherents to use self-reliance as an anchor rather than blindly following what was popular. In his now iconic 1837 address, "The American Scholar," Emerson called on individuals—young men and women in particular—to "walk on our own feet; we will work with our own hands; we will speak our own minds."[4] Americans liked that Pat Tillman was his own man.

For Pat, part of being his own man meant maintaining an age-old sense of duty and honor. But it was complex. He valued loyalty, loved his country, and admired family members who had served in its armed forces. Yet he was skeptical, critical of political leaders, and could seem irreverent. Contributing to his layered nature, he embraced a sort of modern tweak on the masculine virtues espoused by the likes of Hamilton Fish and Teddy Roosevelt in their times. Tillman, as it turns out, could be tough and physical, sensitive and tender, duty-bound and loyal, unconvinced and questioning. Yet no matter how layered the cloth, Tillman spun it himself, and Americans appreciate that. In the popular coverage of Tillman this comes through.

Other interesting things come through in the coverage of Tillman. In contrast to that of Fish, Baker, Kinnick, and Kalsu, Tillman's is more probing of his personal life, religious beliefs, philosophical pursuits, and motivation for joining the military. This in part reflects the digital era's ability to access and disseminate information, and the complex times within which the era has arisen. Also new with the coverage of Tillman is the tendency of some who covered him to apply a postmodern take on his life, such as that by the authorized Tillman biographer Jon Krakauer, who, when asked by the *Wall Street Journal* what Tillman's sacrifice meant, answered that "it didn't mean anything."[5]

Still, there are similarities in the coverage of Tillman as with that of Fish, Baker, Kinnick, and Kalsu, such as respect for volunteerism, freedom, honor, and physical prowess. Tillman's story, then, represents the complicated, intrusive digital era, imbued as it is with postmodernism and relativism, as well as the enduring nature of concepts like duty and honor and the foundational values of liberal democracy.

As people have tried to make sense of the recent Iraq War, as people yearn for answers to life's most difficult questions, as physical relativism mingles with concrete beliefs and technological innovations give people access to vast amounts of information with relative ease, Americans seem hungry for an authentic hero. The widespread admiration Americans have expressed for Tillman suggests he's come as close as anyone to being one.

Alas, maybe we can turn to Alfred Lord Tennyson, a nineteenth-century British poet who turned to the personal to make sense of the startling forces of his day, scientific and industrial, to shed light on modern Americans' admiration for Tillman and what it might tell us about ourselves. *In Memoriam*, Tennyson's tribute to a fallen friend, contains these lines:

> *There lives more faith in honest doubt,*
> *Believe me,*
> *than in half the creeds.*

Through Tillman, might modern Americans be asking: If we strove so admirably in pursuit of truth, could we be better off?

30

FOR MOST OF HIS CHILDHOOD, Patrick Daniel Tillman grew up on the outskirts of Almaden, California, an upper-middle-class neighborhood of just under 40,000 people in the southeastern San Jose region, with his mom Mary (known as "Dannie" to those close to her), a special education teacher; his dad, a lawyer; and his two brothers. The middle Tillman brother, Kevin, was fourteen months younger than Pat, while Richard came along when Pat was four.

When Pat was two years old, he once climbed out of an upstairs window onto the family home's second-floor roof. His mom, having been alerted that something was amiss, rushed upstairs. She found Pat's little brother Kevin on his tiptoes peering out a window, watching his big brother. Hurrying to the window, she found that Pat had somehow unlocked the window and walked onto the roof. As if that wasn't alarming enough, he'd leapt from the roof to a nearby tree, which he was now hugging. Trying not to panic, she eased out onto the roof to try to grab hold of her son. A blustery wind, thankfully, blew the tree to which Pat clung toward the roof, and she pulled him to safety. Back inside, she started to scold him but upon looking "into his intense brown eyes, so full of delight and mischief," she began to cry instead and hugged him. Only later, after her nerves settled, could she talk to him more calmly.[1] The episode reflected a crucial part of Pat's nature. He loved to test himself, to take risks, and seemed to have particularly enjoyed doing so out in nature.

In addition to testing himself physically, from a young age Pat demonstrated an ability to think of others. Another time as a two-year-old, he got worried one afternoon that he and his mom and brother Kevin would be late in returning from the mall to see their Uncle Mike, who was coming to town that day. "Hurwee, Mom! Hurwee!" he urged his mom as they drove home. When they got close, Pat unbuckled his car seat belt, something he'd already learned to do, and poked his head up to the front seat, scanning to find Uncle Mike's car. When he spotted it in the Tillman driveway, his face turned even more worried, thinking that Uncle Mike had been waiting for them. "Here we come, Unka Mike!" he hollered.[2]

The Tillman's home in Almaden sat on the edge of town in a more rural area. Tucked alongside a forested, rocky canyon, the home backed up to the 4,000-acre Quicksilver County Park, which used to feature mercury mines. Trails right near the Tillman home ran through this old-mine-turned-massive-park, and Pat's mother encouraged her sons to explore the trails. A creek ran nearby, too, which she encouraged them to fish. And oak trees stood tall on their property, which she encouraged her boys to climb. They were free-range kids before the term became trendy.[3] And Pat reveled in it. He emanated life, energy, action; played all kinds of sports and played them well, roughhoused and joked.

IN THE FALL OF 1990, Pat started at Leland High, a public school in San Jose. Young for his grade, he arrived for his first day of classes at thirteen years of age, standing only five feet five inches tall and weighing just 120 pounds. But he brought with him his signature confidence. When the baseball coach, Paul Ugenti, told him he'd play on the freshman-sophomore team rather than varsity, Pat quit the sport to focus on football. It was a bold move. Pat had only played organized football for one year, in eighth grade, and he'd broken his tibia that season. An assistant football coach even encouraged Pat not to abandon baseball, a sport in which he'd shown considerable promise, because Pat wasn't "built like a football player." Pat didn't listen.

In addition to choosing football as his main sport during his freshman year, Pat developed a crush on a freshman girl named Marie Ugenti—the daughter of the baseball coach who'd told him he wouldn't be on the varsity. Years later, she would become Pat Tillman's wife.[4]

It took a while for anything romantic to materialize between the two, however. They'd pass each other in the school hallways, and the groups they ran in would sometimes interact outside of school. But, as Marie explained it in *The Letter,* a memoir she wrote eight years after Pat's death, "Like most high school girls, my friends and I paid the most attention to the older boys." Eventually, though, she sensed that Pat had feelings for her, mainly because although he seemingly talked easily with everyone, teachers and classmates alike, he acted shy around her. As their senior year approached, Pat stood several inches taller and weighed nearly sixty pounds more than when he'd started at Leland, and this hadn't gone unnoticed by Marie, either.

Shortly before their senior years, during a game of Capture the Flag with a group of friends, sparks flew between them. In a private moment, they expressed interest in each other, and a month later they went on their first official date, to dinner at a restaurant along the ocean in Santa Cruz. After dinner they went down to the beach, where they sat shoulder to shoulder, looking at the water, talking about their lives. For the next eleven years, through the rest of high school and college—even though they went to different universities—and afterward, they remained together.[5]

Marie brought out Pat's tender side. Early on, friends viewed the relationship as a steadying influence on him. But a week after Pat turned seventeen, in mid-November 1993, just a short time after Pat and Marie started dating, Pat got into a fight outside Round Table Pizza, a popular restaurant at a strip mall in Almaden.

The fight occurred at about 9:00 p.m. The short of it is that Pat and his buddies, some of whom—Pat included—had been drinking earlier that night, were inside Round Table Pizza when one of Pat's closest friends, Jeff Hechtle (who'd been drinking earlier as well), instigated a fight outside. Pat saw himself as a protector, and he was particularly protective of Jeff, who suffered from a rare disease that caused moles to grow on his scalp and for which he'd had several complex and painful procedures to control, leaving the left side of his head covered mainly in scar tissue. So, as Pat came out of Round Table Pizza, having heard there was a fight, and saw that his buddy Jeff was involved, he rushed to aid him, as did others in Pat's group. The group of guys on the opposite side of the ruckus quickly started to retreat. But Pat was livid. He chased down a young man named Darin Rosas, a lanky surfer who actually didn't even like contact sports, let alone fights, under the impression that Rosas was responsible for attacking Jeff.

Tillman knocked Darin out for a few seconds with a blow to the back of the head, then proceeded to kick him and otherwise beat him up. When Pat finally realized that he'd misjudged the situation and saw the damage he'd inflicted upon Rosas, however, he apologized and gave

Rosas his contact information. But by then the police had arrived. Rosas would visit the dentist several times in the ensuing weeks to repair his teeth; Pat would soon learn that he faced a felony charge, later reduced to misdemeanor assault.[6]

Ultimately, upon graduating from Leland High School, Pat served thirty days in a juvenile hall facility, carried out 250 hours of community service, and his family paid $40,000 as a result of the incident.[7]

It was an alarming episode, but Marie viewed it as out of character for Pat and didn't overreact. She considered Pat an "incredibly sensitive, good guy," and she saw how the event impacted him. In her memoir, she wrote that Pat "felt terrible he'd hurt another person. . . . He started spending more time with me, and less time with friends who were prone to getting in trouble."[8]

★ WHEN PAT ENTERED ARIZONA STATE in 1994 as a seventeen-year-old freshman, he arrived as the recipient of the football program's last scholarship of his class. Indeed, without the offer from the Sun Devils, there's a chance he'd have abandoned football altogether, as the only other schools showing strong interest in him had been Brigham Young (the culture of which Pat didn't see as a good fit) and the relatively lowly San Jose State football program. The problem, in recruiters' views, rested with Pat being too small for a linebacker, a hair too slow for the secondary.[9]

Despite landing the team's last scholarship and being looked over by so many other schools, Pat still felt confident enough in himself to speak his mind. Early in Pat's training with the Sun Devils, he had a one-on-one meeting with head coach Bruce Snyder, who told Pat that most freshmen redshirted. As politely as he could, Pat made it clear that redshirting didn't appeal to him. When Coach Snyder said Pat wouldn't likely see time on the field as a freshman, Pat said, "Coach, you can play me or not play me, but I'm only going to be here four years. And then I've got things to do with my life."[10]

On the outside, Tillman gave off this superconfident air. And, in many ways, he was just that. But he held his family close to his heart, and the transition to college life and being away from them challenged him, bringing out his sensitive side. He expressed his feelings in a letter he wrote to him mom and his Uncle Mike, both of whom had come to visit him in Tempe at the start of his freshman year:

> *Mom & Mike,*
>
> *I would have just come out and said this but I know my eyes would have swelled and I would not have been able to talk. I would like to tell you that I am very glad you came to see me. This whole thing is a lot harder to deal with than I ever expected. It makes me feel like a woose every time I begin to cry. However, I can do nothing to change it. I'm sure I will be fine pretty soon. My moods right now change constantly from OK to sad to really sad. Your being here really helped though. It is comforting to know someone cares . . .*

Tillman relied heavily on his high school sweetheart Marie, too, who'd decided to attend the University of California–Santa Barbara. She could have gone to Arizona State but thought better of it; a biology major, she found UC Santa Barbara's strong academics appealing, and she figured it couldn't hurt to let herself and Pat chart individual college paths while attempting to stay together.

As Marie recalled, both felt rocked by life outside Almaden, and yet their bond strengthened as they found comfort in each other. They'd talk on the phone for hours. "Our writing got more intense and frequent," Marie recalled. "We relied less on our family and old friends and relied more on each other. We became coconspirators, each other's point person—the one we would check in with each day and the one with whom we'd talk over decisions large and small." Pat might call for advice on his class schedule or they'd reminisce about what they missed in Almaden, about being homesick.[11] She could open up to him about her shyness and discomfort in social settings, and he didn't mind showing her his sensitive side. "He wasn't insecure about the sensitive side," Marie explained in *Where Men Win Glory*. "He considered both qualities [toughness and sensitivity] important, and didn't see them as irreconcilable in any way."[12]

As for football, Tillman didn't redshirt. And, as Coach Snyder predicted, he saw limited action his freshman year. He played mostly on special teams but did record a sack on his first play from scrimmage in a game at the University of California–Berkeley. On the season, the Arizona State team struggled mightily, however, finishing 3-8.

The next season, Pat's sophomore year, the Sun Devils showed improvement, finishing 6-5, and Tillman became the team's top backup linebacker, finishing seventh on the squad in tackles. To boot, his brother Kevin, recruited by Arizona State to play baseball, joined him in Tempe, making his time there much easier to handle. When Marie would visit Pat on weekends in the spring, they'd go watch Kevin play baseball.

"I loved Pat's loyalty to and support of Kevin," Marie wrote. "It was an attractive quality—sweet and completely true to Pat's nature."[13] The brothers, always close, would end up serving together in Iraq and Afghanistan as US Army Rangers.

At Arizona State, Tillman's penchant to test himself physically out in nature continued. Hiking the rim of Oak Creek Canyon, near the town of Sedona, a rocky paradise about two hours from Tempe, he found a cliff with a forty-foot or so drop to boulders. Some ten feet below and fifteen feet beyond this cliff was an old, dead-looking tree. Pat thought long and hard about it before finally backing up, running to the cliff's edge, and hurtling himself toward the tree. If he missed his mark, death, paralysis, or at a minimum many broken bones loomed. But he hit the tree with a force that knocked all the air from his lungs, and it held up despite its wear while he held on. Tillman also liked to climb up to the top of a tall light tower at Sun Devils Stadium, where he could think and reflect and take in the city views.[14]

During Pat's junior year, the Sun Devils football team arrived on the national scene in a big way, finishing the regular season ranked second in the nation at 11-0 and earning a trip, thanks to a Pac-10 title, to the Rose Bowl for a showdown with the fourth-ranked Ohio State Buckeyes. At the 1 January 1997 Rose Bowl, played in front of over 100,000 fans, Tillman helped lead a stingy Sun Devils defense. Late in the fourth quarter, Ohio State held a slight lead in the low-scoring affair, 14-10. But then Arizona State quarterback, Jake "The Snake" Plummer, threw a touchdown pass to put his team up 17-14 with 1:40 left. Ohio State responded with a dramatic twelve-play scoring drive, capped by a touchdown pass of its own, giving them a 21-17 victory. Still, the game remains only the second Rose Bowl ever played by Arizona State.

On the season, Tillman earned second-team All-Pac-10 recognition and finished second on the team in tackles. The undersized, possibly too slow, last scholarship recipient had turned into quite a force, and not just in football—as a force of nature.

Teammates, classmates, and coaches saw in him a deep thirst for knowledge and a healthy appreciation for debate. He seemed to always carry a book with him. Once he stayed late into the night at an LDS assistant coach's office to talk about Mormonism. The two ended up deciding to read the Book of Mormon so they could discuss it. Legendary Arizona State baseball coach Pat Murphy recalled seeing Pat in the bleachers, attending one of his brother's baseball games, with a book in hand. "He always had a book with him," Murphy said. "Between innings, or anytime there was a lull, he'd have it open and he'd be reading something."[15]

In time, Tillman would digest the Bible and the Koran. After his death, much would be made of his religious views, some considering him an outright atheist, others describing him more as agnostic. In an ESPN article, his mother characterized the family as spiritual but not as adherents of fundamental aspects of organized religion. She also said, "Pat may not have been what you call a Christian. He was about the best person I ever knew. I mean, he was just a good guy. He didn't lie. He was very honest. He was very generous. He was very humble."[16] Tillman purportedly also read *The Communist Manifesto* and *Mein Kampf* and works by different philosophers, in addition to the writing of Ralph Waldo Emerson.[17] To observers he came across as a man chiseled from rock of its own making.

In 1997, Pat's senior year, he earned All-American honors, recognition as the Pac-10's defensive player of the year, and was named Arizona State's MVP. *Sporting News* chose him as the Student-Athlete of the Year, too, for his strong summa cum laude performance in Arizona State's W. P. Carey School of Business, from which he graduated in three and a half years.

At an October game that year in Tempe versus the University of Southern California, sports agent Frank Bauer sat in the stands. He'd come eager to get a look at Pat Tillman's roommate, the six-foot-five, nearly 300-pound yet fleet-of-foot defensive end Jeremy Staat (who, as it happens, would be so inspired by Pat Tillman that he joined the US Marines after his NFL career). As he watched, Bauer found that he liked Staat, as he'd hoped, but another player also caught his eye. Upon saying hello to Staat in the locker room after the game, he sought out that player, Pat Tillman. "Here's this kid with long hair, wearing shorts and flip-flops," Bauer recalled. "I told him, 'Hey, I think you can play in the National Football League.' He looks at me with those eyes of his and he goes, 'Really?'" Tillman was feigning a bit, though. According to Krakauer's *Where Men Win Glory*, he'd already determined he could make it in the National Football League.[18]

31

IN THE 1998 NFL DRAFT, Pat Tillman went in the last round, 226th, to the Arizona Cardinals. He signed a contract offer from the Cardinals with a starting salary of $158,000, provided he could make the team, which was no small feat for a late seventh-round choice. His contract did include a $21,000 signing bonus.

Once he got deep enough into training camp to feel confident he would make the team, Marie joined him in Arizona and the two started a life together there, renting a one-bedroom apartment in Chandler. Tillman had cultivated some relatively Spartan ways, and they lived pretty simply, especially when viewed in the context of major professional sports.[1]

On 29 August 1998, the Cardinals played their last exhibition game, this one versus the Raiders in Oakland, meaning lots of Pat's family and friends could attend. He picked off a pass during the game and, by its end, ranked tops on the team in preseason tackles. Eight days later, in Tillman fashion, the unheralded last pick in the draft for Arizona didn't just make the team; he was named the opening-day starter at safety.

Pat Tillman playing football for the Arizona Cardinals. Courtesy Arizona Cardinals.

Agent Frank Bauer, who'd been unexpectedly impressed by Tillman a year earlier, could hardly believe how quickly he'd made an impact in the NFL. "I always knew Patty would be a fantastic special-teams player in the NFL," he said, "but to be the starting safety as a rookie in his very first game—he fooled the hell out of everybody."[2] To boot, reporters loved that he would ride his bike to practice and have extended philosophical talks with coaches before workouts got under way, a lot like when he'd played at Arizona State.[3]

He started ten games at free safety his rookie season, recording forty-six tackles and one sack. But he lost his starting job by year's end to veteran free safety Kwamie Lassiter. Still, the Cardinals enjoyed unexpected success that season, shocking the Cowboys in the first round of the playoffs—the organization's first playoff win since 1947—before bowing out the following week.

Tillman spent season two in Arizona, now at strong safety, mainly backing up Tommy Bennett and playing special teams. Coming into the year, given the Cardinals' playoff win the season prior, fans carried high hopes, only to see the team trudge through a rough 6-10 campaign. Tillman acquitted himself well enough, however, solidifying his roster spot and his status as a dependable NFL player. The organization embraced his approach and his attitude.

"He had a charisma about him," Larry Marmie, a defensive coach in Arizona, would recall. "The secretaries liked him. The custodians liked him. Little kids gravitated to him."[4] On the field, though, Tillman wanted more.

Tillman entered his 2000 off-season workouts determined to win back his starting role. He worked hard on his body while continuing to read deeply and to travel with Marie, to Paris, Sedona, and elsewhere. To challenge himself, in May 2000, he even ran a marathon, which didn't exactly complement his efforts to get stronger and faster. Nonetheless, he arrived at the Cardinals' July training camp stronger than ever and lighter than any time since high school.[5]

Sure enough, in 2000, Tillman delivered a superproductive season for the Arizona Cardinals, starting all sixteen games and finishing with a franchise record 224 tackles. In the cutthroat world of the NFL, however, Tillman still worried about his job, and he was hard on himself at times. After a close opening season loss to the New York Giants, Tillman wrote in his journal, "I f****** suck. I missed a tackle that resulted in a 78-yard touchdown . . . I'll do better next week." Frustrated, shortly before their next game, he got into a bit of a brawl in practice with a running back. Head coach Vince Tobin summoned Pat to his office as a result and chewed him out, apparently telling Tillman that he didn't constitute a starter in the NFL. Tillman felt like he needed to come up big in the team's next game, versus the Cowboys, or else he'd lose his job to Tommy Bennett once Bennett returned from his injury. So Pat did just that, breaking up several passes and delivering some crucial tackles of the Cowboys' world-class running back Emmitt Smith late in the Cardinals' 32-31 win.[6]

At season's end, having reviewed film of Tillman's season over several days, *Sports Illustrated*'s football writer Paul Zimmerman, known as Dr. Z, put Tillman on his All-Pro Team. He caught some flack, sure, from folks who questioned Tillman's coverage ability. But in April 2001, when the Seattle Seahawks offered Tillman a five-year, $9.6 million contract with $2.6 million guaranteed, people realized Dr. Z must have been on to something. Ecstatic to receive the offer, Pat's agent, Frank Bauer, called Pat with the news. Knowing Arizona wouldn't match, he told his client, "You have to sign it." Pat told him he'd have to think it over. A day or so later, Pat called Bauer back and told him he wasn't going to sign with Seattle.

"Look, Frank," he said, "the Cardinals drafted me in the seventh round. They believed in me. I love the coaches here."

Bauer was incredulous. "Patty, are you nuts?" he asked. "Are you f*****' crazy? The Rams want to pay you $9.6 million!"

Instead, Pat took a one-year deal for just over a half a million dollars from the Cardinals. "You just don't see loyalty like that in sports today," Bauer said later, adding, "He was a once-in-a-lifetime kid."[7]

The 2001 preseason for the Arizona Cardinals ended on August 31 with a win over San Diego. Given a bye in week one of the upcoming NFL schedule, the first Sunday of which was 9 September 2001, Tillman and his mates didn't end up playing their first regular-season game until 23 September 2001. That's because the NFL suspended all week-two games on account of the September 11 terrorist attacks.

The attacks, carried out by members of the radical Islamic terrorist group al-Qaeda, involved the hijacking of four commercial airliners, two of which were flown into New York City's World Trade Center towers, ultimately bringing the towers and surrounding buildings down. Another plane was flown into the Pentagon, home to the US Department of Defense, just outside the nation's capital. Passengers overtook the fourth hijacked plane and were able to divert it from hitting the hijackers' intended target, perhaps the White House, but it ultimately crashed into a field in Pennsylvania, killing all on board. Most of the hijackers who physically carried out the attacks were Saudi nationals, as was al-Qaeda leader Osama bin Laden, who had found a safe haven and training ground in Afghanistan, which was led by a like-minded Islamic fundamentalist political group known as the Taliban. All told, 2,996 people died in the 9/11 attacks, including 415 firefighters and police.

At the time, a lot of Americans didn't know the name al-Qaeda or that of Osama bin Laden. Nearly overnight virtually everyone did. And in the coming weeks and months, Americans learned a great deal about the values and world views held by members of groups like al-Qaeda and the political groups it allied itself with, such as the Taliban, which imposed a rigid take on Sharia, Islamic law.

Under the Taliban, girls were banned from school and women from the workplace. Even after the US response to the September 11 attacks led to the downfall of the Taliban, the political movement carried out an insurgency in Afghanistan. In 2015, fourteen years after the Taliban fell from power, England's *Daily Mail* reported that Afghan schoolgirls had been poisoned by toxic gas, the perpetrators of the crime suspected to be Taliban militants opposed to the education of girls, especially those age ten and older. When in power, the Taliban banned music, film, and television and introduced public executions for adulterers, amputations for thieves.[8] In November 2001, bin Laden described Afghanistan, still under the control of Taliban leader Mullah Omar, as "the only Islamic country" in the Muslim world. The al-Qaeda leader subscribed to the idea of violent jihad and the implementation of Sharia law.[9]

Pat Tillman learned of the attacks when his brother Kevin called him on the morning upon which they occurred. "Get your ass up and turn on the TV," Kevin urged his brother frantically. Pat quickly turned on the television and saw a Boeing 767 fly straight into one of the World Trade Center towers. He watched coverage through much of the day, at home and then at the Cardinals' practice facility. He was moved in particular by images of people who were facing scorching heat and unbearable smoke emanating from the crash below jumping from the World Trade Center Towers to their deaths.[10]

Tillman admired the intellectual giants and freedom defenders Winston Churchill and Abraham Lincoln. And, just as those men had lived through pivotal times, according to Tillman's soon-to-be-wife Marie, after 9/11 he sensed a heightened importance for his time. He'd always embraced the idea of honor, a kind of chivalric code. Now he "did feel called to act," Marie later wrote. He and Marie would soon discuss the prospect of him enlisting and, in time, would do research into which military route seemed best for Pat. But he always intended to finish out his contract with the Cardinals, which he did.[11]

For years, the NFL and the military had enjoyed a close relationship, cultivated in part because both entities share values, attract young men, and figure prominently in American culture. The military has routinely advertised during NFL games, and the NFL holds events that show support for the military. After 9/11, the NFL became an entity through which support for the US military and for the values that underpin America could be expressed. As an example of this, football historian Michael Oriard has written about how the patriotism quotient at the first Super Bowl following 9/11 soared. Fox aired a three-hour pregame show titled *Heroes, Hope, and Homeland*, which ended with a "Tribute to America" by former NFL stars who read the Declaration of Independence while, for background music, the Boston Pops played "Lincoln Portrait."[12]

More subdued but rather poignant, the halftime show of Fox's Super Bowl production featured a live performance by U2 and Bono during which the names of the victims of 9/11 scrolled along a big screen behind the performers. In 2016 a *Rolling Stone* article rated it the best Super Bowl halftime show of all time, stating that through this performance, "U2 created one of the truly great live-TV rock & roll moments of all time."[13]

But Pat wasn't one to make decisions based on such things. He would think deeply about joining and do research on it before signing up. In her memoir years later, Marie recalled when she and Pat first talked about him joining the military. It was not long after the attacks, and Pat's brother Kevin had come to town for a Cardinals game. After the contest, Kevin and a small group of other friends joined the Tillmans at their house. Later in the evening, having turned in, Marie lay in bed listening to the chatter and occasional rise of laughter of her husband, his brother, and their friends. At one point she heard the conversation turn to 9/11. By the time Pat crawled into bed, she was nearly asleep. She put her chest on his head, sensing his mind churning from the night's conversation.

"What if I joined the Army?" he asked. Marie opened her eyes and found her husband staring at the ceiling.

"Are you serious?" she asked.

"I don't know, maybe," he said.[14]

In the immediate days after the September 11 attacks, Pat had given an interview with NFL Films in which he said, "I play football and it just seems so—Goddamn, it is unimportant compared to everything that has taken place. I feel guilty even having the damn interview." Pat talked about his grandfather, who had been stationed at Pearl Harbor, and noted that others in his family had served, while "I really haven't done a damn thing as far as laying myself on the line like that." He also said, "Times like this you stop and think about just how—not only how good we have it, but what kind of a system we live under."[15] As he continued to ponder matters, he would determine he wanted to do something. He chose to join the military.

The Cardinals' last game of the 2001 season took place on 6 January 2002, a makeup date for its matchup with the Washington Redskins, which had originally been scheduled for the Sunday after the 9/11 attacks. Tillman tallied a jaw-dropping eighteen tackles in the game, but it ended in a 20-17 Cardinals defeat. It proved to be the last time he'd ever suit up in the NFL.

He didn't enlist immediately, however. He still needed to think it through. As Marie Tillman recalls, "It wasn't like 9/11 happened and Pat immediately said, 'I'm joining the Army.' He did a lot of research first. He weighed all the pros and cons."[16]

32

BY THE TIME OF THE February 2002 Super Bowl, the US military, under Republican president George W. Bush, had invaded Afghanistan and removed the Taliban—who had balked at handing over bin Laden and other terrorists after the September 11 attacks—from power. An interim Afghan administration, supported by the United Nations and led by Hamid Karzai, came to power and the long process of stabilizing the country for popular elections commenced. Those elections were ultimately held in October 2004 and resulted in Karzai becoming president of the newly named Islamic Republic of Afghanistan.

The US military, meanwhile, by this time formally backed by North Atlantic Treaty Organization (NATO) forces, provided security for the nascent country and battled the Taliban insurgency and likeminded Taliban allies. However, one thing the US Army had not accomplished in removing the Taliban from power was capturing Osama bin Laden.

IN APRIL 2002, the Arizona Cardinals offered Tillman a three-year, $3.6 million contract. Ultimately, Tillman turned it down because he had plans to enlist. On 8 April 2002, a month before his wedding date with Marie, he typed out his views on enlisting in a document titled "Decision," which Krakauer printed in full in his authorized biography of Tillman. In this document, Tillman wrote:

For much of my life I've tried to follow a path I believe important. Sports embodied many of the qualities I deem meaningful: courage, toughness, strength, etc., while at the same time, the attention I received reinforced its seeming importance. In the pursuit of athletics I have picked up a college degree, learned invaluable lessons, met incredible people, and made my journey much more valuable than any destination. However, these last few years, and especially after recent events, I've come to appreciate just how shallow and insignificant my role is. I'm no longer satisfied with the path I've been following . . . it's no longer important.

I'm not sure where this new direction will take my life though I am positive it will include its share of sacrifice and difficulty, most of which falling squarely on Marie's shoulders. Despite this, however, I am equally positive that this new direction will, in the end, make our lives fuller, richer, and more meaningful. My voice is calling me in a different direction. It is up to me whether or not to listen.[1]

In the end, having talked with people who had served and in consultation with Marie, Pat chose to volunteer for the US Army Rangers, where he'd likely be able to live in Fort Lewis, near Seattle.[2]

In May, shortly after Pat and Marie returned from their honeymoon in the South Pacific, the Tillman family and Marie's met with Pat and Kevin in an attempt to convince them not to join the army. Pat agreed to the meeting out of respect and because he felt that they should be able to tell him how they felt, but the decision had already been made.

Still, the meeting got emotional. Pat's mom expressed her concern that one of her boys could get killed. Pat said it wouldn't happen. Marie's father, who loved and respected his son-in-law, tried to appeal to Pat's logical side by coming at the matter from an economic angle. This did not sit well with Pat's mom.

"Why are you talking about *money?*" she demanded. "This isn't about money! Pat and Kevin could get killed!" At that, she broke down sobbing, telling her boys that life presents itself with enough difficulties and asked, "Why do you want to go looking for it?"[3]

In an interview with Krakauer, Marie said she never explicitly asked Pat why he volunteered for the US Army, "Because I understood Pat well enough to already know . . . . If it was right for people to go off and fight a war, he believed he should be part of it." She knew it tore him up that his decision hurt people close to him, including her. Yet she knew he felt strongly about playing a role in the conflict between those who had carried out 9/11 and the United States. And as hard as it might have been, she fully supported him.[4]

Tillman had made sure news of his decision didn't break until after he married Marie in early May—he didn't want it taking away from their wedding day. When Tillman did finally meet with Cardinals' head coach Dave McGinnis to let him know his decision, McGinnis said, "You know, this is going to cause a media storm. How are you going to handle it?"

Tillman flashed a smile at his coach and said, "I'm not. You are."[5]

As expected, when the Arizona Cardinals beat writers heard the news from the Cardinals' organization, they wanted to talk to Pat. They were told, however, that he didn't intend to talk about it, period. Local writer Dan Bickley gave him a call to check anyway.

"Hey, Pat, how are you doing?" Bickley recalls saying.

"I'm doing great, dude," Pat said on the other end of the call, "and I really appreciate you respecting the fact that I'm not going to talk about this with anyone. Not even off the record."

Bickley respected Pat's decision on interviews and, before saying goodbye, thanked him.[6] Tillman never gave an interview from then through his time of service.

PAT AND HIS BROTHER KEVIN, who'd been considering volunteering for the special ops even before the 9/11 attacks, formally enlisted in early June 2002. They headed for boot camp in Georgia in early July.

The brothers spent their first nine days "in-processing" at Georgia's Fort Benning, where they stayed in a concrete "bay" bunkhouse with over 100 other new enlistees. According to Krakauer, Tillman was quickly "astonished, and appalled, by the immaturity of the eighteen- and nineteen-year-olds" there. He and his brother found, not all, but too many of them, to be "indolent whiners" who signed up not out of a sense of duty or even adventure but, instead, because they basically had nothing else to do.[7]

Throughout his time in the military, Tillman sought out people he could relate to better. One such man he and his brother found at Fort Benning was Tulio Tourinho, a married Brazilian national and father who had left his teaching job in Kentucky after 9/11 to volunteer.

It was after midnight one night during this "in-processing" phase at Fort Benning when Tillman determined Tulio was a man he'd like to get to know. Tulio had recently arrived at Fort Benning. He was tired, had just been injected with a bunch of shots by army medical personnel, and his wife hadn't been exactly pleased with his decision to enlist. And now, as he tried to sleep late at night, a bunch of the young enlistees were talking and yelling and "making silly, obnoxious noises." Tulio finally reached his wit's end. He yelled as loud as he could, "Shut the fuck up! I'm thirty years old, I quit my job to serve my country, left a wife pregnant with our first child at home, who I love and miss dearly, and I will be goddamned if I'm gonna let some fucking immature juvenile punks prevent me from getting a good night's sleep!"[8]

Together Tulio and the Tillmans forged a bond that helped each other make it through their time at Fort Benning. Still, it was tough. At boot camp, a mere three weeks into his three-year commitment, Tillman wrote in his journal:

> Everything about my life has completely shifted. Everything. I planned on having kids, continuing my football, and enjoying life as always. Now I'm sitting in a barracks with 53 kids. This path needs to hurry itself up and brighten . . . . I do my best to control it, but sometimes I get so incredibly frustrated around here my fucking jaw muscles collapse my teeth on themselves. Today Marie's letters came and I needed so badly to be with her, hold her, make love to her . . . I can see her writing.[9]

Although he struggled during much of his time at boot camp and afterward at advanced individual training—especially with the military's penchant for giving people "rank" based on time served rather than merit, or with the tendency of higher ranking soldiers to bark seemingly silly orders just for the sake of it—Tillman did develop a certain level of respect for the experience. After completing the final boot camp challenge, a seven-day field training exercise that included a thirty-two-mile march while carrying weighty rucksacks, he wrote in his journal, "Despite what I expected from this basic training, Nub [Pat's nickname for his brother Kevin] and I were pushed a little . . . Tougher than expected in the end, a worthy task . . . These kids have reason to be proud. They weathered the storm . . . I'll give it to this place, it was a good finale, now get me the f*** out."[10] Eight days later, however, he wrote, "It's been almost a month since I've spoken with Marie. If she hasn't run off with anyone, she surely hates my guts . . . The poor girl is such a superhero—actually at this point a Greek tragedy heroine. I need to hurry and put an

American (happy) ending to this story . . . I cannot speak for Kevin, but I feel no sense of accomplishment from finishing this place [boot camp and advanced individual training]. I've learned no ultimate lessons and improved my character in no way."[11]

Things improved at Airborne School and the Ranger Indoctrination Program, known for its brutally difficult tactical training and physical demands. These programs left Tillman feeling like he'd learned and been challenged.

Shortly before Christmas 2002, he and Kevin earned the US Army's tan berets, given to full-fledged members of the 75th Ranger Regiment. They became members of the 2nd Battalion of the 75th Ranger Regiment, a decorated force known as the Black Sheep.

On 6 June 1944, D-Day during World War II, the 2nd Ranger Battalion had scaled the cliffs at Pointe du Hoc. Some of the men from that day were in Normandy forty years later to hear Ronald Reagan say of them, "These are the boys of Pointe du Hoc. These are the men who took the cliffs. These are the champions who helped free a continent. These are the heroes who helped end a war."[12] Now Tillman was ready to contribute to his generation's military challenge.

33

WHILE PAT AND KEVIN went through the initial phases of Ranger training, Marie found a two-bedroom brick bungalow, above Puget Sound, for them to rent. And soon after, for a stretch at least, she and Pat and Kevin settled into their new kind of normal. Pat and Kevin would leave the cottage-like home in the morning, wearing civilian clothes, and head to the base for training, while Marie would set off for the consulting job she eventually landed in downtown Seattle. Sometimes the brothers had to travel to train, but not always. During these stretches Marie felt more a part of things, and their cottage became a kind of separate, happy place, apart from all the uncertainty of the future.[1]

In that home, Tillman kept a picture of Winston Churchill on an important shelf—a bit like Nile Kinnick, who had kept a bust of Churchill on his desk during World War II, some sixty years earlier. Churchill

stood for big ideas—freedom, duty, honor, grit—things which he'd spoken so movingly of during World War II and which had, in part, motivated Tillman to join the military.

Pat Tillman and his brother, Kevin, who enlisted with Pat and served with him as an Army Ranger. Courtesy Pat Tillman Foundation.

Yet Tillman still struggled with day-to-day elements of military life. As his wife Marie explained it, sometimes he'd come home from a day of work at the base frustrated because he'd mowed lawns all day or been messed with by higher-ranking soldiers a bit. Marie recalled that Pat might come and say, "I'm too old for this shit. I can drop to the ground and give them fifty push-ups, but I don't want to, because it's stupid." He'd think, Marie wrote, *Here this horrific thing happened on 9/11, and I have something to contribute, and I'm mowing lawns.*[2] Tillman's frustrations rose further when, a few months later in March 2003, he found himself being shipped to Iraq rather than to Afghanistan, the country that had given safe haven to the terrorists who carried out the 9/11 attacks.

President George W. Bush and his cohort of advisors, including Vice-President Dick Cheney, Secretary of Defense Donald Rumsfeld, and Secretary of State Colin Powell, had argued for war in Iraq unless Saddam Hussein would give up the weapons of mass destruction (WMDs) they thought he had. Hussein, presumably unwilling to admit he had no WMDs so as not to look weak to rivals, particularly Iran, didn't come clean to the United Nations or to the United States. In turn, the United States, along with the United Kingdom and several other allies, launched an invasion of Iraq featuring a "shock and awe" bombing campaign.

But Tillman, like many other Americans, did not find the arguments put forward by the Bush administration for the war in Iraq convincing. Before Tillman left for his deployment, he told his wife Marie, "I'll do my job. But I don't think our role there is virtuous at all."[3] Generally, Marie wrote in her memoir, she used discretion when engaging her husband in debate. She knew he loved debating, everything from how to make a perfect cup of coffee to politics, and that he would sometimes take a position just to get someone fired up and thinking about an issue in a new way. But she did engage him on the Iraq War. Both disagreed with the rationale for it. "We felt it was illegal and unjust," Marie wrote. Yet, she noted, Pat realized that when he'd signed up for the military he'd agreed to follow someone's orders. "He'd made a commitment and felt it wasn't right to back out of a commitment just because it turned out differently than he anticipated," she explained.[4]

In hindsight, Americans know that, though the invasion did lead to the fall of the Saddam Hussein government, the United States by the time

it arrived found only a small amount of old, deserted chemical munitions in Iraq and that the war devolved into a years-long conflict—with
a particularly brutal insurgency against the US military effort in 2004
in Fallujah and elsewhere. Ultimately, a US troop surge that year did
enable the election of a transitional government in 2005 and, in 2006,
an elected permanent Iraqi government.

In 2011, Democratic president Barack Obama announced that all US
troops would exit Iraq by year's end. In 2014, however, with the rise of
the Islamic State of Iraq and the Levant, known widely as ISIS, President
Obama ordered air strikes in Iraq and announced the return of a small
number of US troops to the country.

During Tillman's time in Iraq, he pulled mostly security duty around
the Baghdad airport, searched house-to-house on occasion for men on
the now-infamous fifty-two-card deck featuring Iraq's most wanted, and,
during down time, hanging with his brother Kevin and men like Ranger
pal Russell Baer. With Baer, the Tillman brothers would drink coffee
and form the Baghdad Book Club and talk about philosophy, literature,
life. They talked about things like Noam Chomsky's *Propaganda and the
Public Mind* and Plato's *Republic*, which Baer was reading at the time.
Tillman also made friends in Iraq with a group of Navy SEALs, among
them Kevin White, with whom he enjoyed visiting even if White's politics skewed notably right of Tillman's. Of the SEALs he befriended in
Iraq, Tillman wrote, "They are exactly the type of guys we looked forward
to meeting when we decided to join."[5] But Tillman's views on the Iraq
War didn't change while he served in it.

On the night of 31 March 2004, Pat and his buddy Russell Baer sat
atop a bunker south of Baghdad, waiting at the ready in case their services were needed to help with the planned and now controversial rescue
of Pfc. Jessica Lynch (which ultimately didn't occur until the following
night). Pat and Russell chatted as they watched 155 mm shells light the
desert sky several miles away. By and by the conversation turned to politics and the Iraq War. And this is when, according to Baer, Pat shook his
head and said, "This war is so f****** illegal."[6]

During this time, in his diary, which Krakauer received access to for
his 2009 Tillman biography, Tillman also expressed concerns about the
Lynch rescue that he and Baer were waiting on standby for. He wanted
her saved, of course, and was grateful when he learned she had been. But

he wondered why so many troops, about a thousand, had been tasked with some sort of role in the rescue. As it turned out, his PR suspicions regarding the Lynch rescue proved to have some merit.

Lynch herself said in 2007 congressional hearings that media stories had inaccurately presented her as a "Rambo from the hills of West Virginia" when she had actually not fired a shot before getting captured. (Her gun had jammed, and she'd gotten knocked unconscious when the US military vehicle she was in crashed into another US military vehicle.) Lynch added, "I am still confused as to why they chose to lie and tried to make me a legend when the real heroics of my fellow soldiers that day were, in fact, legendary. People like Lori Piestewa and First Sergeant Dowdy, who picked up fellow soldiers in harm's way. Or people like Patrick Miller and Sergeant Donald Walters, who actually fought until the very end. The bottom line is the American people are capable of determining their own ideals for heroes and they don't need to be told elaborate tales."[7]

Some argue that the media ran with inaccurate elements of the Lynch story without the Pentagon leading the push. Others, like Iraq War critic and Tillman biographer Krakauer, argue that the government spun tales about Lynch to hype her rescue and build morale with the American public for the war effort. He points to Jim Wilkinson, whom he characterizes as the "Bush Administration's top 'perception manager,'" for orchestrating the media response to the Lynch rescue and for making sure specially outfitted troops could film the rescue for extra effect.[8] Krakauer argues that just over a year later, White House perception managers trained by Wilkinson would see Tillman's death as another PR opportunity.

Tillman found ways to cope in Iraq, but he struggled with his misgivings about the effort and with being away from Marie. At one point, he wrote to her:

> It's hard to think about how bad this situation really is sometimes. I hate being away from you, I hate the fact that you're growing into a life so far removed from me . . . I love us, our family, and feel somehow I'm just missing out. What the fuck kind of marriage involves my absence for months at a time? This is truly terrible and I think I may actually be a bad person for putting you through this. It's funny because at the time

I felt that any absence would be tolerable due to the "cause" or whatever concept I deluded myself into believing I was standing for. I'm a fool. How I managed to find a way out of our perfect existence is incredible.[9]

And yet, indicating the complexities inherent within Pat Tillman, while in Iraq he expressed frustration with superiors who kept him out of the hot action, having him instead pull security for parked airplanes. He didn't believe in the war, didn't think the United States should be there, but he wanted tougher assignments. He was, as biographer Krakauer put it, "more than a little ambivalent" about returning from Iraq without a Combat Infantryman Badge (CIB), awarded to infantrymen who participate in direct combat.

Krakauer says that in addition to wanting to feel like he pulled his weight, Tillman "wanted to know firsthand what it was like to have people trying their best to kill him, and perhaps be required to kill in return." Tillman's takes on war, then, as Krakauer notes, were complex, impacted by "sometimes contradictory notions of duty, honor, justice, patriotism, and masculine pride."[10]

In the end, most of Tillman's time in Iraq was actually, from a combat perspective, quite uneventful. He fired his gun only once, and on that occasion just to serve as warning shots to a couple of cars getting too close to a restricted zone. And, although while in Iraq Tillman thought some of his superiors showed less than ideal battlefield sense, and he disagreed with the Bush administration's war effort, he did find things to like about the men with whom he served more directly. A little over two weeks before returning from Iraq, Tillman wrote in his journal, "You know, I have to admit, some of these kids are getting to me. I find myself thinking of things I can do to help their future. As pissed off as I can be with this place, there are some very good people, especially some of these kids. Whether I like it or not, I have a soft spot for some of these little brats."[11]

⭐ TILLMAN CAME HOME FROM IRAQ and reunited with Marie on 19 May 2003. While he was gone, she had started to connect with people through her new job, but it was difficult. When she would hear news of a US helicopter being shot down or a soldier getting killed, she'd immediately worry that Kevin and Pat were involved. If friends or colleagues might ask at the end of a workday if she wanted to meet up for happy hour, she'd think things like, *Sure, Pat and Kevin will be back from their tour in Iraq by then, why not?*[12]

Pat and Kevin's returns allowed them to settle into some semblance of routine again. And in July, with Kevin and Pat receiving two weeks of leave, they managed a trip to Lake Tahoe to relax with old friends.

Back in Washington after their leave, Kevin and Pat prepped for the Rangers' grueling sixty-one-day Ranger School, which, if they could come out of it with passing marks, would get them "tabbed," giving them full-fledged Ranger status. They started the school in late September 2003. Two months later, having been kept awake for twenty hours a day, virtually every day; having carried some ninety pounds of gear on brutal hikes or challenging mountain climbs, rain or shine; having subsisted on 2,400 calories a day while burning more like 5,000; and having lost about half the members of their 253-soldier class, Pat and Kevin earned their tabs. One of Pat's mountain phase coaches during Ranger School summed up Tillman's performance, saying, "Tillman was a stud. He was the real deal."[13]

As the New Year approached, an interesting scenario arose regarding Pat's military service contract. Given that he'd served on active duty in a war, a wrinkle in the contract, provided other certain conditions were met, could allow him to get out of his three-year term of service early. Aware of this wrinkle, the Seattle Seahawks' general manager, Bob Ferguson—who, earlier in his career as an executive with the Cardinals, had helped land Tillman in Arizona and who counted Tillman as his favorite player in his long career—contacted Pat's agent, Frank Bauer. He let Bauer know that the Seattle wanted Tillman in a Seahawks jersey for the 2004 season. "We've checked into it," Ferguson said. "He's already served in a war. He can get out of the service."[14]

Other teams expressed interest, too. And it seems reasonable to assume, given Tillman's iconic status and the close advertising relationship between the NFL and the US military, that, had he asked, Tillman would have received an honorable discharge. But Tillman never asked.

Marie confirmed the NFL offers but added, "We never really discussed it because it just wasn't going to happen. There was no way he was going to bail out of the Army halfway through." He saw it as his duty, no matter how tough or if he disagreed with America's leaders, to finish the three years he'd originally committed to.[15]

34

EARLY IN 2004, back working at Fort Lewis as fully tabbed Rangers, Kevin and Pat were on hand to see a new batch of recruits arrive. One newbie, Josey Boatright, recalled being screamed at and generally messed with. But then a big fellow came up to him and said, "Are you the new guy in Second Platoon? My name is Pat Tillman. Relax, this stuff will pass. It'll be over soon. Nice to meet you." At the time, Boatright didn't realize that this man was the Tillman written about in the press; he simply appreciated the encouragement. "A lot of the Rangers were cocky and arrogant and muscle-bound. They treated new guys like shit. Pat was never like that," Boatright told Tillman biographer Krakauer. "He was always polite. He was a genuinely nice guy."[1]

In the few months Marie got to spend with her husband before he and his fellow Rangers deployed again, in early April, this time to Afghanistan, she sensed growth in her husband. She saw a more sensitive man, unencumbered by past "hang-ups," more attuned to what really mattered in life. While difficult, he told his wife that the military had humbled him and that the emotional challenges it wrought had made him a better person.[2]

Pat, his brother Kevin, and fellow Rangers flew to Afghanistan on 7 April 2004. Their job there would be to root out Taliban fighters in the difficult mountainous border region between Afghanistan and Pakistan. The Taliban had taken refuge just over the Afghan border in Pakistan, in largely self-governed and illiterate Federally Administered Tribal Areas. From there, they would launch attacks into Afghanistan, claiming jihad and hoping to wreak instability. Tillman and his fellow Rangers, then, were part of an effort, dubbed Operation Mountain Storm, to thwart these types of attacks and thereby help deliver the stability needed for Afghanistan's upcoming national elections, originally scheduled for 5

July 2004. The strategy called for unconventional fighting, for small groups of
special ops rather than huge numbers of
ground troops. Helicopters would often
drop these small, quick-tempo special-ops
groups into dangerous areas, and then
the soldiers would go about searching for
and rooting out the enemy. The mission
aligned with what Tillman had envisioned
for himself when he'd decided to enlist.[3]

In mid-April, Pat and his fellow Black
Sheep Rangers landed at Afghanistan's
Forward Operating Base (FOB) Salerno.
They quickly mounted their weapons

Cpl. Patrick Tillman in full uniform. Courtesy Pat Tillman Foundation.

on Humvees and loaded up gear and supplies, including ready-to-eat-
meals, before setting out in Humvees and Toyota Hilux pickups along
the mountainous backcountry of a border town called Spera, in Khost
Province. They drove along riverbeds and goat tracks. A couple days into
their work, they drove to a desolate valley and climbed atop a 9,000-foot
peak, below which they could see Pakistan and a well-worn Taliban pathway from it into Afghanistan. They kept a watch on the path overnight,
enduring cold and rain, before moving on to other nearby terrain.

For six more days, they searched for Taliban in small settlements with
hut-like houses made of stone and mud, but didn't come up with much
other than a small number of weapons. They'd mingle with locals sometimes as they went house to roughshod house digging for tips. Russell
Baer, serving with Pat at this time, recalled him accepting a watermelon
from a local Afghan and savoring it.

The Rangers lived spartanly. At one point, they turned to snake for
protein. All the while, even when mingling, they stayed on guard, aware
that an easy grin or offer of friendship could be a Taliban-inspired ruse
in the guerilla-style conflict.[4]

On 22 April 2004, the Black Sheep Rangers awoke with one final
village to sweep, Manah, before returning to FOB Salerno for much-
needed rest. They'd been living in the mountains for just over a week.
That morning, however, a broken-down Humvee, for which (to no avail)
a new fuel pump had been flown in the night before, impeded their prog-
ress. It took four hours that morning for them to tow the Humvee a mere

five miles through a soggy, winding, descending riverbed trail. By then, the Humvee had endured such a beating—its tie rods snapped, its front wheels flopping—it'd been rendered untowable.[5]

Stuck near a half-dozen or so mud and stone huts known as the village of Magarah, Lt. David Uthlaut, leader of the Black Sheep, called FOB Salerno to ask that a heavy wrecker (recovery) truck come to tow the Humvee back to base, or that a helicopter fly in to sling-load the Humvee and carry it away. It took a while for his requests to work their way through the chain of command. Meanwhile, locals came out to see a rare sight: thirty-five Army Rangers, their vehicles, and several accompanying Afghan Military Force (AMF) soldiers hanging about, waiting. At 1:30 p.m., both requests—for either a heavy wrecker or helicopter to come to them—met denial. Instead, Uthlaut was told that he'd have to somehow get the dilapidated Humvee fifteen additional miles to a paved road, at which point a US Army wrecker truck could bring it to FOB Salerno. Superiors also ruled out abandoning the 6,000-pound vehicle. In the end, Lieutenant Uthlaut hired a local driver with a "jinga," a five-ton diesel truck, to tow the Humvee fifteen miles to pavement.[6]

The tow job would take a while, though, and the Black Sheep still had their final village sweep of Manah on the docket. Lieutenant Uthlaut wondered if that sweep could be canceled or delayed. He contacted FOB Salerno again, using e-mail, to determine how to proceed. Ultimately, after 4:00 p.m., he was ordered—even though he expressed his displeasure at the order—to split his platoon: one portion would follow the jinga and broken Humvee to paved road, while the other would set up an assembly area to ready the sweep of Manah. Lieutenant Uthlaut thought that splitting put his men at unnecessary risk and would achieve virtually nothing since the full-on sweep of Manah wouldn't begin until the two split parts reunited anyway. Again, his concerns weren't heeded.

Tillman biographer Krakauer blames the Bush administration, Secretary of Defense Rumsfeld in particular, for this. Krakauer argues that an unspoken reason for the helicopter sling-load option getting rejected was that the Afghan conflict had become like a "neglected stepchild" compared with US military efforts in Iraq, and therefore Afghanistan faced a dearth of choppers. Krakauer also says Rumsfeld's emphasis on efficiencies led to a basically unnecessary rush to clear villages rather than take a more methodical approach.

But in this instance, Krakauer's apparent political agenda in his Tillman biography distracts from the narrative. Army officer Andrew Exum, a man who led a quick-reaction force of forty Rangers, a lot like Tillman's Black Sheep, and who described himself as "no fan of the Bush administration's decisions," argued in the *Washington Post* that "the errors that led to Tillman's death were all operational and tactical."[7]

As it happened, in quintessential Tillman fashion, by the time Lieutenant Uthlaut had received this final order to split the platoon, Tillman had won a rock-throwing contest against some local Afghan men. It was after 4:00 p.m., dusk loomed, and by this time locals had heard the US troops talk with the Humvee-towing jinga driver about their plans. A local then, if desired, would have had plenty of time to spread word of those plans to others.

Eerily, just before pushing off, an Afghan approached the platoon to deliver a message: a doctor living nearby wanted to have a word. The Black Sheep, however, already faced a tight time line. They left without talking to the doctor. In hindsight, some wondered if perhaps the doctor had wanted to warn them of an ambush.[8]

That soon-to-come ambush has been covered in considerable detail through the course of five military investigations, a *Sports Illustrated* article, a book written by Pat Tillman's mom, the press, Krakauer's biography, a documentary made in part by Pat Tillman's brother, Kevin, and more. The details involved in its retelling get quite complex.

In short, the portion of the split platoon that Pat Tillman was a part of, Serial 1, traveled toward Manah to prep for the planned village sweep. Meanwhile, the other part of the platoon, Serial 2—at the urging of the jinga driver, who said it would be safer and take less time—changed its route to get the broken Humvee to pavement. Instead of driving over a treacherous mountain pass, Serial 2 went around the mountain. This meant it actually would follow about fifteen minutes behind Pat Tillman's group through a steep canyon before veering off near Manah.

The last stretch of this drive along the rutty unpaved route to Manah featured a skinny canyon, through which Humvees and other vehicles could barely fit and during the traversing of which, at least for a time, they lost radio contact. With steep cliffs rising on either side, the ambush-ripe route stirred fears among the Black Sheep. A Ranger in Serial 2 later described the terrain by saying, "The canyon was unbelievably narrow, and the walls just shot straight up. I've never seen anything like it in my life. And the way the sun was setting, the shadows—it was creepy."[9]

Pat's serial made it through unscathed, although it missed a turn to Manah shortly thereafter. As Serial 2 traveled through the gorge, however, it came under mortar fire from the steep cliffs rising above.[10]

Pat and his fellow Black Sheep in Serial 1 heard the fire and realized what was happening. Twelve of their group's twenty men, including Tillman, rushed to higher ground in hopes of providing cover for Serial 2. They hurried along mountainous terrain for several minutes, passing through a cluster of mud and stone houses before reaching "a bald spur," at which point nine of the twelve stopped. Tillman, Bryan O'Neal (an eighteen-year-old Ranger that Tillman had sort of taken under his wing), and one of the Afghan troopers assigned to their serial continued overtop the spur for about sixty yards, where they got a clearer view of the canyon below. They rightly assumed that Serial 2 would come driving into the clearing soon. From this spot they could also see the ridgelines above, from which Taliban fire had emanated.

Fellow Ranger Russell Baer marveled as he watched Pat, carrying all his gear and a SAW, seemingly fly over stone walls and rocky rubble to this area. In debriefs later, some would criticize Tillman for taking this position. But he'd asked a superior for permission to do so and received it. In its three-part series on the saga, ESPN.com's Mike Fisher, having reviewed transcripts of investigations into the matter and having interviewed several Rangers who were there that evening, determined that Tillman's decision to take up the position he did with O'Neal and the Afghan soldier was reasonable.[11]

Meantime, the soldiers in Serial 1 who hadn't run to the spur or joined Tillman beyond it, stayed near their vehicles, two of which worked on radioing in word of the ambush. Then those two, Ranger Jared Lane and Black Sheep Lieutenant Uthlaut, took up a position near a house in Manah. So, at this point, the platoon was fragmented into several parts. Meanwhile, the lead Humvee of Serial 2 pulled out in front of the jinga. Other vehicles in its convoy, however, had gotten notably behind it.

Making matters messier, Sgt. Matthew Weeks, part of the nine who remained at the spur, tried to radio in his group's new position, both to Serial 2 and to aerial support. He got no responses. His transmissions were apparently jammed by others trying to transmit at the same time.

Soon, the nine at the spur started to take fire. At first, they thought it from the enemy. Later, they realized it had more likely been friendly fire from the lead Humvee in Serial 2. In the chaos, Baer's eardrum ruptured from a blast. "It was really f———close," he recalls about the harrowing scene.

Lieutenant Uthlaut, the platoon leader, and soldier Lane, who were now providing cover fire from a position about one hundred yards away from the spur, also took friendly fire. As part of the deluge, a grenade significantly injured Uthlaut's face. About ten seconds or so later, an American bullet tore through Lane's left knee. Meanwhile, Pat and his small group took Taliban fire from atop the canyon they'd recently driven through. They fired back.[12]

Soon thereafter, matters went further awry. When the lead Humvee of the Serial 2 convoy came through the gorge into the relative clear, its troopers continued to fire at what they perceived to be the enemy. They still didn't know the exact whereabouts of Serial 1, let alone Pat's small group.

The lead Humvee's squad leader, Sgt. Greg Baker, has admitted that, upon coming out of the canyon, he mistook the AK-47-wielding Afghan soldier near Tillman and O'Neal for the enemy and shot him dead. The soldiers on Baker's Humvee, as trained—although they are also trained to identify, acquire, and then engage—fired in the same direction as Sergeant Baker. As this massive amount of firepower was unleashed in their direction, Tillman and O'Neal, about ten to fifteen yards from their now-fallen Afghan comrade, took cover behind a couple of low-lying boulders.

"Stop! Friendlies! Cease fire!" they hollered repeatedly. At one point, Pat even raised his arms to wave. But between the noise of the guns, the approaching darkness, and the adrenaline and fog of war, the gunners didn't catch the drift.

Instead, they lit up the entire area, not just Tillman's and O'Neal's positions. Indeed, they nearly killed cover-taking Rangers in the larger group near the spur; Ranger Will Aker was only one of them who nearly got shot. Russell Baer, on the spur too, feared for his life and those of his comrades.

"You could see rounds impacting all around us," he recalled, adding, "They just wouldn't stop shooting. I came *so* close to shooting back at those guys. I knew I would be able to kill every one of them with my

SAW. It didn't seem like anything else was going to stop them. I'm glad I didn't do it, but it definitely crossed my mind."[13]

While the shooters on Serial 2's lead Humvee didn't realize the situation, their driver did. From the front seat of the Humvee, he spotted Serial 1 vehicles ahead and put two and two together, shouting to his gunners, "Friendlies on top!" But they didn't understand him. Apparently, of those who heard him making noise at all, one or more only heard what they took to be a holler from the driver, which they presumed to be the result of him taking incoming fire.

Tillman, having hollered and waved to no avail, eventually set off a purple smoke grenade to alert the firing Rangers that he and O'Neal were friendlies. But rather than help, the smoke was misread as remnants of a Taliban mortar round, and the Rangers below unleashed a barrage of fire on Tillman's position again, hitting Tillman's bulletproof vest at one point and knocking the wind out of him. At some point Tillman also took shrapnel in his left forearm and wrist. Afterward, O'Neal, who considered himself in a more vulnerable position, said that, between waving his arms and setting off the grenade, both of which drew fire, Tillman had likely saved his life.[14]

Investigators later determined, from divots in the boulders around the spot at which Tillman had taken cover, that ammunition from a .50-caliber machine gun, an M249 SAW, and perhaps one or more M4s had been fired at his position.[15]

With the Taliban apparently in retreat and not shooting any longer, there was a lull in the fire. Tillman and O'Neal stood up—they were at this time an estimated fifty yards from the lead Humvee of Serial 2—and the two exchanged words of relief, assuming that finally the Rangers below had figured things out. But then, suddenly, machine gun fire screamed toward Tillman and O'Neal yet again.

"Cease fire, friendlies!" Pat hollered, but the shots continued. Surely exasperated, Tillman shouted words that weren't like him to say, "I am Pat f———Tillman, damn it! I am Pat f———Tillman!"[16]

Moments later, O'Neal, his head buried in the rocky earth just below Tillman's position, heard what sounded like flowing water coming down toward him. He soon realized it was blood. Tillman had been shot in the head and killed.

"Oh, my God!" O'Neal screamed, devastated. "Oh, my God!"[17]

35

JUST UNDER TWO MINUTES after Tillman was killed, calls of "cease-fire" finally got the shooting to stop. Sergeant Weeks, who was up on the spur near where Tillman and O'Neal had taken up position, ordered men around him to keep a watch out for Taliban while he went to check on the screams coming from what turned out to be O'Neal. Weeks said he found O'Neal in a "state of hysteria."

"It was our guys that did it!" O'Neal screamed. "They fucking killed him! We were waving our arms! How did they not know we're here?"

Moments later, another soldier arrived, Mel Ward. Upon processing what happened, he simply fell to his knees and hugged Pat Tillman, crying. They'd pulled guard duty together just hours earlier, while their platoon had waited to figure out what to do with the broken-down Humvee. They'd talked about the future, their wives, their families.[1]

Within a couple minutes or so, the last vehicle of Serial 2, a Humvee upon which Kevin sat in the turret, came out of the canyon and stopped below where Pat had been killed. None of the other Rangers who knew what happened knew what to say. So Kevin kept watch on the turret for nearly an hour in the deepening figurative (and literal) dark as the process of covering Tillman's body and bringing it down the hillside on a kind of stretcher occurred.

The driver of Kevin's Humvee, Sgt. Jason Parsons, eventually stepped out of the vehicle and was told that Tillman had died—he was not told, however, that it had come from friendly fire. After a while, Kevin, getting an increasingly eerie feeling, asked Parson's about his brother's whereabouts. Parsons played ignorant for a time, but after Kevin asked numerous times, he felt that he had to let Kevin know that his brother was dead. Naturally, he didn't mention friendly fire as the cause, because he didn't know it had been.

Upon learning of his brother's death, Kevin went silent for a short while. Then he started walking sort of aimlessly about, screaming. None of the Rangers who knew friendly fire to be the cause communicated this to Kevin.

Fratricide is a terrible thing. And it was as if everyone who knew the cause of death found it too disappointing, too embarrassing, too tragic to tell Pat's brother. Parson's squad leader, Staff Sgt. Jonathan Owens, even got mad at Parsons for telling Kevin that Pat was dead, as if he wouldn't soon figure it out anyway.[2] With the Rangers given orders to stay quiet, Kevin wouldn't find out the cause of Pat's death until five weeks later, after a military investigation into the cause released its findings. He and his family were livid when they found out they'd been misled.

In the swirl of the controversy surrounding the military's botched handling of the aftermath of Tillman's death, some have suggested that perhaps Tillman was murdered by his own troops, maybe by Rangers who resented him or maybe even as part of a conspiracy within the State Department and the army, both of which, some have suggested, wanted him dead because of his lack of support for the Iraq War. In his biography of Tillman, Krakauer, while acknowledging some odd elements within the testimony spanning five military investigations, convincingly debunks these conspiracy theories.

"I investigated them all and, in every case, I realized there was nothing to them," he told the *Daily Beast*. "If the Army wanted to kill Pat Tillman, they would not stage a complicated firefight like the one that claimed his life."[3] Krakauer also noted that, sadly, fratricide happens more often than people outside the army might think. An estimated 41 percent of casualties in the Iraq War resulted from friendly fire, 13 percent in Afghanistan. For World War II, estimates suggest a 21 percent casualty rate, Vietnam 39 percent.[4]

Eventually, on the night of Pat Tillman's death, two Black Hawk helicopters arrived on the scene, one to take away the significantly injured Uthlaut and Lane, the other to evacuate the bodies of Tillman and of the killed AMF soldier. The following morning, while on watch, Black Sheep soldier Brad Jacobson spotted a Chinook flying overhead with a sling-loaded Humvee swinging below—the same broken-down Humvee they'd been ordered to tow. Jacobson later said under oath that the sight of the choppers "was a quiet reminder that perhaps if our leadership had done their job right in Bagram and had gotten that helicopter to us like we asked, none of this would have happened."[5] Similarly frustrating is the decision to order the Black Sheep to split up.

⭐ THE WAY THE US ARMY and Defense Department handled Tillman's death in the days and weeks immediately afterward made the tragic scenario worse. First, even though Black Sheep Rangers knew it was fratricide, higher-ups—namely, Lt. Col. Jeffrey Bailey, commander of the 2nd Ranger Battalion—ordered the Rangers to keep this information from Kevin Tillman. Under these orders, Black Sheep Ranger Baer, who was on the spur during the fire and who had enjoyed a bond with Pat and Kevin, was even tasked with traveling back to the States with Kevin and Pat's body. Baer found it so troubling to do this that he went AWOL for a time after making the trip. "A few days earlier, the guys I worked with had killed Pat and another guy [the Afghan AMF soldier], injured two more, and shot at me, and I wasn't allowed to tell anyone," he told Krakauer.[6]

As noted, it didn't end there with regard to the military fouling up matters. Higher-ups also concocted a story about Pat's death by claiming that while running up a hill to protect his men and forcing the enemy to withdraw, he'd been shot dead by Talibani insurgents. Kevin White, the Navy SEAL who'd befriended Tillman in Iraq, was then asked by the army to rehash this tale as part of the announcement, to be made at the ESPN-broadcast Tillman memorial, that Tillman had been posthumously awarded the prestigious Silver Star.[7]

Of course, White didn't know that the narrative underpinning the granting of this Silver Star—the recommendation for which was expedited by the high-ranking Gen. Stanley McChrystal—was based on questionable "witness accounts": one purportedly from the man closest to Tillman when he died, Bryan O'Neal, and the other from a Ranger who was on the spur near them, Mel Ward. In 2007, at a congressional inquiry, O'Neal was asked if he wrote the sentences attributed to him "claiming that you were engaged with the enemy."

O'Neal replied, "No, sir."

Meanwhile, the other supposed witness, Sergeant Ward, has stated, "When they showed me a Silver Star recommendation that I supposedly wrote for Pat, it was unsigned, which is a big red flag for me, because in the Army you can't submit anything without signing it . . . Besides, it didn't sound like my words . . . It sounded really hokey—something I would never have written." It remains a mystery as to who carried out the embellishment of O'Neal's remark and the conjuring of words attributed to Ward.[8]

Black Sheep Jared Lane recalled that when the two had served together in Iraq, Tillman had told him: "He was afraid that if something were to happen to him, Bush's people would, like, make a big deal out of his death and parade him through the streets. And those were his exact words: 'I don't want them to parade me through the streets.'"[9] The false narrative concocted in the immediate aftermath of Tillman's death makes this concern seem prescient.

With this concern in mind, before heading to Afghanistan, Tillman had—against regulations—even made copies of paperwork that indicated his desire not to have a military funeral in the event he died in service. "I just have a feeling," he'd told Marie, "they might try to go against what I've signed, so you should hold on to these." Marie remembered this when the Army's Casualty Assistance Officer said to her, ". . . and there's going to be his military funeral." She pulled out the paperwork to keep this from happening.[10]

Instead, Tillman's family had his body cremated on April 30. Three days later, the ESPN-broadcast public memorial took place, on the day before what would have been Pat and Marie's second wedding anniversary. The memorial was held at the same location at which Pat and Marie graduated high school, the San Jose Municipal Rose Garden, and some 2,000 people attended. Those on hand and those watching on television heard from family and friends of Pat's, coaches and former teammates, as well as from Navy SEAL Kevin White. National figures such as Arizona senator John McCain and California's first lady, Maria Shriver, whose husband Arnold Schwarzenegger Pat admired, offered words of condolence, too.[11] Celebrated vocalist Darius Rucker sang renditions of "America the Beautiful" and "Amazing Grace."

36

WHILE THE CONCOCTED NARRATIVE presented at the memorial has overshadowed the event itself, the memorial did provide insight into Pat's spirit. Those who knew Pat spoke of his booming laugh and his curiosity, his desire to seek truth, and his valor. There was a quote on the memorial placards from Ralph Waldo Emerson, which read, "What I must do is all that concerns me, not what people think." And there was the request from the Tillman family asking that in lieu of flowers, donations be sent to the Pat Tillman Foundation.[1]

The Ralph Waldo Emerson quote reflected Pat's appreciation for the famous philosopher, a champion of individualism. In her 2012 memoir *The Letter: My Journey through Love, Loss, and Life*, Pat's wife Marie Tillman further highlighted Pat's admiration of Emerson. Indeed, Emerson helped Marie pull through the many dark days that came after Pat's death, days and nights during which she would barely eat, or panic at the thought of forgetting a memory of Pat—memories like which of his eyes "had a fleck of gold near the pupil. What he'd eaten the last time we had dinner together, what the warmth of his skin through a thin white T-shirt felt like."[2]

It became hard for her to make simple decisions, like whether she should eat or watch TV. But one evening at home, having returned from walking for hours and feeling unsure of what do next, she decided to get up out of bed and eat. As she started to get up, she noticed a book stuck between the bed and wall. It was Pat's well-worn copy of Ralph Waldo Emerson's "Self-Reliance".

Holding it, she thought about the time that Pat, back from his Iraq tour, had popped up from reading on the couch and rushed into their bedroom to read Marie passages from it. Tears welled up in her eyes thinking of Pat's enthusiasm. She flipped through the book and saw his underlined passages, one of which stood out: "Nothing can bring you peace but yourself." Another seemed to pop off the page: "Be not the slave to your own past. Plunge into the sublime seas, dive deep and swim far, so you shall come back with self-respect, with new power, with an advanced experience that shall explain and overlook the old."[3]

In the coming weeks, she kept the book with her, returning to it "in my darkest times to find insight, or just to see Pat's pen drawn across the page." And Emerson's work led to more reading. She read for hours—"Thoreau, Jean-Paul Sartre, Nietzsche, Kierkegaard, and Victor Frankl, absorbing the parts that spoke to me, dismissing the rest, and piecing together my own framework to build from."[4] In time, she also found hope in reading about others people's experiences in overcoming adversity.

It didn't happen overnight. A full year after Pat's death, she still engaged only minimally with the outside world. But she did start thinking about the future, of venturing out. She'd read an article on kite surfers at Mt. Hood in Oregon and decided to go see them. She drove for a few hours and found a coffee shop from which she could sip coffee and watch the surfers, propelled by their wind-driven kites, glide across the water. She thought of Pat—how, if he'd traveled with her, he'd have given kite surfing a go, how she'd have snapped photos and cheered him on. Perhaps, she thought, they'd have stayed at a bed-and-breakfast along the shore.

There was sadness, yes, but at least she'd made it out of the cottage to a beautiful spot, she told herself. She watched for only thirty minutes before getting back in her car and making the hours-long drive back home.[5] She sensed, however, that she'd made a big step in trying to do what her late husband had asked of her in the "letter" he'd written her before leaving for Iraq. She would title her memoir after the letter, and it had a difficult but simple message: if he were to die, she needed to live. Pat's regard for Emerson helped her see this through.[6]

Eventually, Marie was brave enough to visit a country to which she'd felt pulled since her husband's death—Afghanistan. There she visited the United Service Organization (USO)'s Pat Tillman Memorial USA Center at Bagram Airfield, a place where soldiers could get online, send e-mails, relax, and sleep. But while it helped, she didn't get complete closure from the trip.

"Grief is messy; grief is complicated; grief is in many ways unending," she wrote.[7] But she did gain more insight and perspective. And

Pat Tillman and his wife, Marie, who heads the Pat Tillman Foundation. Courtesy Pat Tillman Foundation.

she found further inspiration there. At a concert she watched a group of female soldiers try to escape the pressures of war for a few hours by rocking back and forth to music. As she watched, Marie Tillman felt a tremendous sense of pride in them.

"The men and women I met reminded me of what had been at the core of Pat's decision to serve," she wrote, "the purity of it all before lies and Congressional hearings made me grow cynical and suspicious."[8] The female soldiers Marie observed were, after all, in Afghanistan to help it rebuild, to make it so that young Afghan girls could go to school, listen to music, and, if they so chose, dance.

In 2008, Marie Tillman felt ready to take on the lead role with the Pat Tillman Foundation, which, under her guidance, has come to count more than 450 Tillman Scholars among its ranks and has granted over $14 million in academic scholarships and support to them at over 100 different universities. These scholars are chosen for their "extraordinary academic and leadership potential, a true sense of vocation, and a deep commitment to create positive change through their work in the fields of medicine, law, business, education, and the arts."[9]

This mission really does fit Tillman: supporting young adults in seeking knowledge and wisdom in an academic setting that at its best is rigorous, welcomes the free exchange of ideas, and strives for a better understanding while broadening and sharpening the mind. Tillman loved to engage, to learn, to debate, as did his revered Ralph Waldo Emerson, whose renown is in part due to "The American Scholar," in which he argued that a scholar's education came from three main influences: nature, books, and action. He called on scholars to look freshly at the world, to become "man thinking"—informed of, but not overly burdened by, that which came before—so that they could chart their own paths rather than merely follow the masses, all to see the world more clearly.

From an early age, Pat embraced the idea of asserting himself, to strive to be his version of "man thinking." At times, he also expressed ideas that connected with strains of postmodernism. In a *Sports Illustrated* story, "Remember His Name," award-winning writer Gary Smith presented Pat Tillman as only Smith could: dramatically, gut-wrenchingly, colorfully, hauntingly, respectfully. And in this article he attempted to explain Pat's layered nature by writing, "A man could be strong and soft at the same time . . . He could manage fear by looking straight at it, could take charge of a moment in the most unmilitary of ways, without bristling or bellowing."[10] Smith also tried to capture the complexity of the times in which Pat lived by writing,

> *Pat's wisdom quest was too honest, had carried him clean past that plane where good and evil are fixed and far-flung from one another, to a higher ledge up in the swirling fog where a man could see how right and wrong might rotate and trade places. It just became harder and harder to be Braveheart.*[11]

But, in the end, Smith could only conclude by saying that perhaps the best answer to what, he predicted, would be an elusive search to understand Pat Tillman would come from an image of Pat doing a handstand on a roof, shirt off, risk-taking turned on, "doing something he loved to do just because it was hard and scary."[12] Smith couldn't bring himself to write more definitively about Tillman.

Like Smith, biographer Krakauer described Tillman as an "intricate mosaic of personal history." To sketch Tillman, Krakauer drew heavily upon a philosopher, although it wasn't Emerson, as one might expect, but Friedrich Nietzsche, a philosopher Tillman apparently read and who, some argue, is often misunderstood because his sister edited his manuscripts to try to make them align with German nationalist ideology. Philosophers debate Nietzsche's ideas, their meaning and value, and it can get quite nuanced. As for Krakauer, he argues that it is not hard to imagine Nietzsche finding "more than a few" *ubermensch* (translated from German as "overman" or "superman") attributes in Tillman.

"Prominent among such qualities," Krakauer writes, "were Tillman's robust masculinity and its corollary, his willingness to stand up and fight."[13]

In keeping with some of the ideas expressed by Nietzsche, Krakauer argues further that, rather than seeing Tillman's "alpha maleness" as a tragic flaw that led to his downfall, it is more accurate to view Tillman's death as "a function of his stubborn idealism—his insistence on trying to do the right thing. In which case it wasn't a tragic flaw that brought Tillman down, but a tragic virtue."[14]

But in connecting Tillman so tightly with Nietzsche, Krakauer doesn't highlight how traditional values and ideas, like those of freedom and the pursuit of reason and justice, did stir Tillman's soul. Cherishing such enduring values and ideas is not in keeping with Nietzsche's concept of *ubermensch*.

America doesn't always get it right. Its wars don't always sit well with its people. Pat Tillman knew this and still cherished the American experiment. Some 228 years before his death, the values underpinning that experiment were expressed in the Declaration of Independence, a document written by Thomas Jefferson, a man of unorthodox Christian beliefs who loved freedom and feared the power of government. A line can be drawn from Thomas Jefferson's belief in the primacy of the individual to Ralph Waldo Emerson's emphasis on individual liberation, self-reliance, self-government, and aversion to blind social conformity. And from Emerson, one can sketch a connection to Pat Tillman, which now radiates outward from Tillman to others.

These radiating lines have written upon them both the enduring values that have informed American since its inception and newer markings that reflect our ever-changing times.

Pat Tillman died in a town called Manah, which has been translated to refer to a chief Goddess of Mecca known for snatching men away, thereby robbing them of their purpose and value. But Tillman's worldview wouldn't accept that a centuries-old mythological fable had to define someone. It remains up to individuals who encounter Pat Tillman's story to decide if they want to discern meaning from him.

Epilogue

FISH, BAKER, KINNICK, KALSU, AND TILLMAN were all great athletes, and the span of time during which their lives stretched saw the popularity of sports skyrocket. Through sport they became widely known, and the familiarity that most Americans have with sport gave them a connection to these men. Americans cared about Fish, Baker, Kinnick, Kalsu, and Tillman because they saw them shine in the competitive arena and they read about the exploits of the teams on which they played. The military service of these men, even though in Kalsu's case it took a few decades, resonated with Americans. Across the land people were galvanized by the news of their deaths and riveted by the stories of their lives as told through the popular press. They could relate to, or at least marvel at, their fallen ftars.

The lives of the fallen stars cover more than one hundred years, and their stories, collectively, take us across the globe. They came from different types of families, from superelite to ordinary, and from different educational backgrounds, from Ivy League to state schools. They fought on foot, in the air, and, in Kinnick's case, trained at sea. But whatever their background or however they served, they all defended the core values upon which their country was built. Taken together, their lives capture key parts of the American story.

The geography alone of these men gives us insight into the story of America. Take, for instance, the western march of their hometowns. Both Fish and Baker came from the East Coast. Kinnick rose to stardom on the Midwest's Iowa prairies. Kalsu was born and raised a little further west, on the wind-swept Great Plains on the outskirts Oklahoma City. Tillman, of course, was born about as far west as one can get in the contiguous United States. This westward march aligns with a core part of the American story, the impact of the literal and figurative "frontier" on American individuality and innovativeness, and its adventurous spirit.

The geography of the wars in which the men in *Fallen Stars* served shows the increasing role the United States has played on the global stage. The wake of the Spanish-American War put the United States on a course to become the world's preeminent economic and military power. That position proved decisive in ending both World War I and World II. After these wars, the difficulty that comes with discerning how to best wield superpower status came into sharp focus in Vietnam as well as Iraq and Afghanistan.

The religious backgrounds of the men in *Fallen Stars* reflect the diverse religious history of the United States. Ham Fish, from a family with prominent Dutch and English roots, was brought up in the Episcopal faith. His family attended one of the oldest churches in the United States. Hobey Baker came from the established, eastern Episcopalian culture as well. Nile Kinnick, meanwhile, was raised on a New Age faith, Christian Science. Bob Kalsu, of prominent Czech heritage on his dad's side and French-Canadian on his mother's, was Catholic. Pat Tillman, meanwhile, was described by biographer Krakauer, as "agnostic, perhaps even atheist."[1]

Some of the men in *Fallen Stars* came from money, or at least were brought up in elite settings. Hamilton Fish, of course, grew up among the types of families that would find their names on Mrs. William B. Astor's list of society's elite four hundred. Summers in Tuxedo Park, exclusive boarding schools, heirs and heiresses, men's clubs and balls were the kinds of things the Fish circle was familiar with. Money, however, didn't animate Ham Fish. Hobey Baker went to the same storied prep school as Fish and attended an Ivy League school as well. He grew up in part in a leafy Philadelphia suburb, but his family didn't actually have a lot of wealth. Still, through his elite education and athletic exploits, he gained access to the exclusive ranks of America's early twentieth-century smart set.

Kinnick's family was well known among the prairies of Iowa, his grandfather having been governor of the Hawkeye State. But his family didn't come from the type of money that Fish's did. During the Depression, the Kinnicks, facing considerable economic pressure from their farming operation, had to move to Omaha, Nebraska, where Nile Sr.

found salaried work. Kalsu didn't have the kind of political family pedigree of Kinnick and came from pretty modest means, his father a laborer at the Tinker Air Force Base. Tillman was raised in a middle- to upper-middle-class background, his father a lawyer, his mother a teacher. But they didn't consider themselves wealthy, and they didn't raise their kids to think materialistically. Indeed, Pat was almost embarrassed by the money he could make playing football.

The men in *Fallen Stars* had unique personalities yet shared traits, too. Fish was romantic, idealistic, passionate. Baker yearned for adventure and wanted to be liked, to show people that he could do it, that he belonged. Kinnick was intellectual and curious, intensely competitive yet sentimental, idealistic in some ways, pragmatic in others. Bob Kalsu carried himself with a powerful, quiet dignity. He didn't go to Vietnam out of a romantic notion or wisdom quest. He went because he felt duty-bound to support his nation, the core values of which, just as with the other men in *Fallen Stars*, he revered. Tillman had a romantic bent, a lot like Fish, and a deep thirst for knowledge, a lot like Kinnick. Tillman went to war to stand for the American way of life and, as a striver and a thinker, to test himself. At war, he sought to square his ideals with that which his country asked him to do. In Iraq, in particular, he came away disappointed in his nation's leaders. Ultimately, though, he died fighting in exactly the type of hot zone he wanted to confront, an area in which radical Islamists fought against the ideals for which Tillman stood.

The popular press championed some of the same characteristics in all five men: their values, their courage, their athletic prowess, their sacrifice. But in the case of Kalsu, this didn't happen on a national level until decades after his death. With Tillman, the popular press also delved much more deeply into personal matters—his political, religious, and social views. The amount of information that was immediately accessible, through the Internet, to someone interested in the Tillman saga stands in marked contrast to that of earlier eras. That same technology, however, can now enable someone halfway across the globe to quickly pull up the University of Iowa's digitalized copies of Nile Kinnick's World War II letters. It's an intimate experience to read handwritten letters penned by Kinnick from that time.

The men in *Fallen Stars* lived in different eras, served in different wars, and brought their own personalities and backgrounds to their military service. In them, we see indications of the changes that have impacted the American way of life over time. But we also see continuity. Foremost, in their own way, they all felt a commitment to and a willingness to sacrifice for a very basic but transformative American value: freedom.

Folks can disagree over how best to make freedom ring, at home and abroad. But those who embrace the fundamental ideas expressed in the Declaration of Independence and woven into the fabric of America—the right to life, liberty, and the pursuit of happiness—can agree that the willingness of people like Ham Fish, Hobey Baker, Nile Kinnick, Bob Kalsu, and Pat Tillman to stand for a great experiment, that of representative government, is enlightening and soul-stirring.

Notes

INTRODUCTION

1. Dave Caldwell, "A Soldier's Uniform Ranks High in N.F.L. Sales," *New York Times*, 26 November 2006.

2. Roderick Nash, *The Nervous Generation: American Thought, 1917–1930* (Chicago: Elephant Paperbacks, 1990), vii, 2–4.

3. Michael Oriard, *Bowled Over* (Chapel Hill: University of North Carolina Press, 2009), 18. Michael Oriard, "Flag Football: How the NFL Became the American War Game," *Slate*, 17 November 2009, http://www.slate.com/articles/sports/sports_nut/2009/11/flag_football.html, accessed 12 July 2016.

4. Emil R. Salvini, *Hobey Baker: American Legend* (Princeton: Hobey Baker Foundation, 2005), 49.

5. *Washington Post*, 30 December 1918.

6. Michael Oriard, *King Football: Sport and Spectacle in the Golden Age of Radio & Newsreels, Movies & Magazines, the Weekly & the Daily Press* (Chapel Hill: University of North Carolina Press, 2001), 11, 12.

7. William Nack, "A Name on the Wall," *Sports Illustrated* 95, no. 3 (23 July 2001), http://www.vault.sportsillustrated.cnn.com, accessed 18 August 2008.

8. ESPN.com News Services, "Pat Tillman Investigation," 31 March 2007, http://www.espn.com/espn/eticket/story?page=tillmanpart1, accessed 31 March 2007.

CHAPTER 1

1. "Ham Fish Saved a Child," *Gettysburg Compiler*, 9 August 1898, 1.

2. It was often noted that many of Fish's friends were Columbia students and "members of prominent New York families." "Fish Did Not Know Fear," *Los Angeles Times* via *Pittsburgh Dispatch*, 9 July 1898, 8. "Former Salt Laker Killed," *Daily Tribune*, 25 June 1898, 1. "Hamilton Fish, 3D," *Logansport Pharos*, 27 September 1898, 7.

3. "Victims of the First Battle of Our Army on Cuban Soil," *The World*, 26 June 1898, 2. "Fish Did Not Know Fear," 8.

4. "Rush the Growler," *Weekly Gazette & Stockman*, 21 July 1898. "Patriots Form His Family Tree," *Hamilton Daily Republican-News*, 14 July 1898, 7.

5. "Hamilton Fish, Jr.," *Dubuque Herald*, 29 June 1898, 4.

6. "Fish Expected to Die," *Times-Democrat*, 1 July 1898; reprint of *Boston Herald* story.

CHAPTER 2

1. "Columbia Wins by Five Lengths," *Chicago Tribune*, 25 June 1895. "At Columbia's Boat-House," *The World*, 25 June 1895.

2. William Swanson, "The Elco Story," http://www.elcomotoryachts.com/history-of-elco.shtml, accessed 21 August 2009. "On the Observation Train," *The World*, 25 June 1895.

3. "Columbia Wins by Five Lengths."

4. "Yells, Bands, Fireworks," *The World*, 25 June 1895.

5. Ibid.

6. Hamilton Fish, *Hamilton Fish: Memoir of an American Patriot* (Washington, DC: Regnery Gateway, 1991), 10, 11.

7. "Hamilton Fish, 3D," 7.

8. "Of the Members of the Class of 95," *Columbia 1895* (New York: Columbia University Yearbook, 1895), 122.

9. John William Robson, "Traditions and University of Life" and "The Origin of Publications," *Guide to Columbia* (New York: Columbia University Press, 1937), 189, 191. "Peithologian Society," *Columbia 1894* (New York: Columbia University Yearbook, 1894), 59.

10. "No Mollycoddles, Says Roosevelt," *New York Times*, 24 February 1907, 1.

11. "The Denver and Rio Grande Western Railroad, Main Line Thru the Rockies," American-Rails.com, http://www.american-rails.com/denver-and-rio-grande-western.html, accessed 22 December 2009. "Fish Makes Trouble," *Daily Tribune*, 26 August 1896, 8. "Former Salt Laker Killed," *Daily Tribune*, 25 June 1898, 1.

12. "Former Salt Laker Killed," 1.

13. "Hamilton Fish Killed in the Battle at Sevilla," 1 July 1898. "Hamilton Fish, 3D," 7.

14. "Hamilton Fish, Killed in the Battle at Sevilla."

15. "Fish Makes Trouble," 8. Mason Mitchell, "Tribute to Hamilton Fish," *Oregonian* via *New York Sun*), 14 August 1988, 3.

16. "Fish Makes Trouble," 8.

17. "Former Salt Laker Killed," 1.

CHAPTER 3

1. Edward Ranson, "Electing a President, 1896," *History Today*, 1 October 1996, http://www.highbeam.com/doc/1G1–18755134.html, accessed 2 January 2010.

2. Ibid.

3. Ibid.

4. "Cross of Gold, William Jennings Bryan, Campaign Speech, 1896," http://www.pbs.org/wgbh/amex/1900/filmmore/reference/primary/crossof gold.html, accessed 15 January 2010.

5. Ranson, "Electing a President."

6. The Union League supported the Union cause in the Civil War in various ways, including by outfitting two African American regiments. Union League Club, "About the Club," http://www.unionleagueclub.org/default .aspx?p=GenericModuleDefault&NoModResize=1&NoNav=1&ShowFooter =False&ModID=65394&modtype=Aboutnbsp;thenbsp;Club&sl=1&vnf =0&ssid=0&dpageid=205548, accessed 23 August 2009. Gail Lumet Buckley, *American Patriots: The Story of Blacks in the Military from the Revolution to Desert Storm* (New York: Random House, 2002), 191. Union League Club should not be confused with the Union Club. Of all the elite social clubs in the country, the Union Club reigned supreme. Modeled on England's most exclusive clubs, a hereditary connection to Gotham's early founders was hugely important to gain admittance, and even in the Gilded Age, when entering its doors became slightly easier than in earlier decades, no club matched its exclusivity. A streetcar of cash was not enough—J. P. Morgan found this out when he tried to get a friend accepted, as did William K. Vanderbilt when his brother-in-law's application was denied (in turn, the two titans left the Union League and formed the Metropolitan). The Union Club limited access to its Italianate brownstone on the corner of Fifth Avenue and Twenty-first Street to 1,000 people, and from its inception the classic Knickerbocker clans like the Livingstons, Van Rensselaers, and Stuyvesants—to whom Hamilton Fish was connected by lineage—led the ranks. Greg King, *The Court of Mrs. Astor in Gilded Age New York: A Season of Splendor* (Hoboken: John Wiley & Sons, Inc., 2009), 92–93.

7. King, *Court of Mrs. Astor*, 87–92.

8. Legend holds that in the fourth century, St. Nicholas secretly helped a poor man provide dowries for his three daughters. On one occasion, he delivered this gold by dropping it down the family's chimney, and the coins happened to drop right into a stocking that had been hung over the fireplace to dry. The Saint Nicholas Society of the City of New York, "History of the Society," http://www.saintnicholassociety.org/history.htm, accessed 23 August 2009.

9. Ibid.

10. "Fish Did Not Know Fear," *Los Angeles Times* via *Pittsburgh Dispatch*, 9 July 1898, 8.

CHAPTER 4

1. David Trask, *The War with Spain in 1898* (New York: Macmillan, 1981), xiii.

2. "War Exists," *Chicago Tribune*, 26 February 1898, 12. Further indicating the tenseness, once the *Maine* moored in Havana, Capt. Charles D. Sigsbee, unsure about how his ship would be received, kept men on extra watch, made sure that the *Maine's* boilers always had enough steam in the event that they were needed to work the hydraulics for the turrets, and ordered the 328 enlisted men on his ship to stay on board. Charles D. Sigsbee, *The 'Maine': An Account of Her Destruction in Havana Harbor* (New York: Century Co., 1899), 42, 43.

3. As an example, in the days after the *Maine* incident, Queen Maria Cristina had made the US ambassador to Spain feel as if "All Spain has been educated to believe that all help in the insurrection comes from us and that the rebellion only lives because of our sympathy and assistance," regardless of facts. Trask, *War with Spain*, 32.

4. "Fish Did Not Know Fear," *Los Angeles Times* via *Pittsburgh Dispatch*, 9 July 1898, 8.

5. The famous Rough Riders nickname emerged early on, and it came from Buffalo Bill Cody's Congress of Rough Riders Wild West Show. At first Teddy didn't like the name. He didn't want folks thinking his efforts were a "hippodrome affair," he explained. In time, he would recognize how popular it was and embrace it. Paul Andrew Hutton, "Col. Cody, the Rough Riders, and the Spanish American War," *Points West* , Fall 1998, https:// centerofthewest.org/2014/08/06/cody-rough-riders-spanish-american-war/, accessed 28 May 2009.

6. Edmund Morris, *The Rise of Theodore Roosevelt* (New York: Random House, 2001), 642.

7. Teddy did become the colonel of the Rough Riders during the war when Dr. Wood got promoted to brigadier general. Morris, *Rise of Theodore Roosevelt*, 642, 646–48, 652.

8. Ibid.

9. "Ted. Roosevelt's Rough Riders," *San Antonio Light*, 22 May 1898. "Official Identification List," *New York Times*, 26 June 1898, 1.

10. Edward Marshall II, *The Story of the Rough Riders, 1st U.S. Volunteer Cavalry; the Regiment in Camp and on the Battle Field* (New York: G. W. Dillingham co., 1899), 41, 42.

11. "Ted. Roosevelt's Rough Riders."

12. Mason Mitchell, "Tribute to Hamilton Fish," *Oregonian* via *New York Sun*, 14 August 1988, 3.

13. Morris, *Rise of Theodore Roosevelt*, 649.

14. "Ted. Roosevelt's Rough Riders."

15. Ibid.

16. Ibid. "Lieutenant Tiffany Dead," *New York Time*, 26 August 1898, 2.

17. According to the *New York Times*, "Few social events of the younger set were complete without his presence." Yet Tiffany had "gladly grasped the opportunity to join Roosevelt's regiment and to desert the ballrooms for the malarial fields of Cuba." "Lieutenant Tiffany Dead," 2. As with Hamilton, William Tiffany's first trip west occurred before his Rough Rider enlistment. As a teenager he'd spent months in Montana, convalescing from ill health. There he learned to ride bareback and to shoot. Sadly, also like Fish, the Spanish-American War led to his demise. On 25 August 1898, having just returned from Cuba and with his recently affianced, Miss Maud Livingston, and his mother by his side, William Tiffany succumbed to yellow fever. "Ted. Roosevelt's Rough Riders." "Lieutenant Tiffany Dead," 2.

18. It starred in the War of 1812 and remains the oldest commissioned naval vessel in the world. "Ted. Roosevelt's Rough Riders." Theodore Roosevelt, *The Rough Riders* (New York: Charles Scribner's Sons, 1899), 14.

19. John Lyon Collyer, *The B. F. Goodrich Story of Creative Enterprise, 1870–1952: An Address to New York* (Whitefish, MT: Kessinger Publishing, 2006), 9, 10.

20. "Ted. Roosevelt's Rough Riders."

21. Morris, *Rise of Theodore Roosevelt*, 649, 650.

22. Ibid., 649, 50, 52.

23. "Official Identification List," *New York Times*, 26 June 1898, 1.

24. Marshall, *Story of the Rough Riders*, 43.

25. "Official Identification List," 1.

26. "Ted. Roosevelt's Rough Riders."

27. "The Rough Riders," *Daily Light*, 19 May 1898.

CHAPTER 5

1. Edward Marshall II, *The Story of the Rough Riders, 1st U.S. Volunteer Cavalry; the Regiment in Camp and on the Battle Field* (New York: G. W. Dillingham Co., 1899), 47.

2. Ibid., 48–49.

3. Ibid., 49–51.

4. Edmund Morris, *The Rise of Theodore Roosevelt* (New York: Random House, 2001), 653–54.

5. Ibid., 655–57.

6. "How Ham. Fish Died," *San Antonio Light*, 31 July 1898.

7. Ibid. "Official Identification List," *New York Times*, 26 June 1898, 1.

8. "How Ham. Fish Died."

9. "Launch of the Yucatan," *New York Times*, 17 July 1890. Theodore

Roosevelt, "The Rough Riders," *Scribner's Magazine* 25, no. 2 (February 1899): 144–46.

10. "Launch of the Yucatan." Roosevelt, "The Rough Riders," 144–46.

11. Ibid.

12. Marshall, *Story of the Rough Riders*, 55–57.

13. Roosevelt, "The Rough Riders," 148–49. Roosevelt, *Rough Riders*, 62.

14. "How Ham. Fish Died."

15. Joyce Milton, *The Yellow Kids* (New York: Harper & Row, 1989), xii, xiii.

16. Marshall, *Story of the Rough Riders*, 71–73.

17. "How Ham. Fish Died."

18. Morris, *Rise of Theodore Roosevelt*, 670.

19. "How Ham. Fish Died."

20. Ibid.

21. Ibid. "The Battle of Sevilla Heights," *New York Times*, 26 June 1898, 1.

22. "How Ham. Fish Died." "The Battle of Sevilla Heights," 1.

23. "How Ham. Fish Died." "The Battle of Sevilla Heights," 1.

24. Dale L. Walker, *The Boys of '98: Theodore Roosevelt and the Rough Riders* (New York: Forge, 1998,) 179. After the war Isbell would perform in Buffalo Bill Cody's Congress of Rough Riders, the Wild West show from which the press had taken the name "Rough Riders" and applied it to Roosevelt's men—much to the chagrin, initially, of Roosevelt, who thought the name would keep Americans from taking his regiment seriously. Paul Andrew Hutton, "Col. Cody, the Rough Riders, and the Spanish American War," *Points West* , Fall 1998, https://centerofthewest.org/2014/08/06/cody-rough -riders-spanish-american-war/, accessed 28 May 2009.

25. "How Ham. Fish Died."

26. Ibid.

27. Ibid. "Hamilton Fish's Death." *The Times-Democrat*, 28 July 1898, 14.

CHAPTER 6

1. "Bloody Battler Near Santiago," *Cedar Rapids Daily Reporter*, 25 June 1898, 1. "Blood Flows on Cuban Soil," *Nebraska State Journal*, 25 June 1898, 1.

2. "Heroic Rough Riders," *Times Democrat*, 4 July 1898. Joyce Milton, *The Yellow Kids* (New York: Harper & Row, 1989), xii, xiii.

3. "Fish Did Not Know Fear," *Los Angeles Times* via *Pittsburgh Dispatch*, 9 July 1898, 8.

4. Editorial, *Galveston Daily News*, 28 June 1898, 1. Inevitably, the story of how Ham Fish had lost that pewter-based image of St. Joseph, given to him by the mother of the little girl he had saved at Rough Rider camp, spread about America. A different version of this same story ran in the *Des Moines Daily News*. It was told by a woman who claimed to have been in San

Antonio while the Rough Riders trained. She portrayed the Rough Riders as "the embodiment of youthful chivalry and courageous young manhood" and said that, while playing cards in San Antonio, a Catholic man had given Ham Fish a small image of St. Joseph and told him to wear it for safety. "I beg of you not to throw it away, for if you do you will be the first to fall." Back at camp, she claimed, Fish supposedly smiled as he told his fellow Rough Riders about the encounter and then withdrew the amulet from his pocket and chucked it as far as he could. "Around the Evening Lamp," *Des Moines Daily News*, 3 August 1898, 2.

5. "Christian Endeavor," *Eau Claire Leader*, 6 November 1898, 6.

6. The poem originally ran in the *New Orleans Times-Democrat*. "Hamilton Fish Jr.," *San Antonio Daily Light*, 29 June 1898.

7. "The Battle of Sevilla Heights," *New York Times*, 26 June 1898, 1. Theodore Roosevelt, *The Rough Riders* (Boston: Harvard College Library, 1943), 79.

8. Edmund Morris, *The Rise of Theodore Roosevelt* (New York: Random House, 2001), 677.

9. "Rough Riders' Chaplain," *Alton Weekly Telegraph*, 8 September 1898,

10. "The Dead in Cuba," *Dubuque Daily Herald*, 29 July 1898, 4.

10. "Rough Riders' Chaplain." 10.

11. "Grinds," *Columbia 1895* (New York: Columbia University Yearbook, 1895), 137.

12. "Official Identification List," *New York Times*, 26 June 1898, 1.

13. "Hero Hamilton Fish through His Mother's Eyes," *The World*, 3 July 1898, 17.

14. "Official Identification List," 1.

15. "The Dead in Cuba," 4.

16. "Fish's Remains Arrive," *Evening Herald*, 18 July 1898, 2. "Cubans Will Act Alone," *Trenton Evening Times*, 21 July 1898, 1. "Will Bring Bodies of Fish and Capron," *New York Times*, 14 July 1898, 3. "Funeral of Hamilton Fish," *New York Times*, 28 July 1898, 3. "Funeral of Hamilton Fish," *New York Times*, 29 July 1898, 12.

17. The "peg-leg" Dutch governor of New York, Peter Stuyvesant, owned land in the Bowery. "The Bowery Ain't What It Used To Be," *United Press International*, 24 September 2001, http://www.highbeam.com/doc/1P1–47 087287.html, accessed 26 January 2010.

18. "Funeral of Hamilton Fish," 28 July 1898, 3. "Funeral of Hamilton Fish," 29 July 1898, 12.

19. "Short News Stories," *Logansport Journal*, 26 August 1898. "Hamilton Fish's Funeral," *New York Times*, 30 July 1898, 12.

CHAPTER 7

1. "Famous Athlete in Aviation Corps," *Aerial Age Weekly* 3, no. 14 (26

June 1916): 444. "Airship Squad Flies to a Football Game," *New York Times*, 19 November 1916, 8. Emil R. Salvini, *Hobey Baker: American Legend* (Princeton: Hobey Baker Foundation, 2005), 85.

2. *New York Times*, 31 March 1913.

3. *Washington Post*, 30 December 1918.

4. *Washington Post*, 12 January 1918.

5. Salvini, *Hobey Baker*, 49.

6. Baker to Percy Pyne, 12 November 1917, John C. Davies Collection on Hobey Baker, box 1, Princeton University Library, Princeton, NJ.

CHAPTER 8

1. Salvini, *Hobey Baker*, 2, 6–8.

2. Jack Falla, *Open Ice* (Mississauga, Ontario: Wiley, 2008), 200–202.

3. In 1938, *Time* wrote an article about how Thornton had recently completed a 30,000-mile global cruise with his two sons and a crew of three on a seventy-foot schooner. "Businessman's Dream," *Time*, 16 May 1938, http://www.time.com/time/magazine/article/0,9171,759709,00.html?artId =759709?contType=article?chn=us, accessed 19 July 2011.

4. Hobey Baker to Mother, n.d. (likely within a few weeks of Hobey's twelfth birthday on 15 January 1904), from the personal collection of Christo Morse. Hereafter cited as Morse Collection.

5. Hobey Baker to Mother, though hard to read, appears to be dated 10 October 1903, Morse Collection.

6. Hobey Baker to Mother, 27 November 1903, Morse Collection.

7. Ron Fimrite, "A Flame That Burned Too Brightly: Hobey Baker, the Golden Boy of American Sport before World War I, Found Little Worth Living For beyond the Playing Fields of Princeton," *Sports Illustrated*, 18 March 1991, http://sportsillustrated.cnn.com/vault/article/magazine/MAG1118992 /1/index.htm, accessed 15 July 2011.

8. "Everybody's Hero on Skates," *Sports Illustrated*, 16 January 1956, http://sportsillustrated.cnn.com/vault/article/magazine/MAG1131219/index .htm, accessed 16 July 2011.

9. Falla, *Open Ice*, 201.

10. Ibid.

11. Fimrite, "Flame That Burned Too Brightly."

12. "Princeton Coaches Used Baker at End," *Trenton Evening News* (Extra), 10 October 1911, 8. "Stars of Princeton and Harvard Elevens Ready to Clash on Gridiron for First Time in Fifteen Years," *Trenton Evening News* (Extra), 1 November 1911, 8.

13. "Princeton Beats Eli for Gridiron Honor," *Trenton Evening News* (Extra), 18 November 1911, 1.

14. John Sayle Watterson, *College Football: History Spectacle Controversy*

(Baltimore: Johns Hopkins University Press, 2000), 110–11, 128.

15. Damon Runyon, "Princeton Tigers in a Great Game Beat Dartmouth," *Oakland Tribune*, 27 October 1912, 1.

16. Fimrite, "Flame That Burned Too Brightly."

17. Falla, *Open Ice*, 202.

18. Salvini, *Hobey Baker*, 25, 28.

19. Fimrite, "Flame That Burned Too Brightly."

20. Arthur S. Link, "Wilson, Woodrow," Educational Technologies Center, Princeton University, http://etcweb.princeton.edu/CampusWWW/Compan ion/wilson_woodrow.html, accessed 18 July 2011.

21. David Brooks, "The Organization Kid," *The Atlantic*, April 2001, http://www.theatlantic.com/magazine/archive/2001/04/the-organization -kid/2164/, accessed 25July 2011.

22. Fimrite, "Flame That Burned Too Brightly."

CHAPTER 9

1. *New York Times*, 6 July 1914.

2. Salvini, *Hobey Baker*, 64.

3. Cleveland Amory, *Who Killed Society?* (New York: Harper, 1960), 208.

4. "Percy R. Pyne, 2D, Is Bachelor Host," *Trenton Evening Times*, 15 January 1914, 11. "Ball Brilliant Plans Complete," *Indianapolis Star*, 12 April 1914, 28.

5. "Gayety of Social Sets at Home and Abroad," *Washington Post*, 13 November 1914, 7. "Auto Race to Rival Horse Show and Polo," *Indianapolis Star*, 5 September 1915, 44.

6. Salvini, *Hobey Baker*, 64, 66.

7. Ibid., 81.

8. A younger cousin, also named Percy Pyne, signed on as a fighter pilot during World War I. In fact, he took down a Fokker D VII near Don-sur-Meuse in October 1919 flying a Spad XIII—the same plane Hobey often flew. Jon Guttman, *Spad XIII vs. Fokker D VII: Western Front 1916–18*, pt. 7 (New York: Osprey Publishing, 2009), 46.

9. Salvini, *Hobey Baker*, 69.

10. *New York Times*, 19 July 1914, 27 December 1914.

11. "Athletic Notes," *Our Paper* 32, no. 10 (11 March 1916).

12. Salvini, *Hobey Baker*, 78.

13. "Hockey Losing Hold in New York from Fad," *Bakersfield Californian*, 18 February 1916, 9. "Boston Wins Amateur Hockey Title," *New York Times*, 2 April 1916, 22.

14. Fimrite, "Flame That Burned Too Brightly." Francis Scott Fitzgerald, *This Side of Paradise* (New York: Charles Scribner's Sons, 1920), 49.

15. Falla, *Open Ice*, 205.

CHAPTER 10

1. "Famous Athlete in Aviation Corps," *Aerial Age Weekly*, 3, no. 14 (26 June 1916): 444.

2. William McBrien, *Cole Porter: A Biography* (New York: Vintage Books, 2000), 57–58.

3. "'Johnny' Poe Killed Fighting in France," *New York Times*, 30 October 1915, 3.

4. McBrien, *Cole Porter*, 57–58.

5. Peter Hart, *Aces Falling: War above the Trenches, 1918* (London: Phoenix, 2007), 1–2.

6. W. David Lewis, *Eddie Rickenbacker: An American Hero in the Twentieth Century* (Baltimore: Johns Hopkins University Press, 2008), 159.

7. Alan Bott, *An Airman's Outings* (London: William Blackwood and S. Edinburgh, 1917), xiv, http://www.archive.org/stream/airmansoutingsoobot tuoft/airmansoutingsoobottuoft_djvu.txt, accessed 23 September 2011.

CHAPTER 11

1. Baker to Father, 8 August 1917. All Baker letters are from the Morse Collection.

2. Baker to Father, 10 August 1917. Baker to Percy Pyne, 20 August 1917. Baker to Father, 20 August 1917.

3. Baker to Percy Pyne, 20 August 1917. Baker to Father, 20 August 1917.

4. Baker to Father, 17 September 1917. Baker to Percy, 10 September 1917. Baker to Father, 27 September 1917.

5. Baker to Percy Pyne, 3 November 1917. Baker to Percy Pyne, 12 November 1917. Baker to Father, 22 November 1917.

6. Baker to Father, 28 November 1917.

7. Baker to Father, 16 December 1917. Baker to Percy Pyne, 18 December 1917. Baker to Father, 26 December 1917. Baker to Percy 29 December 1917. Baker to Percy Pyne, 30 December 1917. Baker to Aunt Laura, 30 December 1917. Baker to Father, 13 January 1918.

8. Baker to Father, [?] February 1918.

9. "Miss Mimi Scott's War Romance," *Philadelphia Inquirer*, 27 October 1918.

10. Eugene H. Mossman, "Miss Mimi Scott's War Romance," *Washington Post*, 27 October 1918, SM2.

11. Ibid. "Vincent Astor Weds Helen Huntington," *New York Times*, 1 May 1914, 13.

12. Mossman, "Miss Mimi Scott's War Romance," SM2.

13. "Ball at the Ritz for Miss Mimi Scott," *New York Times*, 31 December 1918.

14. "Miss Mimi Scott in Vertical Stripes and Miss Sands in Horizontal Stripes," *Tulsa World*, 12 September 1915.

15. "A-Tour in the Smart World of Point Lace and Diamonds," *Washington Post*, 20 June 1914, 6.

16. Greg King, *The Court of Mrs. Astor in Gilded Age New York: A Season of Splendor* (Hoboken: John Wiley & Sons, 2009), 453–55.

17. Mossman, "Miss Mimi Scott's War Romance," SM2.

18. "Automobile Run to the Races," *New York Times*, 19 May 1901, 10. "Testing the Automobiles," 1 April 1900, 19. "In the Automobile World," *New York Times*, 9 September 1900, 19.

19. Mossman, "Miss Mimi Scott's War Romance," SM2.

20. "Stats Organizing Aviation Sections," *Aerial Age Weekly* 2, no. 13 (13 December 1915): 307.

21. Mossman, "Miss Mimi Scott's War Romance," SM2.

22. Ibid. "Vincent Astor Weds Helen Huntington," 13. Salvini, *Hobey Baker*, 100.

23. Nora Saltonstall, *"Out Here at the Front"*: *The World War I Letters of Nora Saltonstall* , ed. by Judith S. Graham (Boston: Northeastern University Press), 103, 142. "Elegance on the Run," *New York Times*, 16 February 1958, 50.

24. Saltonstall, *"Out Here at the Front,"* 92.

25. Ibid., 159.

26. Charles A. Riley, *The Jazz Age in France* (New York: Harry N. Abrams, 2004), 61.

27. Baker to Father, [?] February 1918.

28. Baker to Percy Pyne, 21 April 1918. Baker to Father, 23 May 1918.

CHAPTER 12

1. Salvini, *Hobey Baker*, 100.

2. Baker to Percy Pyne, 21 February 1918. Baker to Father, 15 February 1918. Salvini, *Hobey Baker*, 98–108.

3. Baker to Father, 8 March 1918. Baker to Percy, 9 March 1918.

4. Baker to Percy Pyne, 4 April 1918.

5. Baker to Father, 12 April 1918.

6. Ibid.

7. Ibid. Baker to Percy Pyne, 21 April 1918.

8. Baker to Father, 28 May 1918.

9. Baker to Percy Pyne, 17 May 1918. Baker to Father, 18 May 1918. Baker to Father, 20 May 1918.

10. Baker to Father, 21 May 1918.

11. Baker to Father, 23 May 1918.

12. Baker to Percy Pyne, 23 May 1918.

13. Baker to Father, 29 May 1918. Baker to Father, 31 May 1918. Baker to Father, 13 June 1918.

14. Baker to Percy Pyne, 9 July 1918.

15. Salvini, *Hobey Baker*, 98–108.

16. Baker to Percy Pyne, 17 July 1918. Baker to Father, 20 July 1918. Baker to Father, 23 July 1918.

17. Baker to Father, 27 July 1918. Baker to Percy Pyne, 26 July 1918.

18. Baker to Father, 8 August 1918 (but written on 12 August 1918).

19. Baker to Father, 29–31 August 1918.

20. Ibid. Baker to Father, 1–3 September 1918.

21. Baker to Father, 30–31 August 1918 and 1–3 September 1918.

22. Baker to Father, 30–31 August 1918 and 1–3 September 1918.

23. Baker to Father, 30–31 August 1918 and 1–3 September 1918. Hobey proposed either late at night on Sunday, 1 September 1918, or perhaps before sunrise on Tuesday, 2 September 1918.

CHAPTER 13

1. Baker to Percy Pyne, 4 September 1918.

2. Charles John Biddle, *The Way of the Eagle* (New York: Charles Scribner's Sons: 1919), 274, 275.

3. Baker to Father, 15–18 September 1918.

4. Baker to Father, 26 September 1918.

5. Baker to Percy Pyne, 25 September 1918.

6. Baker to Father, 12 October 1918.

7. Baker to Father, 13–20 October 1918.

8. Baker to Father, 13–20 October 1918.

9. Mossman, "Miss Mimi Scott's War Romance," SM2.

10. Ibid.

11. Ibid. "Sport Snap Shots," *Lima Sunday News*, 8 December 1918, 24.

12. Mossman, "Miss Mimi Scott's War Romance," SM2.

CHAPTER 14

1. Baker to Father, 23 October 1918. He's stationed at a place where he can go into Nancy, France, for dinner.

2. Baker to Father, 28 October 1918. Hobey to Percy Pyne, 15 November 1918.

3. Baker to Father, 29 October 1918. Hobey to Percy Pyne, 1 November 1918.

4. Baker to Father, 2 November 1918. Hobey to Percy Pyne, 1 November 1918.

5. Baker to Father, 11 November 1918. Hobey to Percy Pyne, 15 November 1918.

6. Baker to Father, 11 November 1918.

7. Ibid.

8. Baker to Percy Pyne, 15 November 1918.

9. Christopher Phelps, "The Sexuality of Malcolm X," *Journal of American Studies*, http://eprints.nottingham.ac.uk/34331/1/Phelps%20-%20The%20Sexuality%20°0?of?f%20Malcolm%20X.pdf, accessed 26 August 2016.

10. Baker to Father, 21 November 1918. Phelps, "Sexuality of Malcolm X."

11. Albert E. George and Edwin H. Cooper, *Pictorial History of the 26th Division United States Army* (Boston: Ball Publishing, 1920), 41.

12. *Washington Post*, 30 December 1918.

13. *Washington Post*, 13 September 1919.

14. Morris Miller, "Sport Snap Shots," *Janesville Gazette*, 7 January 1919, 10.

15. Salvini, *Hobey Baker*, 100.

16. Falla, *Open Ice*, 215.

17. Robert Cantwell, "The Gallant Life of Princeton's Hobey Baker Poses Enigmas for the Literary," *Sports Illustrated* 12 September 1966, http://cnnsi.printthis.clicability.com/pt/cpt?expire=&title=The+Gallant+Life+Of+Princeton%27s+Hobey+Baker+Poses+Enigmas+-+09.12.66+-+SI+Vault&urlID=413119967&action=cpt&partnerID=289881&fb=Y&url=http%3A%2F%2Fsportsillustrated.cnn.com%2Fvault%2Farticle%2Fmagazine%2FMAG1078970%2Findex.htm, accessed 16 July 2011.

18. Quoted in Salvini, *Hobey Baker*, 102.

19. Cantwell, "Gallant Life."

20. "Last Tribute Paid to 'Hobey' Baker," *Philadelphia Inquirer*, 20 July 1921.

CHAPTER 15

1. William D. Richardson, "Kinnick, Iowa Ace, Gets Trophy Here," *New York Times*, 7 December 1939, 39.

2. Wanda Montz, "Hitler and Queen Elizabeth Are Outstanding Personalities of the Year in Cedar Rapids Ballot," *Cedar Rapids Gazette*, 31 December 1939, 7.

3. Scott M. Fisher, *The Ironmen: The 1939 Hawkeyes* (Lincoln: Media Publishing, 1989), 2–3.

4. Ibid., 3–4.

5. Ron Fimrite, "Nile Kinnick: With the Wartime Death of the '39 Heisman Winner, America Lost a Leader," *Sports Illustrated*, 31 August 1987, http://www.si.com/vault/1987/08/31/116008/nile-kinnick-with-the-war-time-death-of-the-39-heisman-winner-america-lost-a-leader, accessed 9 June 2016.

6. Quoted in Paul Baender, ed., *A Hero Perished: The Diary & Selected Letters of Nile Kinnick* (Iowa City: University of Iowa Press, 1991), xviii.

7. University of Iowa, "Iowa's Nile Kinnick," 1944, University of Iowa Libraries, https://www.youtube.com/watch?v=Hg-taYNIjjo&feature=youtu.be, accessed 9 June 2016.

8. Al Grady, "Nile Kinnick Stadium: For Those Too Young to Remember," *Iowa City Press Citizen*, 20 June 1972.

9. Baender, *A Hero Perished*, 151. D. W. Stump, *Kinnick: The Man and the Legend* (Iowa City: University of Iowa, 1975), 83.

10. Michael Oriard, *King Football: Sport and Spectacle in the Golden Age of Radio & Newsreels, Movies & Magazines, the Weekly & the Daily Press* (Chapel Hill, University of North Carolina Press, 2001), 11, 12.

CHAPTER 16

1. Baender, *A Hero Perished*, xiii.
2. Ibid., 104.
3. Ibid., 51–52.
4. Ibid., xv–xvi.
5. Stump, *Kinnick*, 30–33.
6. Mike Chapman, "Ironman: The Nile Kinnick Story," *Iowa History Journal*, iowahistoryjournal.com/ironman-nile-kinnick-story/, accessed 3 June 2016.
7. Ibid.
8. Stump, *Kinnick*, 39–41.
9. Ibid., 39, 44.
10. Ibid., 44.
11. Fisher, *Ironmen*, 8.
12. Fimrite, "Nile Kinnick."
13. Fisher, *Ironmen*, 24.
14. Kinnick to Mother, 4 December 1939, in Baender, *A Hero Perished*, 33.
15. Stump, *Kinnick*, 44–45.
16. Ibid., 47.
17. Ibid., 45.
18. Ibid.
19. Ibid., 46.

CHAPTER 17

1. Fisher, *Ironmen*, 13.
2. Stump, *Kinnick*, 48–49.
3. Kinnick to Dear Family, 7–8 January 1939, in Baender, *A Hero Perished*, 15.
4. Ibid., 17, 18.
5. Ibid.
6. Francis Wallace, "Pigskin Preview of 1939," *Saturday Evening Post* 212 (23 September 1939): 42. Fisher, *Ironmen*, 34.
7. Wallace, "Pigskin Preview of 1939," 42. Fisher, *Ironmen*, 33.
8. Fisher, *Ironmen*, 17, 25–26.
9. Stump, *Kinnick*, 55.

10. Fisher, *Ironmen*, 22.

11. Stump, *Kinnick*, 51.

12. Ibid., 55.

13. Fisher, *Ironmen*, 47.

14. Stump, *Kinnick*, 58.

15. Fimrite, "Nile Kinnick."

16. Fisher, *Ironmen*, 72.

17. "Kinnick, Seven Other Hawkeyes Play 60 Minutes to Beat Irish," *Chicago Sunday Tribune*, 12 November 1939, pt. 2, p. 1.

18. "Iowa Ahead of Notre Dame 7-0 at End of Half," *Mason City Globe-Gazette*, 11 November 1939, 1.

19. Fimrite, "Nile Kinnick."

20. Fisher, *Ironmen*, 99.

21. Stump, *Kinnick*, 64–65.

22. Fimrite, "Nile Kinnick."

CHAPTER 18

1. Baender, *A Hero Perished*, 30. Kinnick to Mother, 4 December 1939, in Baender, *A Hero Perished*, 32–33.

2. "Cardinals Draft George Cafego; Brooklyn Claims Nile Kinnick," *Chicago Tribune*, 10 December 1939, B1.

3. Baender, *A Hero Perished*, 40.

4. Kinnick to Mother, 4 December 1939, in Baender, *A Hero Perished*, 33.

5. "Iowa Star Receives Walter Camp Today," *Berkeley Daily Gazette*, 17 January 1940, sports sec., 1.

6. "Nile Kinnick Adds Camp Trophy to His Collection," *Wisconsin State Journal*, 17 January 1940, sports section, 2.

7. Baender, *A Hero Perished*, xix, 35, 36.

8. Ibid., 54.

9. Kinnick to Mother, 26 May 1940, in Baender, *A Hero Perished*, 38–40.

10. Baender, *A Hero Perished*, 41–44.

11. Franklin D. Roosevelt, "127—Campaign Address at Boston, Massachusetts," 30 October 1940, *American Presidency Project*, www.presidency.ucsb.edu/ws/?pid=15887, accessed 13 May 2016.

12. Baender, *A Hero Perished*, 44–45.

13. Ibid.

CHAPTER 19

1. "Packers Beat All-Stars, 45-28, in Aerial Duel" and ". . . Henry J. McCormick Means No Foolin'!" *Wisconsin State Journal*, 30 August 1940, sports section, 1.

2. Stump, *Kinnick*, 78–79.

3. "SUI's Nile Kinnick Dies in Action," *Globe Gazette*, 4 June 1943, http://digital.lib.uiowa.edu/cdm/compoundobject/collection/kinnick/id/3296/rec/1, accessed 10 June 2016.

4. Quoted in Stump, *Kinnick*, 81.

5. Kinnick diary, in Baender, *A Hero Perished*, 151.

6. Kinnick diary, 1 February 1942, in ibid., 184.

7. Stump, *Kinnick*, 86–87.

8. Ibid.

9. Ibid.

10. Kinnick diary, 11 April and 24 July 1942, in Baender, *A Hero Perished*, 224, 253.

11. Kinnick diary, 4 and 5 April 1942, in ibid., 221.

12. Kinnick diary, 24 and 25 June 1942, in ibid., 244.

13. Kinnick diary, 4 July 1942, in ibid., 247.

14. Kinnick diary, 12, 14, 17, 22, and 25 July 1942, in ibid., 250–53.

15. Kinnick diary, 4 July 1942, in ibid., 247.

16. Kinnick diary, 13 August 1942, in ibid., 257–58.

17. Kinnick diary, 5 and 7 May 1943, in ibid., 263–64.

18. Baender, *A Hero Perished*, 133, 151–52.

19. Kinnick diary, 5 and 7 May 1943, in ibid., 263–64.

20. Fimrite, "Nile Kinnick."

CHAPTER 20

1. Kinnick to Parents, 1 September 1942, Nile Kinnick Correspondence, September–November 1942, Nile Kinnick Digital Collection, University of Iowa Libraries, Iowa Digital Library, http://digital.lib.uiowa.edu/cdm/compoundobject/collection/kinnick/id/1933/rec/10, accessed 4 June 2016. Hereafter cited as Kinnick Digital Collection.

2. Kinnick to Folks, 25 September 1942. Baender, *A Hero Perished*, 91–92.

3. Kinnick to Uncle Chas, Nile Kinnick Correspondence, March–October 1943, Kinnick Digital Collection, http://digital.lib.uiowa.edu/cdm/compoundobject/collection/kinnick/id/2234/rec/11, accessed 10 June 2016.

4. Kinnick to Brother George, 4 March 1943, ibid.

5. Kinnick to Parents, 8 March 1943, ibid.

6. Kinnick to Parents, 13 March 1943, ibid.

7. Ibid.

8. Eric Bergerud, e-mail to author, 17 June 2016.

9. Bill Reitter to Nile Kinnick Sr., 12 June 1943, Nile Kinnick Airplane Crash Correspondence, 1943–1972, Kinnick Digital Collection, http://digital.lib.uiowa.edu/cdm/compoundobject/collection/kinnick/id/2672, accessed 3 June 2016.

10. Baender, *A Hero Perished*, 115–17.

11. Reitter to Nile Kinnick Sr. Fisher, *Ironmen*, 122. Bergerud, e-mail to author.

12. Baender, *A Hero Perished*, 115–17.

13. Eric C. Wilson, "In Memoriam," 5 June 1943, University News Service; "Nile Kinnick Killed in Action; Former Iowa All-American," *Times Davenport*, 4 June 1943; "Nile Kinnick, Iowa Grid Great, Killed," *Courier Waterloo*, 4 June 1943; "Had Served as Pilot on Plane Carrier," *Globe Gazette*, 4 June 1943; Kinnick Digital Collection, http://digital.lib.uiowa.edu/cdm/com poundobject/collection/kinnick/id/3296/rec/1, accessed 10 June 2016.

14. Baender, *A Hero Perished*, 271.

15. Ibid., 275.

16. Kinnick to Celia Pears, 31 May 1943, facsimile copy, in Baender, *A Hero Perished*, 138–39.

17. "Kinnick's Brother Missing on Flight over New Ireland," *Cedar Rapids Gazette*, 14 November 1944, 10.

18. Gillett, "All in the Game."

CHAPTER 21

1. Kevin Carroll, *Dr. Eddie Anderson, Hall of Fame College Football Coach: A Biography* (Jefferson, NC: McFarland & Company, 2007), 185.

2. "All-American Leaves Widow, Two Children," *San Antonio Light*, 21 December 1944, 6.

3. "Speculating in Sports," *Hammond Times*, 27 March 1945, 10. "Jack Chevigny, Famed Irish Grid Star, Ex-Texas U. Coach, Killed," *Abilene Reporter-News*, 25 March 1945, 13.

4. *New York Times*, 28 May 1942, 8.

CHAPTER 22

1. Jan Kalsu, phone interview by author.

2. Ibid. William Nack, "A Name on the Wall," *Sports Illustrated* 95, no. 3 (23 July 2001), http://www.si.com/nfl/2014/09/04/name-wall-si-60-william -nack-bob-kalsu, accessed 9 December 2016.

3. Kalsu, phone interview.

4. Ibid.

5. Ibid. Scott Pitoniak, "Remembering a Buffalo Bill who gave his life for his country," 28 May 2012, http://scottpitoniak.blogspot.com/2012/05 /remembering-former-buffalo-bill-who.html, accessed 13 July 2016.

6. Kalsu, phone interview. Nack, "A Name on the Wall."

7. Laura Palmer, *Shrapnel in the Heart* (New York: Vintage, 1988), 151–52.

8. Kalsu, phone interview.

9. Robert F. Lewis, *Smart Ball: Marketing the Myth and Managing the Reality of Major League Baseball* (Jackson: University Press of Mississippi, 2010), 29.

10. Nack, "A Name on the Wall."

11. NFL Films, "Remembering Bob Kalsu," http://www.nfl.com/videos /buffalo-bills/09000d5d8294caf8/Films-Encore-Remembering-Bob-Kalsu, accessed 12 July 2016.

CHAPTER 23

1. Jan Kalsu, interview by author, 18 August 2016.

2. Ibid.

3. John Underwood, "The House That Earnie Built," *Sports Illustrated*, 3 January 1972, http://www.si.com/vault/1972/01/03/576291/the-house-that -earnie-built, accessed 14 July 2016.

4. Michael Oriard, "Flag Football," *Slate*, 17 November 2009, http://www. slate.com/articles/sports/sports_nut/2009/11/flag_football.html, accessed 12 July 2016. Underwood, "The House That Earnie Built."

5. Nack, "A Name on the Wall."

6. NBC Sports, video of 1968 Orange Bowl Game, Oklahoma vs. Tennessee, https://www.youtube.com/watch?v=-MfyrINYySo.

7. Kalsu interview.

8. Ibid.

9. Ibid.

10. Ibid.

11. Ibid.

12. Matt Warren, "Bob Kalsu's Sacrifice Rooted in His Oklahoma Upbringing," *SB Nation*, 25 May 2014, http://www.buffalorumblings. com/2014/5/25/5748648/bob-kalsu-vietnam-oklahoma-memorial-day, accessed 10 July 2016.

CHAPTER 24

1. Christian Clark, "Bob Kalsu Honored in Del City for Service in Vietnam," *The Oklahoman*, 6 February 2016, http://newsok.com/article/547 7168, accessed 7 July 2016.

2. Nack, "A Name on the Wall."

3. Ibid.

4. NFL Films, "Remembering Bob Kalsu."

5. David Halberstam, *The Best and the Brightest* (New York: Ballantine Books, 1992), 298.

6. James S. Olson and Randy W. Roberts, *Where the Domino Fell: America and Vietnam 1945–2010* (West Sussex: Wiley Blackwell, 2014), x.

CHAPTER 25

1. V. Larry Alford and James Riley, phone interviews by author, 19–20 July 2016.

2. Steven A. Coleman, phone interview by author, 7 July 2016.

3. Ibid.

4. Nack, "A Name on the Wall."

5. Ibid.

6. Ibid.

7. Kalsu interview.

8. Ibid.

9. James H. Willbanks, "Tet 1968: The Turning Point," *Foreign Policy Research Institute*, 15 May 2012, http://www.fpri.org/article/2012/05/tet-1968 -the-turning-point/, accessed 10 July 2016.

10. NPR, "Final Words: Cronkite's Vietnam Commentary," 18 July 2009, http://www.npr.org/templates/story/story.php?storyId=106775685, accessed 9 December 2016.

11. Chester Pach, "The Way It Wasn't: Cronkite and Vietnam," History News Network, 21 July 2009, http://historynewsnetwork.org/article/104635, accessed 9 December 2016.

12. Daniel C. Hallin, *The Uncensored War: The Media and Vietnam* (New York: Oxford University Press, 1986), 162.

13. Ibid., 106.

14. Willbanks, "Tet 1968."

CHAPTER 26

1. Kalsu interview, 18 August 2016.

2. Nack, "A Name on the Wall."

3. Bob Finnigan, "Athletes and War—Call Recalled—War in Iraq Brings Back Memories Players Tried To Forget," *Seattle Times*, 20 January 1991, http://community.seattletimes.nwsource.com/archive/?-date=19910120&slug=1261583, accessed 6 July 2016.

4. "Rhino Den Interviews: Rocky Bleier," *RhinoDen*, 25 November 2012, http://rhinoden.rangerup.com/rhino-den-interviews-rocky-bleier/, accessed 6 July 2016.

5. Nack, "A Name on the Wall."

6. James Riley, interview by author, 25 July 2016.

7. Kalsu interview. Nack, "A Name on the Wall."

8. Kalsu interview.

9. Ibid.

10. Ibid.

CHAPTER 27

1. Keith W. Nolan, *Ripcord: Screaming Eagles under Siege, Vietnam 1970* (New York: Ballantine Books, 2000), 1–4.

2. Ibid., 10–12.

3. Lewis Sorley, *A Better War* (New York: Harcourt, 1999), xii–xv. Lewis Sorley, "The Real Afghan Lessons from Vietnam," *Wall Street Journal*, 11 October 2009, http://www.wsj.com/articles/SB10001424052748703746604 5744630241506223I0, accessed 2 July 2016.

4. Nolan, *Ripcord*, 6.

5. Ibid., 369.

6. Nack, "A Name on the Wall."

7. Ibid., 369. Nack, "A Name on the Wall."

8. Nolan, *Ripcord*, 369.

9. Ibid., 344.

10. NFL Films, "Remembering Bob Kalsu."

11. Nolan, *Ripcord*, 13–14, 344.

12. Ibid., 13–14.

13. Ibid., 14.

14. Ibid., 366, 368.

15. Ibid., 366.

16. Ibid., 365.

17. Nack, "A Name on the Wall."

18. Nolan, *Ripcord*, 368.

19. Ibid., 16–17.

CHAPTER 28

1. Kalsu interview.

2. Ibid. Nack, "A Name on the Wall."

3. Palmer, *Shrapnel in the Heart*, 152.

4. Ibid., 157.

5. Ibid., 152.

6. Nack, "A Name on the Wall."

7. Clark, "Bob Kalsu Honored in Del City."

CHAPTER 29

1. ESPN.com News Services, "Pat Tillman Investigation."

2. Ann Coulter, "2004: Highlights and Lowlifes," 29 December 2004, http://www.anncoulter.com/columns/2004-12-29.html.

3. Dave Zirin, "Pat Tillman, Our Hero," *The Nation*, 24 October 2005, https://www.thenation.com/article/pat-tillman-our-hero/.

4. Ralph Waldo Emerson, "The American Scholar," *Ralph Waldo Emerson*

Texts, http://www.emersoncentral.com/amscholar.htm, accessed 26 July 2016.

5. Jeffrey A. Trachtenberg, "Jon Krakauer's Inside Story of Pat Tillman," *Wall Street Journal,* 11 September 2009.

CHAPTER 30

1. Mary Tillman, with Narda Zacchino, *Boots on the Ground By Dusk: My Tribute to Pat Tillman* (New York: Modern Times, 2008), 7.

2. Ibid., 3, 5.

3. Ibid., 3. Marie Tillman, *The Letter: My Journey through Love, Loss, and Life* (New York: Grand Central Publishing, 2012), 24.

4. Jon Krakauer, *Where Men Win Glory: The Odyssey of Pat Tillman* (New York: Doubleday, 2009), 4.

5. Tillman, *The Letter,* 20–22.

6. Krakauer, *Where Men Win Glory,* 38–42, 45. Gary Smith, "Remember His Name," *Sports Illustrated,* 11 September 2006, http://www.si.com /vault/2006/09/11/8386263/remember-his-name, accessed 27 July 2016.

7. Krakauer, *Where Men Win Glory,* 38–42.

8. Tillman, *The Letter,* 25–28.

9. Krakauer, *Where Men Win Glory,* 44–45.

10. Ibid., 62.

11. Tillman, *The Letter,* 30–31.

12. Ibid., 31–32. Krakauer, *Where Men Win Glory,* 63.

13. Tillman, *The Letter,* 55.

14. Smith, "Remember His Name." Krakauer, *Where Men Win Glory,* 90.

15. Krakauer, *Where Men Win Glory,* 115.

16. Mike Fish, "An Un-American Tragedy, Part One: Pat Tillman's Uncertain Death," http://www.espn.com/espn/eticket/story?page=tillmanpart1, accessed 30 August 2016.

17. Smith, "Remember His Name."

18. Krakauer, *Where Men Win Glory,* 73–74.

CHAPTER 31

1. Tillman, *The Letter,* 38–39.

2. Krakauer, *Where Men Win Glory,* 77–78.

3. "For Cardinals, Pat Tillman Loss Was Hardest of All," *Arizona Republic,* 24 April 2004, http://www.azcentral.com/story/sports/2014/04/22/pat-till man-for-cards-this-loss-is-hardest-of-all/7838363/, accessed 5 August 2016.

4. Ibid.

5. Krakauer, *Where Men Win Glory,* 93, 98, 100–101.

6. "For Cardinals, Pat Tillman Loss Was Hardest of All." Krakauer, *Where Men Win Glory,* 102–4.

7. Krakauer, *Where Men Win Glory*, 111–13.

8. "Hundreds of Afghan Girls Poisoned by Toxic Gas at Two Schools in Suspected Attacks by Taliban Militants Opposed to Their Education," DailyMail.com, 3 September 2015, http://www.dailymail.co.uk/news/article -3221073/Hundreds-Afghan-girls-poisoned-toxic-gas-two-schools-suspected -attacks-Taliban-militants-opposed-education.html, accessed 6 August 2016.

9. "Osama bin Laden Had an 'Extensive' Porn Collection—But Officials Are Refusing to Release Details because of Its 'Nature,'" DailyMail.com, 20 May 2015, http://www.dailymail.co.uk/news/article-3090394/Officials-re fuse-release-Osama-bin-Laden-s-extensive-porn-collection-nature.html, accessed 6 August 2016.

10. Krakauer, *Where Men Win Glory*, 119.

11. Tillman, *The Letter*, 81–82.

12. Michael Oriard, "Flag Football," *Slate*, 17 November 2009, http://www .slate.com/articles/sports/sports_nut/2009/11/flag_football.html, accessed 9 August 2016.

13. Rob Sheffield, "Super Bowl Halftime Shows Ranked: From Worst to Best," *Rolling Stone*, 4 February 2016, http://www.rollingstone.com/music /pictures/super-bowl-halftime-shows-ranked-from-worst-to-best-20140128 /1-u2-2002-0479328, 9 August 2016.

14. Tillman, *The Letter*, 80.

15. Ibid., 81. Krakauer, *Where Men Win Glory*, 120.

16. Krakauer, *Where Men Win Glory*, 136.

CHAPTER 32

1. Krakauer, *Where Men Win Glory*, 138.

2. Tillman, *The Letter*, 81–82.

3. Krakauer, *Where Men Win Glory*, 141–42.

4. Ibid., 136, 142.

5. "For Cardinals, Pat Tillman Loss Was Hardest of All."

6. Dan Bickley, "Pat Tillman: No Words, Lasting Message," *Arizona Republic*, 24 April 2004, http://www.azcentral.com/story/sports/2014 /04/22/pat-tillman-no-words-lasting-message-bickley/7837697/, accessed 10 August 2016.

7. Krakauer, *Where Men Win Glory*, 138, 145.

8. Ibid., 146.

9. Ibid., 145–46, 149.

10. Ibid., 159.

11. Ibid., 160.

12. "President Reagan's Address at a Ceremony Commemorating the 40th Anniversary of the Normandy Invasion, D-Day," 6 June 1984, Ronald Reagan Presidential Library, https://www.youtube.com/watch?v=eEIqdcHbc 8I, accessed 11 August 2016. Krakauer, *Where Men Win Glory*, 162.

CHAPTER 33

1. Krakauer, *Where Men Win Glory*, 165, 166.

2. Tillman, *The Letter*, 94–95.

3. Ibid., 98.

4. Ibid., 97–98.

5. Krakauer, *Where Men Win Glory*, 213–214.

6. Smith, "Remember His Name." Krakauer, *Where Men Win Glory*, 227–28.

7. US House of Representatives, Committee on Oversight and Government Reform, Testimony of Jessica Lynch, 24 April 2007, http://web.archive.org/web/20090220085535/http://oversight.house.gov/documents/20070424110022.pdf, accessed 12 August 2016.

8. Krakauer, *Where Men Win Glory*, 180–83.

9. Tillman, *The Letter*, 100.

10. Krakauer, *Where Men Win Glory*, 216.

11. Ibid., 214, 216–17.

12. Tillman, *The Letter*, 56.

13. Krakauer, *Where Men Win Glory*, 218, 220.

14. Ibid., 256.

15. Ibid., 221–22.

CHAPTER 34

1. Krakauer, *Where Men Win Glory*, 225.

2. Ibid., 225, 228.

3. Ron Synovitz, "Afghanistan: U.S.-led Commando Teams Fight Taliban with Unconventional Warfare," Radio Free Europe, Radio Liberty, 15 March 2004, http://www.rferl.org/a/1051894.html, accessed 15 August 2016. Krakauer, *Where Men Win Glory*, 233.

4. Smith, "Remember His Name." Krakauer, *Where Men Win Glory*, 234–35.

5. Smith, "Remember His Name." Krakauer, *Where Men Win Glory*, 242–43.

6. Smith, "Remember His Name." Krakauer, *Where Men Win Glory*, 242–43.

7. Andrew Exum, "Andrew Exum Reviews Jon Krakauer's Book on Pat Tillman, 'Where Men Win Glory,'" *Washington Post*, 13 September 2009.

8. Smith, "Remember His Name." Krakauer, *Where Men Win Glory*, 242–45.

9. Krakauer, *Where Men Win Glory*, 254.

10. Fish, "An Un-American Tragedy." Smith, "Remember His Name." Krakauer, *Where Men Win Glory*, 253, 254.

11. Fish, "An Un-American Tragedy."

12. Smith, "Remember His Name." Fish, "An Un-American Tragedy."

13. Krakauer, *Where Men Win Glory*, 257–68.

14. Fish, "An Un-American Tragedy." Smith, "Remember His Name." Krakauer, *Where Men Win Glory*, 257–68, 274.

15. Smith, "Remember His Name." Krakauer, *Where Men Win Glory*, 257–68, 274.

16. Smith, "Remember His Name."

17. Ibid. Krakauer, *Where Men Win Glory*, 257–68.

CHAPTER 35

1. Krakauer, *Where Men Win Glory*, 276–77.

2. Ibid., 279–81.

3. John Douglas Marshall, "Pat Tillman, Anti-War Hero," *Daily Beast*, 13 September 2009, http://www.thedailybeast.com/articles/2009/09/13/pat -tillman-anti-war-hero.html, accessed 17 August 2016.

4. Krakauer, *Where Men Win Glory*, 343.

5. Ibid., 280, 281.

6. Ibid., 289–93.

7. "What Really Happened to Pat Tillman?" *60 Minutes*, 1 May 2008, http://www.cbsnews.com/news/what-really-happened-to-pat-tillman/, accessed 22 August 2016. Krakauer, *Where Men Win Glory*, 289–93, 301–2.

8. "What Really Happened to Pat Tillman?" Krakauer, *Where Men Win Glory*, 296–99.

9. Krakauer, *Where Men Win Glory*, 295.

10. Tillman, *The Letter*, 124–26.

11. Ibid., 60.

CHAPTER 36

1. Marco R. della Cava, "Tillman Memorialized in Hometown," *USA Today*, 3 May 2004, http://usatoday30.usatoday.com/sports/football/nfl /2004–05–03-tillman-service_x.htm, accessed 24 August 2016.

2. Tillman, *The Letter*, 106.

3. Ibid., 109.

4. Ibid., 109–10.

5. Ibid., 113–14.

6. Ibid., 107–9.

7. Ibid., 106.

8. Ibid., 245.

9. Pat Tillman Foundation, "Our Mission," www.pattillmanfoundation .org/our-story/, accessed 29 July 2016.

10. Smith, "Remember His Name."

11. Ibid.

12. Ibid.

13. Krakauer, *Where Men Win Glory*, 343–44.

14. Ibid., 343–44.

EPILOGUE

1. Krakauer, *Where Men Win Glory*, 116.

Index

Page numbers in *italic* refer to illustrations.